Ethnicity in Asia

Since 1991, ethnic division has been among the most important sources of conflict and war throughout the world. Although the countries of East and Southeast Asia have not experienced anything quite as horrendous as the wars in the former Yugoslavia in the early 1990s, they have had their share of conflict due to ethnicity. Indonesia is the most illustrative example, but there have also been serious divisions in Burma, China, the Philippines and Vietnam among others.

This book is designed as a comprehensive comparative introduction to ethnicity in East and Southeast Asia since 1945. The Introduction takes up some theoretical issues concerning ethnicity in Asia. Each following chapter covers a particular country and gives a brief historical background before addressing topics such as:

- how to define each ethnic group;
- ethnic identification in the individual country;
- governmental policy towards ethnic groups;
- economies of the ethnic groups in relation to the national economy;
- social issues such as gender and education;
- problems of national integration;
- the impact of ethnic issues on the country's foreign policy.

This text is the first to bring together a coherent study of ethnicity in the region as a whole, allowing the contributors to build on the ideas developed for each country to form broader themes applicable more generally to East and Southeast Asia as a whole. With maps of all countries, and suggestions for further reading, this well illustrated textbook is essential reading for all students studying the communities of East and Southeast Asia, as well as a valuable resource for specialists in the area.

Colin Mackerras is Professor in the School of Asian and International Studies, Griffith University, Australia. In 1999 he was elected Fellow of the Australian Academy of the Humanities and won an award for achievements in Australia–China cultural relations. He is a well known specialist on China with particular research interests in China's ethnic minorities, Chinese history and politics, and Chinese theatre.

Asia's transformations
Edited by Mark Selden
Binghamton University and Cornell University, USA

The books in this series explore the political, social, economic and cultural consequences of Asia's transformations in the twentieth and twenty-first centuries. The series emphasizes the tumultuous interplay of local, national, regional and global forces as Asia bids to become the hub of the world economy. While focusing on the contemporary, it also looks back to analyze the antecedents of Asia's contested rise. This series comprises several strands:

Asia's Transformations aims to address the needs of students and teachers, and the titles will be published in hardback and paperback. Titles include:

Asia's Great Cities: each volume aims to capture the heartbeat of the contemporary city from multiple perspectives emblematic of the authors' own deep familiarity with the distinctive faces of the city, its history, society, culture, politics and economics, and its evolving position in national, regional and global frameworks. While most volumes emphasize urban developments since the Second World War, some pay close attention to the legacy of the longue durée in shaping the contemporary. Thematic and comparative volumes address such themes as urbanization, economic and financial linkages, architecture and space, wealth and power, gendered relationships, planning and anarchy, and ethnographies in national and regional perspective. Titles include:

Hong Kong
Global city
Stephen Chiu and Tai-Lok Lui

Shanghai
Global city
Jeff Wasserstrom

Singapore
Carl Trocki

Beijing in the Modern World
David Strand and Madeline Yue Dong

Bangkok
Place, practice and representation
Marc Askew

Asia.com is a series which focuses on the ways in which new information and communication technologies are influencing politics, society and culture in Asia. Titles include:

Asia.com
Asia encounters the Internet
Edited by K.C. Ho, Randolph Kluver and Kenneth C.C. Yang

Japanese Cybercultures
Edited by Mark McLelland and Nanette Gottlieb

RoutledgeCurzon Studies in Asia's Transformations is a forum for innovative new research intended for a high-level specialist readership, and the titles will be available in hardback only. Titles include:

1. Chinese Media, Global Contexts
Edited by Chin-Chuan Lee

2. Imperialism in South East Asia
'A fleeting, passing phase'
Nicholas Tarling

3. Internationalizing the Pacific
The United States, Japan and the Institute of Pacific Relations in war and peace, 1919–1945
Tomoko Akami

4. Koreans in Japan
Critical voices from the margin
Edited by Sonia Ryang

5. The American Occupation of Japan and Okinawa*
Literature and memory
Michael Molasky
* Now available in paperback

Critical Asian Scholarship is a series intended to showcase the most important individual contributions to scholarship in Asian studies. Each of the volumes presents a leading Asian scholar addressing themes that are central to his or her most significant and lasting contribution to Asian studies. The series is committed to the rich variety of research and writing on Asia, and is not restricted to any particular discipline, theoretical approach or geographical expertise.

China's Past, China's Future
Energy, food, environment
Vaclav Smil

China Unbound
Evolving perspectives on the Chinese past
Paul A. Cohen

Women and the Family in Chinese History
Patricia Buckley Ebrey

Southeast Asia
A testament
George McT. Kahin

Ethnicity in Asia

Edited by Colin Mackerras

RoutledgeCurzon
Taylor & Francis Group

LONDON AND NEW YORK

First published 2003
by RoutledgeCurzon
11 New Fetter Lane, London EC4P 4EE

Simultaneously published in the USA and Canada
by RoutledgeCurzon
29 West 35th Street, New York, NY 10001

RoutledgeCurzon is an imprint of the Taylor & Francis Group

Typeset in 10/12pt Mono Baskerville by Graphicraft Limited,
Hong Kong
Printed and bound in Great Britain by The Cromwell Press,
Trowbridge, Wiltshire

British Library Cataloguing in Publication Data
A catalogue record for this book is available from the British Library

Library of Congress Cataloging in Publication Data
Ethnicity in Asia / edited by Colin Mackerras.
    p. cm. – (Asia's transformations)
  1. Ethnicity–Asia, Southeastern.   2. Ethnology–Asia, Southeastern.
  3. Asia, Southeastern–Politics and government–1945–
  4. Ethnicity–East Asia.   5. Ethnology–East Asia.   6. East Asia–Politics
  and government.   I. Mackerras, Colin.   II. Series.

DS523.3.E87 2003
305.8′0095–dc21

                                                         2003005288

ISBN 0–415–25816–2 (hbk)
ISBN 0–415–25817–0 (pbk)

Contents

Illustrations

Maps

Plates

Tables

Contributors

Chua Beng Huat is Professor of Sociology, and concurrently the coordinator of Southeast Asian Studies Programme, at the National University of Singapore. He has done extensive research in urban planning and public housing, comparative politics in Southeast Asia and the emerging consumerism across Asia. He has held visiting professorships at universities in Malaysia, Hong Kong, Taiwan, Germany, Australia and the United States. His political analysis of Singapore is published as *Communitarian Ideology and Democracy in Singapore* (London and New York: Routledge, 1995). His analysis of public housing policy is published in *Political Legitimacy and Housing: Stakeholding in Singapore* (London and New York: Routledge, 1997). He is editor of *Consumption in Asia: Lifestyles and Identities* (London and New York: Routledge, 2000). He is founding co-executive editor of the journal *Inter-Asia Cultural Studies* published by Routledge in London.

Grant Evans is a Reader in Anthropology at the University of Hong Kong. He has written widely on Southeast Asia, and besides writing on minorities in Laos he has also contributed to discussions of minorities in Vietnam and southern China. More recently his research has been oriented towards history and anthropology. Among his books is *A Short History of Laos: The Land In-Between* (Allen & Unwin, 2002).

Gerry van Klinken has taught at universities in Malaysia, Indonesia and Australia, and is currently researching post-New Order ethnic conflict in Indonesia at the Royal Institute of Linguistics and Anthropology (KITLV) in the Netherlands. He has recently published papers or chapters on the Moluccan and the Central Kalimantan conflicts, as well as on post-New Order interpretations of history and on the perpetrators of the 1999 destruction of East Timor. He is a research adviser to the Commission for Reception, Truth and Reconciliation in East Timor, and coordinating editor of the Australian quarterly *Inside Indonesia* magazine.

Pinkaew Laungaramsri is Lecturer at the Regional Center for Social Science and Sustainable Development, Faculty of Social Sciences, Chiang Mai University. She is the author of *Redefining Nature: Karen Ecological Knowledge and the*

Challenge to the Modern Conservation Paradigm (Earthworm Books, Chennai, India: 2001). She is currently conducting a research project on Shan women and their ambivalent identity along the Thai-Burmese border.

Leong H. Liew is Malaysian by birth and Associate Professor in the School of International Business and Asian Studies, Griffith University, Brisbane, Australia. An economist, he gained his BEc and PhD from Monash University, Melbourne. He has published widely on East and Southeast Asian matters, especially in the economic field. His publications include some thirty articles in refereed journals and book chapters. His books include, as author, *The Chinese Economy in Transition: From Plan to Market* (Edward Elgar, 1997) and, as editor jointly with C.L. Chiou, *Uncertain Future: Taiwan–Hong Kong–China Relations in the Aftermath of the Return of Hong Kong to Chinese Sovereignty* (Aldershot: Ashgate, 2000).

Bertil Lintner is a senior writer for the *Far Eastern Economic Review* and the *Wall Street Journal*. He also writes for the Swedish daily newspaper *Svenska Dagbladet* and *Jane's Intelligence Review* in the United Kingdom. Lintner was born in Sweden but has been in Asia since 1975 (and in Thailand since 1980) and is a recognized expert on ethnic minorities, insurgencies and narcotics in Southeast and South Asia. He has written five books about Burma, including *Burma in Revolt: Opium and Insurgency Since 1948* (Bangkok: White Lotus, Boulder: Westview, 1994), which tells the story of the ethnic and communist insurgency in Burma, and the intertwined Golden Triangle opium trade. His sixth and latest book, *Blood Brothers: Crime, Business and Politics in Asia* (Sydney: Allen & Unwin, 2002) covers organized crime and the Asia-Pacific region. He is married to Hseng Noung Lintner, a Shan national from Burma, and they have one daughter. They now live in Chiang Mai in northern Thailand.

Colin Mackerras is Foundation Professor in the School of International Business and Asian Studies, Griffith University, Brisbane, Australia. He has written numerous books and scholarly articles on Chinese politics, history and culture, especially on its minority nationalities, theatre and international relations. Among his many books are *China's Ethnic Minorities and Globalisation* (London: RoutledgeCurzon, 2003), *China's Minority Cultures, Identities and Integration since 1912* (Melbourne: Longman and New York: St Martin's Press, 1995), and *China's Minorities, Integration and Modernization in the Twentieth Century* (Hong Kong: Oxford University Press, 1994). He is the editor-in-chief of the journal *Asian Ethnicity*, which comes out three times a year from Taylor & Francis in the United Kingdom.

R.J. May is a Senior Fellow in the Department of Political and Social Change, Research School of Pacific and Asian Studies, and convenor of the Centre for Conflict and Post-Conflict Studies, Asia-Pacific at the Australian National University. He is an associate of the Peter Gowing Memorial Center, Dansalan College, Marawi City in the Philippines and has authored or edited numerous books, book chapters and articles on the politics of the Philippines, Papua New Guinea, and comparative ethnic conflict.

Jan Ovesen is Associate Professor of Anthropology in the Department of Cultural Anthropology at Uppsala University, Sweden. He did fieldwork in Afghanistan in the 1970s, in Burkina Faso in the 1980s and, since 1993, he has been engaged in anthropological research and consultancy work in Laos and Cambodia.

A. Terry Rambo is a Professor of the Center for Southeast Asian Studies, Kyoto University, and was previously the East-West Center's Representative in Vietnam. An anthropologist (PhD, University of Hawaii), he has carried out extensive field research in Vietnam and Malaysia. Major publications include *The Challenges of Highland Development in Vietnam* (Honolulu, HI: East-West Center, 1995), *Too Many People, Too Little Land: The Human Ecology of a Wet Rice-Growing Village in the Red River Delta of Vietnam* (Honolulu, HI: East-West Center, Program on Environment, 1993) and *Ethnic Diversity and the Control of Natural Resources in Southeast Asia* (Michigan: Center for South and Southeast Asian Studies, University of Michigan, 1988).

Kirsten Refsing is Professor and Head of the Department of Japanese Studies, The University of Hong Kong. She earned her BA, MA and PhD in Japanese studies at the University of Copenhagen, Denmark. In 1986, she further earned the Danish Post-doctoral Degree of Philosophy for her book *The Ainu Language: The Morphology and Syntax of the Shizunai Dialect*. Her recent publications include a series of twenty-five volumes entitled *The Ainu Library* (Richmond, Surrey: Curzon, 1996, 1998, 2000, 2002), which presents and analyses early Western writings on the Ainu language and culture.

Ing-Britt Trankell is Reader in Cultural Anthropology at Uppsala University, Sweden. She did her doctoral research in Northern Thailand in 1981–3 and, since the mid-1990s, has done research in Laos and Cambodia. Her publications include *On the Road in Laos: An Anthropological Study of Road Construction and Rural Communities* (Uppsala: Dept of Cultural Anthropology, Uppsala University, 1993); and as co-editor, *Facets of Power and its Limitations: Political Culture in Southeast Asia* (Uppsala: Dept of Cultural Anthropology, Uppsala University, 1998).

Preface

This book aims to impart general information and insights into issues relating to ethnicity in East and Southeast Asia. Other than the Introduction, all chapters are based on political nation-states in the contemporary world. It is not designed as a path-breaking study, but does aim to provide a scholarly coverage that takes account of the main new ideas on this controversial topic, and individual authors may be presenting new material. The authors hope that it will prove useful and interesting to the general reader, including journalists, workers in government and undergraduate students. All chapters except the Introduction include guidance on 'further reading'.

The book takes up one particular part of the world, namely East and Southeast Asia. There are several reasons for this choice. One is that the area is a particularly important part of the world for its large area and population, and likely to become more so in the twenty-first century. Second, the comparative literature concerning ethnicity in various countries of East and Southeast Asia is very sparse, most of the existing works dealing with such regions as Europe or America. Third, East and Southeast Asia are countries with extremely interesting and important ethnic mosaics.

Although not all topics are covered in every chapter, there are several major themes in this book. These are:

- the development of ethnicity in East and Southeast Asia;
- state policies towards ethnic minorities of the various countries of East and Southeast Asia, as well as realities of the lives of ethnic minorities;
- some discussions of individual ethnic minorities, and/or groups of ethnic minorities; and
- ethnic conflict within states.

The time focus is the period since the end of the Second World War, with the precise time coverage depending on the country. However, the past continues to weigh heavily and in a subject of this kind it is totally inappropriate to ignore earlier history altogether. In general, the coverage is thickest for the last decades of the twentieth century.

It is my pleasure to thank my fellow contributors, who have been very cooperative and professional. I also offer my appreciation to Mark Selden, the general editor of the series to which this book belongs. His help and support have been very useful in the compilation of this volume.

Professor Colin Mackerras
February 2003

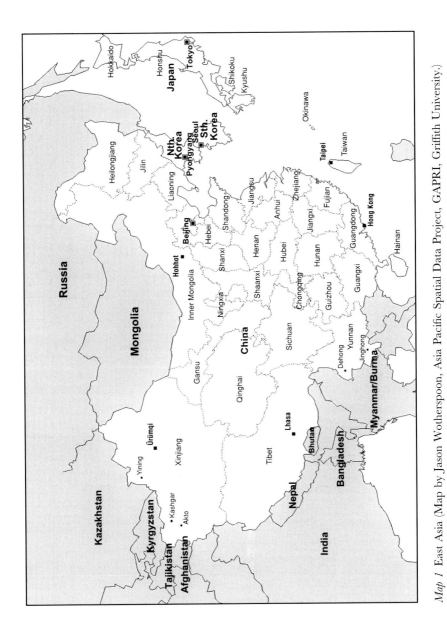

Map 1 East Asia (Map by Jason Wotherspoon, Asia Pacific Spatial Data Project, GAPRI, Griffith University.)

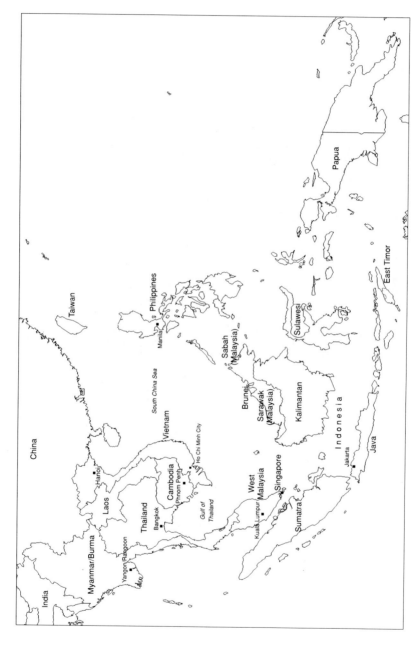

Map 2 Southeast Asia (Map by Jason Wotherspoon, Asia Pacific Spatial Data Project, GAPRI, Griffith University.)

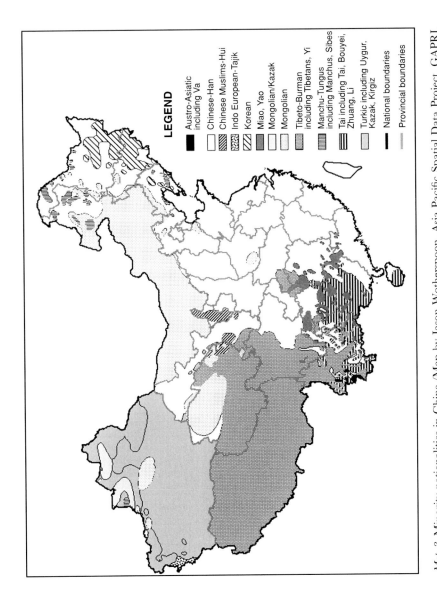

Map 3 Minority nationalities in China (Map by Jason Wotherspoon, Asia Pacific Spatial Data Project, GAPRI, Griffith University.)

LEGEND

- Austro-Asiatic including Va
- Chinese-Han
- Chinese Muslims-Hui
- Indo European-Tajik
- Korean
- Miao, Yao
- Mongolian/Kazak
- Mongolian
- Tibeto-Burman including Tibetans, Yi
- Manchu-Tungus including Manchus, Sibes
- Tai including Tai, Bouyei, Zhuang, Li
- Turkic including Uygur, Kazak, Kirgiz
- National boundaries
- Provincial boundaries

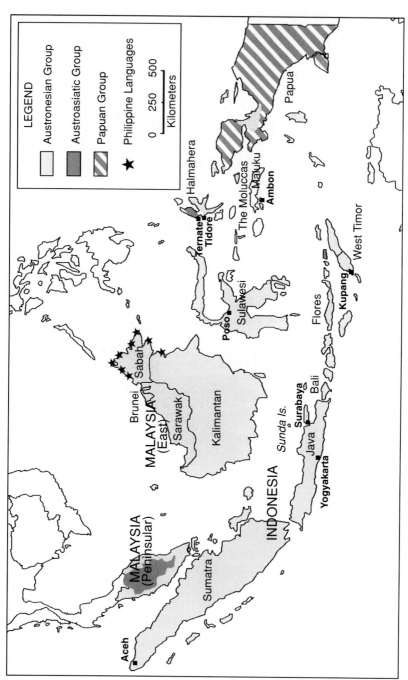

Map 4 Ethnolinguistic map of Indonesia and Malaysia (Map by Jason Wotherspoon, Asia Pacific Spatial Data Project, GAPRI, Griffith University.)

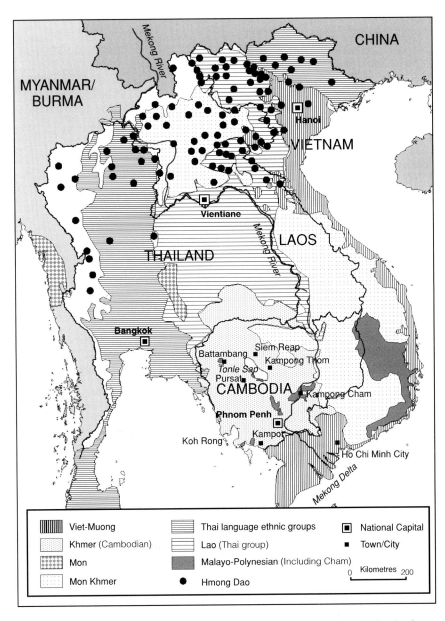

Map 5 Ethnolinguistic map of Vietnam, Laos, Cambodia and Thailand (Map by Jason Wotherspoon, Asia Pacific Spatial Data Project, GAPRI, Griffith University.)

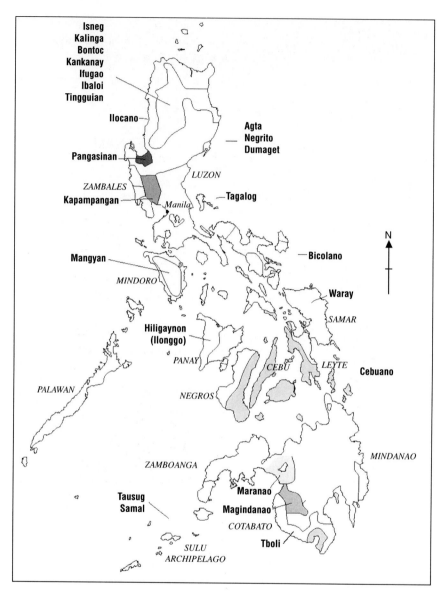

Isneg
Kalinga
Bontoc
Kankanay
Ifugao
Ibaloi
Tingguian

Ilocano

Agta
Negrito
Dumaget

Pangasinan

LUZON

ZAMBALES

Kapampangan

Manila

Tagalog

N

Mangyan

Bicolano

MINDORO

Waray

SAMAR

Hiligaynon
(Ilonggo)

PANAY

CEBU

LEYTE

Cebuano

PALAWAN

NEGROS

MINDANAO

ZAMBOANGA

Tausug
Samal

Maranao

Magindanao

COTABATO

Tboli

SULU
ARCHIPELAGO

Map 6 Language map of the Philippines (Map by Alan Robson, Australian National University.)

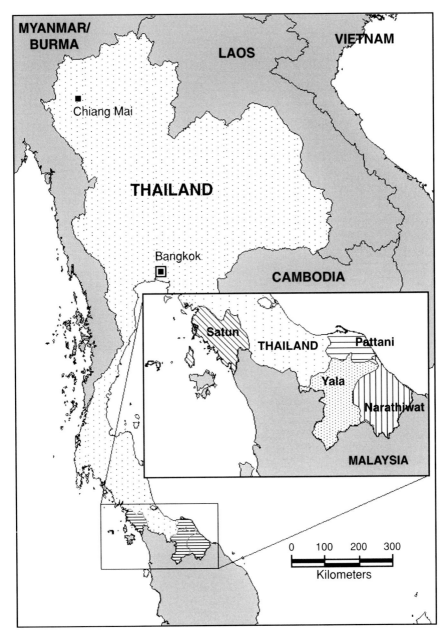

Map 7 Thailand (Map by Jason Wotherspoon, Asia Pacific Spatial Data Project, GAPRI, Griffith University.)

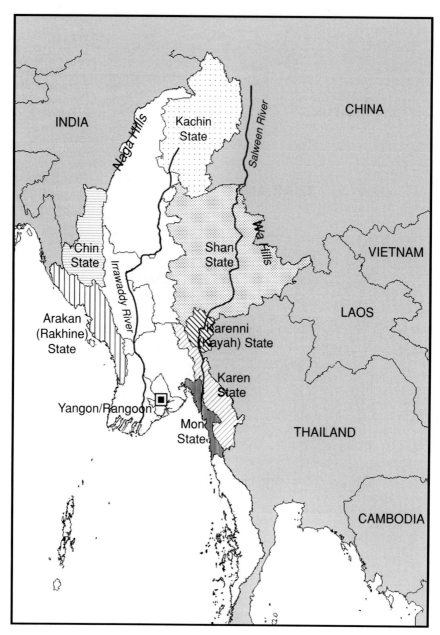

Map 8 Ethnolinguistic divisions of Myanmar/Burma (Map by Jason Wotherspoon, Asia Pacific Spatial Data Project, GAPRI, Griffith University.)

1 Introduction

Colin Mackerras

With the collapse of the Soviet Union at the end of 1991 and the end of the Cold War at about the same time, the ideological divide between Marxism and capitalism lost its major impetus as an arena of world conflict. Although a few countries, notably China and Vietnam, were still run by political parties claiming to adhere to Marxism-Leninism, they too were already on the track of market reform, and did not pose nearly the same challenge to liberal capitalism as had been the case during the decades of the Cold War. Liberal capitalism, as represented mainly by the countries of North America and Western Europe, seemed triumphant. Many countries formerly socialist or neutral went over to the side of capitalism, some though by no means all of them adopting the form of government most strongly advocated by the main capitalist states, namely liberal democracy. The United States and its allies had won the Cold War.

Ethnicity and ethnic conflict in the contemporary world

However, it did not take long for other issues to replace the ideological ones to stoke the fires of conflict. Among these issues, a particularly important one was ethnic divisions and tensions. Of course, these were hardly new when the Cold War ended. In many places throughout the world they had been endemic for decades or centuries. What shocked the world, however, was that the splintering of states like the Soviet Union and Yugoslavia involved terrible ethnic warfare and conflict. When Yugoslavia, which many had once considered a model both of socialism and ethnic harmony, split apart, several wars broke out in succession throughout the 1990s. The most serious was in Bosnia-Herzegovina. No sooner did this country declare itself independent on 5 April 1992 than an extremely savage war broke out between Serb, Croat and Muslim communities, which had earlier appeared to get on with each other reasonably, if not very, well. The war saw human rights abuses of a severity not seen in Europe since the end of the Second World War, and lasted until 1995.

Meanwhile, ethnic conflict seemed to spread to many other parts of the globe. The worst case was in the tiny Central African state of Rwanda, where the minority Tutsis came under attack from the majority Hutus, who comprised about 90 per cent of the total population. Ethnic war amounting to genocide raged there from April to June 1994. It is estimated that throughout 1994 over one million people were killed in genocide or civil war, with even larger numbers fleeing into neighbouring countries. According to the 1991 census, the total population of Rwanda was 7,164,994, but a 1996 estimate showed only about 5.1 million.[1] The conflict had taken the lives of a gigantic proportion of the total population.

Although Asia saw no example as savage as the Rwanda genocide or the war in Bosnia-Herzegovina, it was by no means free of ethnic conflict. In Central Asia, several wars followed the collapse of the Soviet Union, including some fuelled by ethnic hostilities. The independence of Tajikistan, which formerly belonged to the Soviet Union, was followed by a very bitter war lasting from 1992 to 1997. In Indonesia the small territory of East Timor fought a long and violent secessionist struggle. The fall of Suharto in 1998 led on to its independence, though only after further violence and bitter conflict, while anti-Chinese rioting swept Java, ethnic and sectarian violence erupted in several parts of Indonesia, notably Aceh and the Moluccas, and the long-simmering independence struggle of Papua grew in intensity. Myanmar has seen a whole series of insurgencies based on ethnicity. Indeed, very few of the countries of East and Southeast Asia have been completely free of ethnic conflict or tensions.

In Sri Lanka, the Tamils have long been struggling for a separate homeland, and ethnic violence amounting to civil war began in the 1980s, continuing with enormous bloodshed and casualties until a ceasefire came into effect in February 2002. One of the features of this civil war was the Tamil use of suicide bombing, a factor that has become a prominent feature of world news since terrorists hijacked aircraft and flew them into the World Trade Center in New York on 11 September 2001, destroying the two towers of the Center and killing not only themselves but nearly 3,000 other people as well.

Despite examples such as the Tamil war in Sri Lanka, most ethnic conflict does not involve war. One could cite many examples from the countries discussed in the present book. Xinjiang, Tibet and Inner Mongolia have seen periodic ethnic rioting since the 1980s, but it has been sporadic and hardly amounts to anything one could describe as warfare. In Indonesia, we find no generalized civil war, despite the severity of the ethnic problems in some places.

The fact that ethnic conflict has to a large extent replaced ideological conflict since the end of the Cold War makes it of enormous importance for understanding the contemporary world. Despite the fascinating ethnic tapestry of East and Southeast Asia, the region has rarely been studied through the lens of ethnicity and ethnic conflict. The importance of the topic and the lack of literature covering it are the main reasons for writing this book.

There are several extremely important general issues that flow from the rise of ethnic conflict in the wake of the end of the Cold War. One of them is the way dominant ethnic groups look down on, discriminate against and even persecute minorities. In most of the countries discussed in this book, there is a tendency for the majority ethnic group to conceptualize the nation-state with its own culture as the highest and most important, with the minorities holding the function of 'essentializing' the majority, as one scholar has described the relations between Han and minorities in China.[2] Many other examples illustrate the point, such as Kinh Vietnamese nationalism in relation to minorities and Japanese nationalism with respect to Koreans, *burakumin* or Ainu.

One way in which this majority nationalism often expresses itself is through migration into minority areas. We shall see several examples of this phenomenon in the pages of this volume, such as in China and Vietnam. The majority may see such migration as both sensible and their right. After all, the minority areas are, on the whole, much less thickly populated than the majority ones, and this is 'our' country, so obviously it is fine for us to send our people there. Also, the majority is more advanced and can render useful assistance to the minority areas in economic and other terms. On the other hand, the minorities may not see it that way at all. They may think their land is being taken away from them, and that the 'majority nationality' is more like an invader than a friendly assistant. What is perfectly clear is that these migrations of majority peoples into minority areas often cause immense resentment.

Another issue, which is to some extent fuelled by this chauvinism of the majority, is the growth of 'ethnonationalism'. This means the pride and sense of identity that people feel in belonging to a particular ethnic group within a larger nation-state. Nationalism has long been a feature of world politics. During and after the Second World War it was a major factor leading to the independence of a host of colonies throughout Asia and Africa. And nationalism is still very much alive at the beginning of the twenty-first century. But since the end of the Cold War, ethnonationalism has come to the fore. In other words, the nationalism of ethnic minorities within larger nation-states has become a factor, in some cases rivalling the nationalism of nation-states themselves.[3]

Ethnonationalism leads not only to a strengthening of ethnic identities. In many places it has also resulted in a strong feeling that ethnic minorities wish to separate themselves from the larger nation-state and set up their own independent nation-state. Generally, the larger nation-state begins by resisting this pressure, because no state wishes to accept division, and all of them fear that if one ethnic group secedes, then others will wish to follow suit. The examples of the Soviet Union and Yugoslavia suggest that there is some basis to this fear. On the other hand, the separation of East Timor from Indonesia has not so far led to a cascade of further independent nation-states once part of Indonesia. To be sure, Chapter 4 shows that there are several wishing to follow the example of East Timor.

States usually respond to attempts at secession by sending in troops to suppress the disturbances, and Indonesia is among several states considered in this book to fall into that category. Even democratic states sometimes react in this way, as the case of British troops sent into Northern Ireland shows. These wars sometimes do lead to the independence of a new nation-state. Prominent examples are Eritrea in northeastern Africa and East Timor in the southeast corner of Asia. In Eritrea, independence from Ethiopia and sovereignty for the new state was proclaimed in May 1993 after victory in a long and bloody war. In this case, bitter wars followed with Ethiopia. East Timor formally became a sovereign state in May 2002 after centuries as a Portuguese colony and twenty-four years as part of Indonesia.

Wars nation-states regard as secessionist, but which the ethnic proponents call independence struggles, do not necessarily lead to the result either party desires. A prominent example is the Tamils of Sri Lanka. The military suppression of the Tamil independence movement by the Sri Lankan state led in 2002 to a political compromise in which a ceasefire led to negotiations implying a form of autonomy that left both sides without their basic goals satisfied. On the whole, the only guarantee of such wars is that many innocent people will get killed.

In the modern world, populations have also had a strong tendency to become more mixed than was the case in the past. Majority populations in large nation-states have tended to move into the areas inhabited by ethnic minorities and tried to dominate them. What this means is that new nation-states that establish themselves on part of an older and much larger nation-state or empire, are usually much more ethnically mixed than the same area had been decades or centuries earlier. Even the emergence of a new nation-state does not foreclose the possibility of renewed ethnic conflict. We have already noted the example of Bosnia-Herzegovina, and many others could be cited.

Since the dissolution of the Soviet Union, the process of national splitting has mostly been violent. The most significant exception to this pattern in the 1990s was Czechoslovakia, which divided peacefully into the Czech Republic and Slovakia in January 1993.

It is necessary to emphasize that most ethnic minorities throughout the world are not at all interested in independence. They simply want a better deal for the people belonging to their ethnic group. They want better jobs, and more of the good things that a decent economy brings. They may feel discrimination, and there are many examples covered in the present book, but the solution is not necessarily independence. They may seek better policy and treatment from the states where they live. We shall see many illustrative examples in the chapters of this book.

One alternative option to independence, and fitting into the category of better policy, is a system of autonomy for ethnic minorities. While these do not necessarily solve the problems of ethnic conflict or discrimination, they can represent and be part of a process of negotiation between states and ethnic minorities that is highly preferable to open violence and fighting. Diverse forms of autonomy have been tried in various parts of the world,[4] and a few are considered in the present book.

The discourse of rights

The role of ethnicity in public policy and its potential for conflict amply demonstrate its significance in the contemporary world. Another reason why ethnicity is so important is because of its association with the discourse of rights. The strengthening of human rights discourse in international relations was undoubtedly one of the most important features of the late twentieth century.

Discourse in human rights took many forms, including civil, political and democratic rights.[5] The United Nations sponsored the World Conference on Human Rights, held in Vienna in 1993. In the diplomacy of the last remaining superpower, the United States, human rights came to assume a major place in its relations with other countries. In the cases of quite a few countries, such as China, they came to be a highly significant factor in bilateral relations. At the same time, human rights came to occupy a far more prominent role in the discourse of commentary on international relations, including in scholarly literature.

Of course, there is much disagreement over the nature and ideals of human rights. Two prominent schools of thought are the universalist or individualistic and the culturalist or communitarian. The former is dominant among relevant non-government organizations like Amnesty International and Western social human rights movements, and also Western governments. It also enjoys considerable support among ordinary people, including journalists and scholars, outside the West. It argues that human rights are universal and should focus on all people as individuals, because they are human beings.

The culturalist or communitarian view, espoused by many governments in Asia and elsewhere, and with considerable social support both in their own countries and outside, argues that it is more sensible to see human rights not in terms of the rights of individuals but of communities as a whole. What matters most is not what happens to individuals but to large groups of people. This view argues that the universalist attitude, having grown out of Western experience, takes insufficient account of the culture of Asian countries, and the unusually difficult histories to which they have been subjected, often by the European powers and the United States themselves.

There is a strong dimension of power in this debate. Proponents of the universalist view tend to see governments arguing the alternative opinion for opportunistic purposes, especially to maintain their own authority and grip on power. On the other hand, advocates of the communitarian viewpoint often charge universalists with cultural imperialism.[6] By its very nature the universalist approach is applicable everywhere, making those who depart from it open to criticism on the grounds of human rights abuses. Because many Asian governments advocate the culturalist or communitarian view, many have dubbed this controversy 'the Asian values debate'.[7]

Of all forms of human rights the one with the greatest relevance to the present book is obviously ethnic rights. These attracted enormous scholarly and political attention during the late years of the twentieth century and continue to do so in the twenty-first. The United Nations declared 1993 the International Year of the World's Indigenous Peoples, showing the importance the world body attached to this issue. The collapse of the Soviet Union and of the ideological divide between liberal capitalism and Marxism-Leninism was one reason for the attention given to ethnic matters. Another was the renewed struggle against racism, symbolized by the continuing attacks on apartheid in South Africa, the struggle attaining a triumphant victory with the election of Nelson Mandela as the first black President on 9 May 1994. Meanwhile, revulsion against the Holocaust of the Jews under the explicitly racist German Nazi regime lost none of its momentum, even though it had occurred half a century before.

The scholarly discourse that accompanied these political developments adopted various views. Although most scholars were very happy at the victory of Nelson Mandela and favoured the establishment of multiculturalism in democratic countries, many remained deeply sceptical of the intentions of states, even democratic ones. There was a common belief that the changes had not gone nearly far enough towards accommodating minority rights.

One important area is the political one. Support in Western countries for secessionist movements in other parts of the world has tended to be strong, with human rights activists loud in their view that minorities are being suppressed. The implication is clearly that Western governments should support such independence movements. In the 1990s, a very prominent example was the movement in Chechnya. Long ruled as part of Russia, the Chechnyans actually declared independence in November 1991, but brought down on their heads the ire and savage intervention of successive Russian governments, including those of Boris Yeltsin (president of the independent Russian Federation from 1991 to 1999) and his successor Vladimir Putin, who became president in 2000.

Support for independence movements is frequently promoted by diasporas living in the West or somewhere else outside their original homeland, but hailing from the region seeking independence. Such diasporas often collect money for the independence cause. In some cases, support is much more obvious and widespread than in others. A very good example of a people with an independence movement supported very strongly outside the homeland is the Tibetans. The Dalai Lama lives in India, but frequently visits Western and other countries, where he enjoys enormous veneration. Tibetans living in the West and India are a major element providing inspiration and support for the Tibetan independence movement as it exists outside Tibet itself.

Scholars frequently see it as a task to provide an intellectual basis for the idea of secession or sovereignty of minorities, or for individual separatist claims. There are issues that deal with law, morality, cultural separateness, land rights and other matters of very great importance for a people seeking independence.[8] Scholars, activists and members of diasporas frequently overlap, with universities being common sites of activism on behalf of ethnic rights and independence movements.

It is not only politics that is so important. Another area of scholarly discourse is culture. A common complaint against states is that they suppress minority cultures. One prominent scholar in the field of ethnic rights, Will Kymlicka, has argued that the liberal tradition was too individualist to accord any status to ethnic groups that lay between the individual and the state, but also sharply criticized socialism as hostile to minority rights because of its commitment to internationalism. He continues:

So it seems that liberal individualism and socialist internationalism have both led to a denial of the rights of minority cultures. In both cases, however, this denial is exacerbated by an ethnocentric denigration of small cultures, and a belief that progress requires assimilating them into larger cultures.[9]

The point about culture shows that the dimension of the discussion was in no way confined to politics and matters such as political independence. It extended to all the facets of minority peoples. In fact, despite the views of those like Kymlicka, most Western and quite a few other countries have tried to show some sympathy for, and allow some space to, the cultures of minorities living within their country. Where he is definitely right, however, is that minority cultures are nowhere near becoming part of the mainstream of national cultures.

One of the most important of all sources of division is the inequitable distribution of wealth and resources. The discourse of rights has clearly placed a great deal of weight on equality. And it tends strongly to be minorities who are the poorest members of societies. Of course there are exceptions to this, such as in South Africa; and in Southeast Asia minorities of Chinese are not notably poor by the national standards of the countries where they reside, and even include the richest people in some countries. But it still remains true that minorities bitterly resent the perception and/or reality of being largely shut out from the benefits of economic growth. And if urban minorities are less able to get good jobs than the majority population, ethnic conflict is likely to be inflamed.

The destruction of the World Trade Center and damage done to the Pentagon on 11 September 2001, as well as the succeeding 'war against terrorism', added several new dimensions to the issue of minority rights. They can be summed up as follows:

- Both in the West and elsewhere, they put virtually all independence struggles involving violence under suspicion of being terrorist.
- They made more or less any Islamic movement suspect along with Islamic fundamentalism.
- They won more support for powerful states over non-government or social agencies.
- They highlighted suicide attacks, making them more or less inseparable from terrorism.

Terrorism involves targeting civilians violently for political purposes. But the war against terrorism did not solve the traditional paradox that one person's terrorist is another person's freedom-fighter. What it did do, however, was to blur the gap between the two, a trend that did not help those engaged in violent struggles of any kind.

In launching its attack against terrorism, the American administration made a careful attempt to distinguish between mainstream Islam and that kind of fundamentalist Islam led by Osama bin Laden and his al-Qaida network that had been responsible for the destruction of the World Trade Center and damage to the Pentagon. It was also careful to state that the war against terrorism did not justify any oppression of minorities. However, the fact that the great majority of those attacked as terrorists were in fact Muslims could not help but blur the lines between terrorism on the one hand and Islam and Islamic ethnic struggles on the other.

The war against terrorism aroused great divisions among Muslims. Though many supported the campaign, many others saw it as aimed against themselves. Certainly, the war fanned anti-American and anti-Western feeling among many Muslims and Muslim ethnic groups. The rise of suspicion in the West, especially in the United States, of people in their own countries 'with Middle Eastern appearance' did nothing to dispel this feeling. Not long after the 11 September incident, the United States introduced new immigration rules that appeared to discriminate against Muslims, especially men aged between 16 and 45.[10] In the international arena, the continuing and worsening conflict in the Middle East between the Palestinian Arabs and the Jews could only intensify mutual hostility between Islamic and non-Islamic peoples.

The discourse on human and ethnic rights had been distinctly hostile to states since the 1990s. The era of globalization led many to suspect that the role of the state in international relations was in decline. One school of thought even believed a new era was dawning in which 'the state' would vanish as a major player on the international stage.

But the war against terrorism saw states cooperating against an essentially non-state force in a way that had not happened for a very long time. It saw Muslim states like Pakistan take part in the war against terrorism even as many of the people there continued to support Muslim fundamentalism, while the Indian state continued to accuse the Pakistan government of involvement in terrorism. It seemed as though the state as an institution benefited considerably from the destruction of the World Trade Center.

Human rights activists continued to warn against using the horror of the 11 September incidents as a reason for clamping down on ethnic dissent, especially that by Muslim ethnic groups. Chinese attacks on separatism by the Islamic Uygur ethnic minorities have been a particular target of their criticism relevant to this book. But all over the world they found themselves more at odds with states, including democratic ones, than they had been before. States introduced unnecessarily draconian anti-terrorist laws, which many Muslims saw as primarily aimed at themselves, and won much more support from their own people than would have been the case before 2001.

Because the terrorists who carried out the attacks were prepared to kill themselves as they flew the aircraft they had hijacked into the twin towers of the World Trade Center and into the Pentagon, it was unavoidable that the issue of suicide bombing should lift itself enormously into the public eye. This was particularly the case when a series of suicide bombings occurred in Israel and elsewhere, all carried out by Islamic resistance groups, even including young women. Suicide terrorism was nothing new in 2001. But its profile certainly rose enormously as a result of the 11 September incidents.

What's in a name? Some definitions and concepts

Various words and names have been given to the groups of people that are the subject of this book. Most of them have implications and are worth discussing here.

The term 'indigenous peoples' has come to hold a good deal of currency in everyday usage and international law.[11] As noted above, the United Nations General Assembly declared the year 1993 the International Year of the World's Indigenous Peoples, which means that the United Nations has accepted the term as valid. However, it also has some problems. It was on the American continent that 'indigenous' movements sprang up, moving on to the international agenda in the 1980s. The participants in the United Nations Working Group on Indigenous Populations in 1985 were mainly from North America and Australia, with some attendance from Central and South America, only later taking on much broader participation from Asia.[12] The term 'indigenous' peoples is clearly appropriate to colonized countries where large numbers of colonizers have settled, such as America and Australia. But are not the French indigenous to France, the Japanese to Japan, or the Chinese to China?

Precisely for this reason, in recent and United Nations discourse, the term 'indigenous peoples' has come to carry connotations not only of place of origin but of power relations as well. In other words, the term specifically excludes majority or dominant peoples, such as the French, the Japanese or the Chinese, but only includes peoples considered to have been exploited or oppressed, or driven by conquerors from their native land. In this understanding, the Japanese cannot be considered an 'indigenous people'. While I acknowledge the currency of the term, I have serious reservations about it, for the reasons given above.

Of course, whether one considers a people 'indigenous' depends on how far back in the past one wants to go. History has seen conquests by outside peoples in most parts of the globe, and these have usually seen emergent mixtures of cultures and ethnicities. The French adopted much of their culture from the Roman conquest of Gaul and from the Christian religion they inherited from the Romans. There were pre-existing peoples and cultures, but they were largely destroyed through Roman domination over a long period. Because even being indigenous involves judgements over precisely how long a people has lived in a particular location, some have adopted the term 'first nations' as a sign of claims to ownership dating back to an indefinite past.

In countries governed by political parties espousing Marxism-Leninism, the term 'nationality' is in common usage. It derives from a definition Stalin put forward in 1913. He described a nationality as 'a historically constituted, stable community of people, formed on the basis of a common language, territory, economic life, and psychological make-up manifested in a common culture'. Moreover, he was specific that the nationality ceases to be so if even one of the characteristics is lacking.[13] The term 'nationality' is confusing in the sense that in English a person's 'nationality' is also a legally valid term denoting country of citizenship. A 'nationality' is not necessarily a minority, as a result of which countries with Marxist-Leninist parties in control usually adopt the term 'minority nationality'. While this is a perfectly reasonable term if defined, it is not used much outside such countries.

Among the countries under consideration in this book, three are still ruled by Marxist-Leninist parties. However, it is very striking that the official understanding of the term 'nationality' is slightly different between China and Vietnam. The Vietnamese authorities consider 'a self-conscious identification as belonging to that specific group' as a criterion for belonging to a nationality (see Chapter 7), whereas the Chinese do not.

One term that is not in general use nowadays is 'race'. The reason is because it implies giving first priority to biology, and most specialists see no sense or validity in categorizing peoples in such a way. The term has connections with the term 'racism', which the world almost universally regards as among the greatest of evils. It is, however, worth remembering that the term 'race' was once in very common usage. Moreover, as noted in Chapter 6, it remains in common use in Singapore, where it is the preferred term of the Singaporean government, and to some extent in Malaysia.

Another term that is much less used at the beginning of the twenty-first century than was once the case is 'tribe'. This is because it has overtones of the primitive and can be seen as insulting. However, there are contexts where the term has valid use. One instance is in Thailand, where some minorities are referred to as 'hill tribes'.

The term 'ethnicity' or 'ethnic' group has become very widespread in recent literature. However, some even complain about these terms. One view has it that the term 'ethnicity' has a ring of quaintness to it. As Malcolm Chapman puts it, 'it [ethnicity] has settled into the vocabulary as a marker of strangeness and unfamiliarity'.[14] However, I do not accept this view, believing it an unreasonable and one-sided view of a term that in most contexts is perfectly respectable. Where the term is used in this book, it certainly does not imply anything 'quaint'.

The term 'minority' is a useful one and is usually quite applicable. However, it does have a couple of disadvantages. One is that unless it is further specified, such as by adding 'ethnic' in front of it, it could refer to different kinds of minorities, for example people who hold an unpopular opinion. Another issue is that in some countries there is no ethnic group that forms more than half the population, so that all peoples would necessarily become minorities.

Some peoples do not accept the tag of 'ethnic minority' and consider it demeaning and insulting. It seems likely that many Tibetans, to take but one example, do not accept the discourse that locates them as an 'ethnic minority' within China. Rather, some see their homeland as occupied by a foreign power. Such an understanding can be the basis for an independence movement. There are also Tibetans who see their best future in terms of a higher level of autonomy within the People's Republic of China (PRC) than exists at present.

Japan presents a case of a social group whom people regard as being outside the collectivity of Japanese-ness, and consequently non-Japanese, but who are not actually different ethnically from the Japanese. These are the *burakumin*, discussed in Chapter 3 on Japan. Kirsten Refsing claims there that mainstream Japanese regard these people as 'ritually impure because of traditional occupations to do with slaughtering of animals, leatherwork and night-soil collection, which required the people involved to live apart from other citizens'. They could be described as a minority, but not an ethnic one.

'Ethnic group' is a vague and general term. In this discussion, I have deliberately stated that some terms are more appropriate to some countries than to others, and it is not my intention to adopt a universal term that all chapters will unswervingly follow. However, I believe that the terms 'ethnic group' or 'ethnic minority' are valid in the great majority of circumstances.

The following is a definition of the term 'ethnic group':

> An ethnic group is defined here as a collectivity within a larger society having real or putative common ancestry, memories of a shared historical past, and a cultural focus on one or more symbolic elements defined as the epitome of their peoplehood. Examples of such symbolic elements are: kinship patterns, physical contiguity (as in localism or sectionalism), religious affiliation, language or dialect forms, tribal affiliation, nationality, phenotypical features, or any combination of these. A necessary accompaniment is some consciousness of kind among members of the group.[15]

Despite the differences in terminology, most of the features of an 'ethnic group' contained in this definition apply across the board. Shared language or dialect, religion, kinship, history, common ancestry, and physical contiguity or common territory are to be expected in the case of a recognizable group of people.

There are, however, problems. In the modern world, diasporas have become very common and often adopt the language of their new home. Diasporas by their very nature do not share any common territory with the people they have left, yet still belong to the same ethnic group. In the modern world, not all people of the same ethnic group necessarily share a religion. One does have to exercise care in being too rigid about applying definitions. In my opinion, the inclusion of the warning in the definition of an 'ethnic group' given above, about 'any combination' of the features it has listed, is very apt.

One very interesting feature of this definition is the emphasis on consciousness. If a group of people wishes to regard itself as belonging to a particular ethnic group, then that is one reason why others should accept their claim. In the contemporary world, the emphasis on consciousness has grown considerably. In many parts of the world where once people might have hidden their ethnic identity through fear of discrimination, the trend is now in the opposite direction. In other words, people point to their own ethnic identity with pride and seek out membership of a minority ethnic group, even if their claim looks suspect to outside observers.

Other definitions with enough significance to warrant mention here are those that express state policies and underpin relations between majorities and ethnic minorities. Like those for ethnic groups, these terms have ramifications and imply value judgements. One term is 'assimilation', which in one definition 'implies that members of minority groups have absorbed the characteristics of the dominant group to the exclusion of their own and become indistinguishable from members of the majority'. This definition is neutral, but at one time many people regarded 'assimilation' as a good thing if the dominant group was the superior teacher or the home group, rather than the inferior minorities or the immigrants. Many thought that their own culture was superior and that both minorities and immigrants should accept it, losing their own culture and becoming 'assimilated'. Since the last few decades of the twentieth century, however, more and more societies have come to eschew 'assimilation' in favour of other patterns in which minorities or immigrants maintain their own culture and add it to the culture of the whole society.

The term 'multiculturalism' expresses this idea in general terms, though different countries have varied understandings of precisely what it means. Another term is pluralism, a majority–minority relationship or state policy 'in which the various ethnic groups follow their own system and maintain their own characteristics quite freely in a relationship of mutual interdependence, respect and equality'.[16] This is the most liberal and democratic of the various majority–minority relationships and state policies. It also raises difficult questions in cases where border ethnic groups have a long-standing hostility to the majority, based on discrimination and wish to secede, because states of this kind generally think that an excessively liberal policy will simply result in more demands from minorities. Still, experience has also shown that, where there is a modicum of goodwill and trust, there is much to be said for negotiations between majorities and minorities on the basis of mutual respect and equality. The problem is to build up such goodwill and trust in the first place.

A policy and majority–minority relationship that in some ways sits between the two discussed above is 'integration', which one scholar has defined as 'the process whereby ethnic groups come to shift their loyalties, expectations, and political activities toward a new center'.[17] There is no necessary implication of repression, such as frequently exists in 'assimilation', nor does the process leave complete freedom to the minorities, as implied in 'pluralism'. The definition takes account of the desire of all states, especially those coming out of a colonial or semi-colonial situation, that the minorities should relate well enough both with the majority and the state to build a viable political order and strong economy. Certainly, in a well 'integrated' state, one would expect the wish of minorities to secede to be weak or non-existent.

A perennial debate in many fields of scholarship is how many characteristics are essential to being a human being and how many are instilled into people through culture or education. Obviously, both 'nature' and 'nurture' are important, but the balance is very far from obvious. For ethnic groups the issue divides basically between those who favour an essentialist or primordial view and those who lean more towards instrumentalism or constructivism. The former opinion sees ethnic groups as based on an essential nature which goes back through the mists of time, while the latter sees them as more shaped by their surroundings and by forces outside their own ethnic group. Ethnonationalists are tempted to adhere to the primordialist view, because it emphasizes the distinctiveness and age of their culture. It also tends to glorify an age before the onslaught of colonialism, sometimes setting up an imaginary bright past that never corresponded to any historical reality. One of the problems with this view, however, is that it does not allow as much room for change as instrumentalism. In the modern world, change is more rapid and wide-ranging than at any time in the era preceding that of European colonialism. Moreover, the very process of modernization affects both states and minorities, as well as how both states and majorities relate to ethnic minorities.

Conclusion

There is no doubt about the importance of ethnicity in the contemporary world. After a period of comparative respite, it revived as an issue in the last decade or so of the twentieth century, largely because of the collapse of the Cold War based on the ideological divide between liberal capitalism and Marxism-Leninism. It brought with it far-reaching implications that were not obvious when the Cold War ended. Not all these implications are welcome to the main stakeholders in the international order, but what is clear is that ethnic issues have forced themselves into the consciousness of governments and peoples all over the world.

Ethnic questions are fraught with controversy. They are very difficult to handle, because the rights and wrongs are rarely obvious. Ethnic issues are also very important, and appear to be getting more so in the contemporary world. People feel very strongly about ethnic questions, especially those relating to their own ethnic identity. What flows from this is that, unless negotiations occur while there is still goodwill on both sides, ethnic disagreements can easily lead to conflict. The history of the world since the end of the Cold War suggests that such conflict can be extremely bitter and bloody, with even the victors facing extremely serious problems of poverty and state-building.

Notes

1 See the figures in Barry Turner (ed.), *The Statesman's Yearbook: The Politics, Cultures and Economies of the World 2002*, Houndmills, Basingstoke, Hampshire and New York: Palgrave Publishers, 2001, p. 1354.
2 Dru C. Gladney, 'Representing nationality in China: Refiguring majority/minority identities', *Journal of Asian Studies*, 1994, vol. 53, no. 1, p. 98.
3 For a major study of ethnonationalism, see W. Connor, *Ethnonationalism: The Quest for Understanding*, Princeton, NJ: Princeton University Press, 1994.
4 For one excellent account of this topic, see Yash Ghai (ed.), *Autonomy and Ethnicity: Negotiating Competing Claims in Multi-Ethnic States*, Cambridge Studies in Law and Society, Cambridge: Cambridge University Press, 2000. It deals with current autonomies as different from each other as India, China, South Africa and Spain, the 'failed autonomy' of Yugoslavia, and countries where ethnic minorities are 'seeking autonomy', such as Sri Lanka, Bougainville and Australia.

5 For a good, brief and simple run-down of issues connected with human rights, especially as applied in Asia, see Aat Vervoorn, *Re Orient: Change in Asian Societies*, Oxford: Oxford University Press, 2nd edn, 2002, pp. 64–81. The notes to this chapter, pp. 306–8, contain references to some major relevant material.

6 See William A. Callahan, 'Challenging the political order: Social movements', in Richard Maidment, David Goldblatt and Jeremy Mitchell (eds), *Governance in the Asia-Pacific*, London and New York: Routledge, in association with the Open University, 1998, pp. 165–6.

7 For one rundown of the controversy, see Stephanie Lawson, 'The culture of politics', in Richard Maidment and Colin Mackerras (eds), *Culture and Society in the Asia-Pacific*, London and New York: Routledge in association with the Open University, 1998, pp. 245–9. Lawson definitely stands on the 'universalist' side of the debate. See also Peter Van Ness (ed.), *Debating Human Rights: Critical Essays from the United States and Asia*, London, New York: Routledge, 1999.

8 See a good example in Allen Buchanan, 'The morality of secession', in Will Kymlicka (ed.), *The Rights of Minority Cultures*, Oxford: Oxford University Press, 1995, pp. 350–74.

9 Will Kymlicka, 'Introduction', in Will Kymlicka (ed.), *The Rights of Minority Cultures*, p. 5.

10 See Murray Hiebert, 'Less welcome', *Far Eastern Economic Review*, 25 July 2002, vol. 165, no. 29, p. 18.

11 See the discussion in Benedict Kingsbury, ' "Indigenous peoples" as an international legal concept', in R.H. Barnes, Andrew Gray and Benedict Kingsbury (eds), *Indigenous Peoples of Asia*, Monograph and Occasional Paper Series, No. 48, Michigan: Association of Asian Studies, 1995, pp. 13–34.

12 R.H. Barnes, 'Introduction', in Barnes *et al.* (eds), *Indigenous Peoples of Asia*, pp. 1–2.

13 J.V. Stalin, 'Marxism and the national question', *Works*, vol. II, Moscow: Foreign Languages Publishing House, 1953, p. 307.

14 In the introduction to M. Chapman, M. McDonald and E. Tarkin (eds), *History and Ethnicity*, London: Routledge, 1989, p. 16.

15 Richard Schermerhorn, 'Ethnicity and minority groups', in John Hutchinson and Anthony D. Smith (eds), *Ethnicity*, Oxford and New York: Oxford University Press, 1996, p. 17. Cited from *Comparative Ethnic Relations*, Random House, New York, 1970.

16 Patrick Thornberry, *Minorities and Human Rights Law*, London: Minority Rights Group, May 1987, p. 4.

17 June Teufel Dreyer, *China's Forty Millions*, Cambridge, MA and London: Harvard University Press, 1976, p. 1.

2 Ethnic minorities in China

Colin Mackerras

The overwhelming majority of people in China belong to an ethnic group the Chinese state calls Han. The term appears to have originated through a desire to unite the Chinese against the Manchus when the latter ruled China under the Qing dynasty (1644–1911), but most people nowadays normally equate the Han with 'the Chinese'. They are themselves anything but uniform and demonstrate great linguistic and cultural diversity. Cantonese, the language spoken by the people of Guangdong, Hong Kong and other parts of the south of China, is totally incomprehensible to a speaker of Modern Standard Chinese (Mandarin), which is based on Beijing pronunciation. At the same time, the written language of Chinese characters does not depend on region and is understood by literate Chinese all over the country, though it is true that Taiwan and Hong Kong still use the traditional full-form characters, whereas other parts of China have adopted simplified characters. The written language is perhaps the most important of many aspects of consistency among Han Chinese.

In addition to the Han, there are in China fifty-five state-recognized ethnic minorities, which are the subject of this chapter. The Chinese term for these ethnic groups is *shaoshu minzu*, which means literally 'minority nationalities', and it derives from Stalin's definition of the 'nationality', explained in the Introduction. These ethnic minorities make up fewer than one in ten of China's total population but take up about five-eighths of China's total area, including most of the sensitive border areas. Location near such border areas is a product of history and is similar to several other countries discussed in this volume, notably Vietnam. In many cases there are members of the same ethnic group on the other side of China's borders, several running their own nation-states, such as the Koreans, Mongolians, Kirghiz, Kazakhs and Tajiks. Although most seem to be quite happy to remain part of China, there have been separatist movements among a few of them, which have created serious challenges for the Chinese state. Some have highly distinctive cultures, languages and religions very different from those of the Han Chinese. For these and other reasons, the minorities are actually considerably more important to China than the small proportion of their population would suggest.

Because of the general nature of this work, it is necessary to consider China's minorities here as a whole. This is a perfectly valid scholarly exercise. The government has a similar or identical policy towards all of them and they have many commonalities. At the same time, one of the most important points to remember about China's ethnic minorities is their diversity. Their languages belong to a range of different families and branches, the families ranging from Sino-Tibetan, through Altaic to Indo-European. Some follow religions derived from the Chinese or practised for centuries among the Han, while others believe in religions not normally associated with the Han. The enormous diversity of religions will become clear in the relevant section below. The minorities range from peoples who are not very different culturally or ethnically from the Han to those who are very different indeed. There are even groups classified as a single minority nationality that are very different from each other and speak different languages.

Among those quite similar to the Chinese nowadays are the Tujia and the Manchus. The Tujia, most of whom live in Western Hunan Province in Central China, are very similar to the Han and it has been suggested that their Tujia ethnicity is more an outside construct than something meaningful to the people themselves.[1] The Manchus, whose main population concentrations are in north-east China, actually ruled China during its last imperial dynasty, the Qing. It is one of the ironies of history that this experience encouraged them to take over the culture of those they had conquered. This contrasts with the more usual alternative pattern whereby conquerors induce or force their subjects to adopt the culture and language of the rulers. At the beginning of the twenty-first century hardly any Manchus still speak Manchu and the Manchu script is all but extinct. Although some aspects of Manchu tradition survive, they are weak and most Manchus are barely distinguishable from Han Chinese. On the whole, ethnicity is not an issue in relations between Manchus and Chinese.

Among those groups at the opposite extreme, that is, totally different from the Han, are the Uygurs and Kazakhs who live in Xinjiang in far northwest China. These peoples are Turkic ethnically, their language is similar to Turkish, they are Muslims and their arts are more Turkish than Chinese. Most are instantly recognizable as having different features to the Chinese. Ethnicity is frequently a major issue in relations between Uygurs and Han, and there is strong support for a nation-state separate from China among them. On the other hand, the Kazakhs get on reasonably well with the Han and, despite proximity to Kazakhstan, the pressure to secede from China and join up with Kazakhstan is not particularly strong.

There are also many groups in between these two extremes. Two of particular interest and importance are the Koreans of northeast China and the Tibetans inhabiting vast areas of the country's southwest. The Korean language belongs to a different family from Chinese, and the Koreans of China insist on its use. However, they are strongly influenced by Chinese Confucian culture, and, largely because Japanese occupation forced them to resistance and hence cooperation with the Chinese Communist Party (CCP), they accepted Marxism-Leninism much more readily than most other minorities. On the whole, relations with the Han Chinese are good and there are very few who would like to secede from China and join up with Korea.

Plate 2.1 The long-street banquet is a feature of the Hani culture. Hundreds of small square tables laden with food are placed along one or more kilometres through the town. This one was held in a township in Yuanyang County, Honghe Hani and Yi Autonomous Prefecture, Yunnan Province (December 2002)

Plate 2.2 Three Tibetan musicians at the Tibetan restaurant in Lhasa (June 2002)

Plate 2.3 A general view of the Potala Palace (June 2002)

Plate 2.4 A young Hani man swings in the traditional way in a Hani village in Yuanyang County, Honghe Hani and Yi Autonomous Prefecture, Yunnan Province, China. In the background are terraced fields, which the Hani claim to have created some 2,000 years ago and are still a feature of their agriculture (December 2002)

The Tibetans are in a very different situation. The Tibetan language is actually in the same family as Chinese, namely the Sino-Tibetan. Over the centuries the Chinese have influenced them economically and culturally. Their religion, Tibetan Buddhism, is part of the Mahayana tradition found among large numbers of Han Chinese. On the other hand, they are still strongly committed to this religion, which has many features separating it from the Mahayana forms practised elsewhere in China. Despite considerable influence over the centuries, the Tibetan culture is still both strong and highly individual, and very different from Han Chinese culture.

History

The fall of the Manchu Qing dynasty at the end of 1911 brought about a considerable degree of instability in China. Successive warlord governments in north China were most concerned with their own fate and had no time for minority affairs. Yuan Shikai (1859–1916), who was president of the Republic of China from 1912 until his death, declared in April 1912 that there were five nationalities in China (the Han, Mongols, Manchus, Tibetans and Muslims) and that Mongolia, including Outer Mongolia, Tibet and Xinjiang were integral parts of China's territory. Constitutions of 1912 and 1914 enshrined the principal of equality for all nationalities before the law. However, the principal concern of all governments at that time was the unity of China. This meant that ethnic issues were always viewed primarily from the perspective of strengthening national unity.

Sun Yatsen (1866–1925) is regarded as the leader of the 1911 revolution that overthrew the Qing dynasty, and both Taiwan and the People's Republic of China (PRC) look on him as *guofu* (the 'father of the nation'). However, his tenure on power was quite short and very insecure, being chiefly restricted to leading a series of governments based in Guangzhou in the south from 1917 to his death. Like Yuan Shikai, Sun believed that China had five nationalities, the Han, Mongols, Manchus, Tibetans and Muslim Turks and the original flag of his Republic of China had five colours, representing these five ethnic groups.

Chiang Kaishek (1887–1975) led the Nationalist Party government of China from 1927 to 1949. He also believed in five nationalities: the Han, Manchus, Mongols, Muslims and Tibetans. But given the fact that the Japanese invasion threw China into war from 1937 to 1945, Chiang's top priority at all times was national unity, and he never gave much attention to the concerns of minorities. Indeed, he was not even really convinced of the existence of the main nationalities. In his book, *China's Destiny*, first published in March 1943, he argues that all five nationalities belong to the same racial stock and share a common ancestry. In the revised edition of January 1944 he states that 'the differentiation among China's five peoples is due to regional and religious factors, and not to race or blood'.[2]

From 1935 on, the main leader of the Chinese Communist Party was Mao Zedong (1893–1976), and it was the CCP that Chiang rightly regarded as the main long-term threat to his rule. Mao's policies on minorities were more inclusive than those of Chiang Kaishek and he took account not only of the five named above but of numerous others, including many living in the south like the Miao and Yao. The November 1931 Constitution adopted by the CCP even allowed for secession for minorities. However, the Japanese attempts to woo minorities like the Mongols away from China made him change his mind completely and permanently. Yet, Mao and the CCP made a genuine effort to win over the minorities through whose regions they passed in their famous Long March of 1934 to 1935, and cooperated with the ethnic minorities in resisting Japan. Mao Zedong also saw advantage in his minorities' policy from the point of view of winning support against Chiang Kaishek's government.

There was a good deal of substance to the worries about national unity. Various imperialist powers were establishing major influence in parts of China. The Japanese invaded Manchuria in 1931 and there set up the puppet state of Manchuguo, putting at the head of it the former (and last) Manchu emperor of all China. This state lasted until the Japanese were themselves defeated in 1945. They also encroached on other areas of China, including minority areas. In those areas they occupied, especially in Manchuria and the CCP's base areas of the northwest, the Japanese occupation exerted a powerful impact on minority relations, in most cases provoking Han and minorities to unite to resist them.

Meanwhile, both Tibet and Mongolia had formally seceded from China with the collapse of the Qing dynasty. Successive Chinese governments refused to recognize either Tibetan or Mongolian independence. In February 1929, Chiang Kaishek even established a Mongolian and Tibetan Affairs Commission, which was aimed at running Tibetan and Mongolian areas, with Tibet and Mongolia both regarded as 'special territories'. The reality was that Chinese control in Tibet had always been minimal, while the British were able to exert substantial influence over Tibetan affairs and society.

In the case of Mongolia, Soviet intervention had brought about the establishment of the Mongolian People's Republic in November 1924. Successive Chinese governments resisted recognizing Mongolian independence, and Inner Mongolia remained part of Chinese territory. At the end of the war against Japan, Chiang Kaishek's government signed a treaty with the Soviet Union, by which a referendum in Mongolia would decide the future there. The people voted overwhelmingly in favour of independence. Although Chiang Kaishek accepted this at the time, he went back on his agreement once he was defeated and set up government in Taiwan, continuing to claim Mongolia as part of China until his death in 1975. Meanwhile, Soviet influence had made the CCP accept Mongolian independence, and, despite high tensions on the Mongol border from the 1960s onward, it has never challenged Mongolian independence.

All Chinese governments regarded Xinjiang as a province of China. However, there were regimes there which governed semi-independently of China, the most important of these being that of Sheng Shicai, a Han Chinese who ruled Xinjiang from 1933 to 1944. Actually, Soviet economic and political influence remained enormous in Xinjiang right down to the time the CCP came to power and beyond, and impacted more on Sheng Shicai during most of his rule than the central Chinese government. At the same time, there were numerous rebellions by Uygurs for independence from the 1920s to the 1940s, with many people killed in their suppression. The most important was probably the East Turkestan Republic, which was announced in November 1944. One scholar has dubbed the leadership of this Republic 'a feudal Moslem nationalist regime which was encouraged, supported, and controlled by the Soviet Union'.[3] People in theory representing Chiang Kaishek's government succeeded in negotiating a deal with the East Turkestan Republic, but not until the victory of the CCP was Xinjiang firmly secured as part of China.

Policy

The PRC was formally established on 1 October 1949, led by Mao Zedong and his CCP. Policy was at first revolutionary but moderate, but Mao later implemented much more radical policies. In particular, his Cultural Revolution (1966–76) saw a total obsession with class struggle that provided a context for an assault on minority nationalities including all aspects of their culture, but also producing many deaths, especially among groups suspected of separatism, such as the Mongolians and Tibetans. After Mao's death, new reformist policies were introduced under Deng Xiaoping (1904–97). These negated Mao's Revolution, brought China into the world mainstream, and drastically improved China's economy and its people's living standards. Jiang Zemin, appointed general secretary of the CCP in June 1989 in the wake of a major political crisis, continued Deng Xiaoping's policies.

From the outset, the PRC implemented two basic policies towards its ethnic minorities:

1   China is a unitary state made up of numerous politically equal, ethnic groups, the implication being that no minority has any right to secede from China.
2   The minorities have the right of autonomy, including to practise and develop their own cultures and religions, and use their own languages.

This set of policies was introduced in the PRC's interim Constitution called 'The Common Programme' on 29 September 1949, that is just two days before the PRC itself was established. The extent to which it has been implemented in practice has varied sharply over the years the CCP has been in power. The early to mid-1950s were a very good period for these policies and for minorities in general. But various factors in the late 1950s, especially a large-scale rebellion in Tibet in March 1959, led to a reduction in autonomy. The Cultural Revolution's obsession with class struggle implied a negation of the importance of ethnicity. The result was not only the downgrading of autonomy but severe persecutions against minorities, and their religions and cultures, as feudal and backward. The period of reform has seen the reinstatement of autonomy, which has tended to gain in strength since the 1980s, although with some variations and inconsistencies. It has also seen a vast improvement in the livelihood of the overwhelming majority of Chinese, including the minorities, as discussed in much more detail below. At the same time, there has been a long-term trend in the spread of Han Chinese language and culture in the minority areas, at the expense of those of the minorities.

The policy of autonomy has resulted in the establishment of five autonomous regions, equivalent in status to provinces, and, at the end of the twentieth century, 152 autonomous prefectures, counties and banners (as counties are termed in Inner Mongolia). The earliest autonomous region to be set up was the Inner Mongolian, in May 1947, in fact over two years before the PRC itself was set up. The other four, with their dates of establishment in parentheses, are the Xinjiang Uygur Autonomous Region (October 1955), Guangxi Zhuang Autonomous Region (March 1958), Ningxia Hui Autonomous Region (October 1958) and Tibet Autonomous Region (September 1965).[1]

Because China is a unitary state, the authorities have at all times opposed suggestion that any of the ethnic groups might secede from China. The goal of national unity and integration, which has always been at the forefront of Chinese official thinking, is totally at odds with any form of separatism. All separatist rebellions have been crushed immediately and brutally. Other than the rebellion in Tibet in 1959, most of these have been in the period of reform. Separatist activities in Inner Mongolia are reported to have resulted in clashes with casualties in May 1990, but there is no doubt that Tibet and Xinjiang in the far west are the areas most affected by separatism, for which they are considered separately below.

The policy of autonomy has been laid down in detail in several legal documents, especially *The Law of Regional Autonomy* of 1984,[5] which was itself slightly amended in February 2001.[6] Both versions of this law state, in Article 17, that the leader of an autonomous area 'shall be a citizen of the nationality exercising regional autonomy' and that other posts in the government should also be assumed by people of the nationality exercising regional autonomy, and of other minority nationalities in the area concerned. However, it makes no reference to CCP positions. The law gives ethnic areas quite extensive control over their own budgets and allows them to pass laws applicable in their own territory, although these require approval by the Beijing-based National People's Congress before going into effect. Article 23 ordains 'priority to minority nationalities' in the recruitment of personnel in enterprises and institutions. A series of 'preferential policies' (*youhui zhengce*) has been developed following on from the government's ideas on autonomy. On the other hand, Article 7 specifies that the organs of self-government 'shall place the interests of the state as a whole above everything'.

It is important to evaluate autonomy in a balanced way. In no sense is it equivalent to independence, nor does it pretend to be. The CCP holds firm sway over all the ethnic areas, and it is not necessary for members of the local ethnic groups to take any leadership role in the CCP branches. There are no restrictions on the setting up of military garrisons in ethnic areas. On the other hand, the preferential policies and respect for local languages and cultures, and the prescriptions that members of the relevant ethnic minorities should head government organs, have made a difference to the extent of minority identities, including the number of minority people holding government jobs and overall ethnic consciousness. Several members of the minorities have reached very high levels of leadership with the PRC and the CCP, the most notable being the Mongolian Ulanhu (1906–88). Focusing on one ethnic group of southwestern China, one scholar has shown 'how elite members of the Yao nationality have been active agents in the making of a modern socialist and, more recently, postsocialist Yao identity'.[7] Another scholar has written a book arguing that the state's policies have vastly increased the political consciousness of China's most populous minority, the Zhuang, even to the extent of entitling her book *Creating the Zhuang*. She concludes, however, that the result at the end of the twentieth century was that the Zhuang were 'demanding greater inclusion, rather than independence, from the Chinese state'.[8] Ethnic consciousness can be in tension, even conflict, with national integration, but it does not have to be.

Identification

Stalin's definition (see p. 9) assumes the following criteria for determining a 'nationality': history, territory, language, economic life and culture. From 1953 the PRC government sent out groups to check the claims to 'nationality' status of those that applied. By 1955 there were over 400 of these. In 1956 the government established sixteen teams with the task of carrying out a thorough investigation of which groups belonged to which nationalities. The members were asked to eat, live and work with the members of the minorities, as well as train ethnologists from among them to continue the work.

In the 1964 census, there were 183 nationalities registered, but the government recognized only 54 of them. In 1979, the Juno of Yunnan Province were added to make 55. Since that time, authorities have strongly resisted all attempts to add further nationalities.

Most Chinese scholars accept Stalin's definition of a nationality. According to one study, 'in our country's academic circles, there were some in the late 1970s and early 1980s who put forward suggestions to "supplement" or "revise" this or that' in Stalin's definition, but hardly any gained support 'because the great majority of scholars up to now still consider that Stalin's definition of a nationality is basically scientific'.[9] Official thinking still typically dubs it 'a complete and scientific definition'.[10] The official identifications of minority nationalities, population and other statistics, and other major details take it as their basis. Yet it definitely raises some problems, especially when we remember that Stalin is clear that the lack of even one of his criteria disqualifies a group of people from being called a nationality.

As noted above, hardly any Manchus still speak, let alone write or read, Manchu. Are they thereby no longer Manchu? The Hui are the Chinese Muslims, and defined mainly by their religion. These people are actually very diverse, but the great majority are Chinese-speaking and, other than their religion, differ but little from Han neighbours. There are even some who are defined through having Muslim ancestors, even though they themselves do not believe in Islam and no longer abstain from pork.[11] Are such narrow differences enough to mark these people out as a nationality?

On the other hand, there are several instances of peoples who might be considered a separate nationality but are not. The most important example is the Hakkas. They were traditionally marked out from other Han in several respects, including that their women were more independent and did not bind their feet. However, it would be politically very contentious to categorize them as their own nationality, and all attempts in that direction have ended in total failure.

Another example is the Mosuo, of whom there were at the end of the twentieth century about 40,000 living near the Lugu Lake on the border between Yunnan and Sichuan Provinces. They are currently regarded by the state as a branch of the Naxi of Yunnan. However, many Mosuo regard themselves as a different nationality. They practise a matrilinear system whereby inheritance goes through the woman, not the man, and the status of their women is higher than among the Naxi. Moreover, their language and religion are very different from those of the Naxi. However, repeated applications to be classified separately from the Naxi have failed.

The examples of the Hakkas and Mosuo raise the very interesting issue of consciousness, which most Western scholars and states nowadays accept as a criterion for ethnicity. Stalin's definition ignores consciousness, which means that for a group to *believe* it is a nationality is just not evidence. On the other hand, the Chinese authorities do give some leeway both to groups and individuals to determine to which nationality they belong, and such pressure has changed classifications. We shall see below that quite significant numbers of people have in fact changed ethnic registration.

In the light of facts such as these, Chinese authorities and specialists have been forced to acknowledge that, while Stalin's definition still stands, it should be applied 'flexibly and creatively'.[12] Some acknowledge that not all the criteria must be fulfilled to warrant a nationality, and others are prepared to give space to consciousness. One writer, Yang Kun, in an admittedly unusual interpretation of Stalin's definition, states that 'shared psychological makeup is shared national consciousness and national feelings; these are very important and without them there is no possibility of becoming a nationality'.[13]

Another issue is the distinction between nationalities in different historical stages, especially the modern era. Industrialization has not affected all China's minorities equally by any means, but its overall impact is to reduce the differences in 'economic life' among peoples, of whatever nationality or country. In an age where migrations have been so large in scale and over such long distances, and the intermingling of peoples of different nationalities so extensive, the requirement for a specific territory becomes more problematic. There are representatives of most of the minorities of China outside their own territory. Uygurs go all over China, even to Hainan at the very opposite end of the country from their home, in order to sell their produce and make money. In an age where a knowledge of Chinese is more and more necessary for high social status, the great majority of urban minorities know Chinese and quite a few have even stopped speaking their own mother tongue. Do they lose their nationality for that? The answer is clearly no. In fact, re-registration has been towards the minorities, not away from them.

Population

There have been five national censuses in the PRC. The first four refer to 1 July of the years 1953, 1964, 1982 and 1990, and the last to 1 November 2000. The table below shows the combined populations of the minorities, plus some other relevant data.[14]

The minority population has tended to grow under the PRC, all five censuses showing a rise in absolute numbers. The proportion of the minorities to the total fell between 1953 and 1964 but has gone up at every census since then, and at a rate that appears to demand explanation.

The rise both in absolute figures and proportions since 1964 can be attributed mainly to the following three factors:

- improvements in the standard of living;
- more lenient population policy since the 1980s; and
- re-registration.

Since the PRC was established the general trend has been for the standard of living to rise. By far the most important exception to this pattern was the massive famine of the late 1950s and early 1960s. The biggest improvements in the minorities' standard of living have occurred since the late 1970s, with population rises greater then than earlier. The rise in the standard of living has included several matters especially relevant to survival, such as vaccination, improved sanitation and better water supply.

It is well known that China has followed a one-child-per-couple family planning policy since the early 1980s, though two children have usually been possible for rural households in which the first child was a girl. However, this policy has been much more flexibly applied towards the minorities, with each region

Table 2.1 Census figures for China's minorities

Year of census	Total population	Minority population	Minority %
1953	582,603,417	34,013,782	5.89
1964	694,581,759	39,883,909	5.77
1982	1,008,175,288	66,434,341	6.62
1990	1,133,682,501	90,567,245	8.01
2000	1,265,830,000	106,456,300	8.41

having some right to determine its own regulations. Most minority regions did not adopt restrictive policies until the late 1980s, although the trend from then until the end of the twentieth century was towards greater rigidity.

In general, the more remote the minority and the nearer an international border, the slacker the regulations are likely to be. The minorities with the smallest populations have no regulations at all. But in 1988 the government of the Guangxi Zhuang Autonomous Region adopted a rule whereby the Zhuang were generally allowed only one child, but a second if the first one was a girl, a rule applying not only to the countryside but to the cities as well. The 1992 regulations of the Xinjiang Uygur Autonomous Region allow one child per family for urban Han and two for urban minorities, while in the countryside most minorities are permitted three children.[15] In practice, these rules are frequently flouted. During a visit to Xinjiang in 1999, I found two random Uygur families with nine children each, one of them in an urban district and both with several children born since 1992. The 1992 regulations of the Tibet Autonomous Region (TAR) are more flexible than those of Xinjiang: while they specify one child only per family for urban Han people and two children for urban Tibetans, there are no restrictions at all imposed on Tibetans in remote rural areas.[16]

There are obviously political, as well as demographic, reasons for the more flexible policies towards minorities, especially those with regard to Xinjiang and Tibet. The Chinese government has enough problems with these peoples without further irritating them with restrictions on so intimate a matter as the size of their family.

The third reason for the rise in China's minority population, re-registration, means that many people who were previously regarded as belonging to one nationality, generally Han, changed to become a member of another one. The change in the Manchu population between the 1982 and 1990 censuses is a particularly good example, the population more than doubling from 4,304,160 to 9,821,180 over these eight years. As noted above, there is not much difference between the Han and Manchus nowadays, and some Han with Manchu background obviously found it in their interests to re-register as Manchus, because of the preferential policies in education, jobs and so on.[17] This factor of re-registration is found in many countries, not only China, and appears to be associated with the change in attitude towards ethnic minorities in many parts of the world.

One of the most controversial matters connected with population under the PRC has been Han migration to minority areas, especially to Xinjiang and Tibet but also to Inner Mongolia. There has been very significant Han immigration to Xinjiang under the PRC. The proportion of Han to the total population of Xinjiang reached its height in 1978, when, with 5.13 million people, the Han were 41.6 per cent of the total population of 12.33 million,[18] one of the reasons for the fall after that being greater minority natural increase owing to the population policy. However, one specialist claims that from 1987 some 250,000 'self-drifter' Hans, that is those who go to Xinjiang on their own without official permission, 'have poured into Xinjiang each year to look for work'.[19] Official figures claim that the number of Han rose by 2.12 per cent annually, from

5,695,626 to 6,601,297 over the period from 1990 to 1997,[20] while the 2000 census put the Han population at about 7.5 million,[21] which is 39 per cent of the 19.25 million the census gives for the Autonomous Region as a whole.[22] Immigration was clearly very substantial during the 1990s, but about 180,000 per year, not 250,000. Explanations for the discrepancies include either that the official figures or the figure of 250,000 are incorrect, or that a significant proportion of the Han immigrants did not stay in Xinjiang long, or a combination of these.

Han immigration to Tibet has also been significant. Visits to the TAR capital Lhasa in 1985, 1990, 1997 and 2002 suggested to me that the city had undergone rapid Sinicization over the period, especially in the 1990s, and in all four years several Tibetans complained to me about the large number of Han immigrants. Yet the 1990 and 2000 censuses showed the Han proportion in the TAR as a whole to be, respectively 3.68 and 5.9 per cent, by far the lowest of the main minority areas.[23] While there is some justification for the claim of Han immigration to the cities of the TAR, and cities in other Tibetan areas of China, such PRC and impressional data suggest that there is very little indeed to the rural areas. One scholar has shown that many immigrants go to the TAR without their families and return home when they have finished the task that took them to Tibet in the first place.[24]

Economy

In accordance with the autonomy policy, there is a certain leeway for minorities to influence the development of their own areas but, as in other areas of policy, with severe restrictions. Economic policy must be carried under state plans, and it should give priority to the interests of the state as a whole, rather than to individual ethnic areas. It is well known that China's main nuclear sites are in Xinjiang, an ethnic area, and that this has had a cumulatively deleterious impact on the environment of the region.

The nature of economic life among the minorities has changed enormously under the PRC. The tendency has been for them to be integrated into the national economy and to follow the priorities and policies of the central government. The traditional economies by which ethnologists identify ethnic groups still persist. For instance, some Kazakhs and Mongols are still nomadic, and many girls of the southwestern minorities such as the Zhuang and Yao still learn national batik weaving. However, these traditions are coming under increasing challenge from modern economic patterns.

Communications such as telephones and postage have improved drastically, though they are still inferior to the eastern areas of China, and the Internet is beginning to spread to the minority areas. Infrastructure, though still backward, has been greatly improved; railways and roads have been built in most ethnic areas, effectively linking them with the rest of the country. There were still no railways in Tibet in 2001, but a decision had been taken to build one. Industry, which was non-existent or very backward in 1949, has expanded greatly in the minority areas. Calculating from 1980 constant prices, total agricultural

Plate 2.5 Yaks assist in cultivating fields between Lhasa and Shigatse, two boys look on (June 2002)

Plate 2.6 Shamans at a Li-Miao village in central Hainan Province. The village has been made into a tourist attraction as a kind of theme park, with the various traditions displayed. The villagers wear traditional clothing especially for the tourists. The village makes a great deal of money from the tourist trade (January 2000)

Plates 2.7 Traditional Li dancing in the Li-Miao village in central Hainan Province. The dances are put on by amateurs especially for the tourists

and industrial output value in these areas grew by 23.6 times between 1945 and 1990, agriculture by 8.1 times and industry by 135.5 times.[25]

As in the rest of China, the beginnings of modernization have brought about a tremendous rise in the standard of living of the minorities. In extensive interviewing over many ethnic areas I have found such a comment made more often than any other connected with economics. Poverty remains much more serious in the minority areas than elsewhere in China, but, correspondingly, poverty alleviation programmes sponsored by the government and bodies such as the World Bank have focused more attention on them than on other areas.

There are wide disparities in China both between the poorer minority areas and the Han areas, and within the ethnic areas. Moreover, these have grown during the period of reform. Despite rapid economic growth in the minority areas, the growth along the eastern seaboard and in the Han areas has generally been considerably more rapid still, and from a much higher base. At the same time, state intervention in the economy has tended to weaken all over the country, because of the trend towards privatization which has characterized the reform-era policies. One specialist claims that, despite the wish for autonomy, 'most of the minorities, with the exception of many Tibetans and some Muslim groups in the northwest, are demanding *more* central government involvement in minority areas', not less.[26] One of the reasons for this is that excessive free enterprise has the effect of widening inequalities.

Partly to counter this trend, the government in 2000 launched a new and stronger strategy to develop the west more quickly, and shifted the focus of economic development from the east to the west where, as it happens, the great majority of the ethnic minorities live. This change in policy involved pumping large sums of money into the western regions, including a drastic increase in foreign investment; consolidating and increasing the extent of poverty alleviation; and attempting to halt ecological deterioration. It remains to be seen how successful this policy will be, but there are huge problems with implementing it, and most observers are struck by the fact that the environment has, up to now, been one of the casualties of economic growth.

It is also notable that some minorities are doing much better than others economically. The Koreans of Jilin Province stand at the upper end of prosperity. Admittedly, the level of industry and infrastructure they enjoyed in 1949 was higher than most of the other ethnic areas. However, they have adopted the techniques of modernization and economic growth much more actively than perhaps any of China's other ethnic groups. On the other hand, many of the minorities of Yunnan or Guizhou Provinces are almost totally lacking in industry and still follow traditional patterns of livelihood, inducing or failing to solve poverty. Among the best-known minorities, the Mongols and Manchus are at the upper end of prosperity, the Tibetans at the lower, with the Uygurs somewhere in between.

We conclude this section with reference to the problem of how well modernization processes mesh with traditional ethnic cultures. Do they weaken these cultures and does this have a harmful effect on the livelihood of the peoples

Plate 2.8 A corner of the Potala Palace, with the modernized square below (June 2002)

Plate 2.9 A corner of the Potala Palace, with the modernized buildings of Lhasa below (June 2002)

concerned? One controversial example illustrates the problem and is especially important because it centres on the Tibetans, the people with the highest international profile among China's ethnic minorities. In July 2000 the World Bank Board of Executive Directors rejected an allocation of US$160 million towards the Chinese Western Poverty Reduction Project on the grounds that the resettlement programme involved in the Qinghai component might harm the interests of local Tibetans in the host area and damage the environment. China was bitter over the rejection, saying that it would persist with the project anyway. But the example shows the priority the World Bank places on the effect on ethnic groups and their environment. In fact, Chinese policy does give some weight to traditional medicines and traditional economic patterns. But in the long term, economic modernization and globalization are likely to weaken traditions anyway. And globalization processes are likely to affect China's minority areas with accelerating force since China's accession to the World Trade Organization at the end of 2001.

Education

The policy of modernization, which the Chinese state advocates so enthusiastically, requires that as many citizens as possible be educated or at least literate in Chinese. The system encourages people to be loyal to the state, and that includes minorities, because it is a primary aim of education to secure national integration. There is a national curriculum that applies to all areas and ethnic groups. But the CCP does pay at least lip service towards preserving ethnic cultures and allows minorities some say in the forms and content of the education system.

In some respects, the CCP has done very well in terms of the education of the minorities. The actual number who receive schooling has gone up dramatically. For example, the number of minority students enrolled at primary level rose from 1.474 million in 1952 to 7.686 million in 1978 and 12.483 million in 1997, while the number of minority teachers at primary level rose from 59,800 in 1952 to 310,200 in 1978 and 633,000 in 1997.[27]

However, there are quite a few problems in the condition of schooling. One is inequality. In remote or mountainous areas, where many minorities live, standards of education and literacy are far lower than in urban regions. There are also inequalities by nationality and gender. Among the most populous ethnic groups, the one with the lowest rate of adult illiteracy is the Koreans. The 1990 census counted this rate at only 7 per cent, far lower than the 21.5 per cent which it gave for the majority Han. At the opposite end, among the most populous nationalities, the one with the highest rate of adult illiteracy is the Tibetans, the 1990 census showing a rate of 69.4 per cent.[28] On gender, I found in many minority and Han areas that girls go to school less and stay for shorter periods than do boys. However, the situation appears to be improving. One account found that '[e]xcept in Tibet, the illiteracy gender gap has narrowed in all province-level territories during the 1980s' and predicted that 'the illiteracy gender gap will continue to narrow, but will not totally vanish'.[29] It is also notable that the preferential policies mentioned in the section on the economy apply to education, especially at university level. One study found that preferential admissions for members of minorities are 'among the most valued of "positive discrimination" measures accorded minorities in China'.[30]

Article 36 of *The Law of Regional Autonomy* of 1984 gives the minorities some say over the curricula in the schools and some, including the Tibetans, Uygurs and Dong, have developed textbooks which concern the cultures of the relevant minorities. However, any study of local cultures is undertaken *in addition* to the national curriculum, not instead of it. Moreover, the textbooks convey the message the state advocates. Those used by the Uygurs obviously mention Islam, which is central to Uygur culture, but are generally critical of the role of religion. All such textbooks push the unity of the Chinese state and condemn separatism.

One of the most crucial issues here is language. Article 37 of the 1984 law states that minorities should, wherever possible, use textbooks in their own languages and conduct classes in their own languages. However, it is my impression from explorations in schools in many ethnic areas of China that this article is not followed at all closely in most ethnic areas, and that many places use Chinese much more commonly. On the whole, the local language is used for children just beginning school, as most do not understand Chinese. The higher the grade, the more likely it is that the language of instruction will be Chinese.

The main reason for this is that the Chinese state considers that one way to effect national integration is to have all citizens able to speak the national language, which is Modern Standard Chinese. If there is a clash between preservation of ethnic cultures and knowledge of the national language, then the latter will take a higher priority than the former. Looking at the situation from the minorities' point of view, learning minority languages will help to preserve them other than in the private sphere of the home. On the other hand, to be properly employable in contemporary China, one must know the Chinese language very well. For members of ethnic minorities, to fail to learn Chinese is to render them unqualified for the best jobs society has to offer and can only keep them low in status.

To be fair, the Chinese government has invested a good deal of money in training teachers from the minorities, as the figures given above show. That helps towards having teachers and students belonging to the same ethnic group. However, teachers are sometimes brought in from outside. In a Dai village near Jinghong, which I visited in September 2000, a teacher interviewed belonged to a minority, but to the Hani, not to the Dai. She told me she uses only Chinese in class, because she does not know enough Dai to communicate properly.

The state education system in China is entirely secular. Religion is mentioned only as a cultural phenomenon, and is usually criticized. But, on the other hand, among some of the minorities, traditional religion still exercises some impact on the education of children, especially boys. Among the Dai of Xishuangbanna, many boys enter monasteries temporarily, one of the reasons being to learn the Dai written language and to learn more about Buddhism. In Tibetan areas, monasteries are still centres of traditional learning and culture, and many boys still become monks, at least in part to preserve this tradition. However, nowadays they are allowed to enter monasteries only *after* at least a few years of schooling in the state's education system.

Plate 2.10 Two Tibetan monks at the Tashilhunbo Monastery, one young, one old (June 2002)

Society

Since society encompasses so much, space compels me to restrict coverage. I have chosen two aspects that seem to me of paramount importance, namely religion and family.

Religion

Many minorities are considerably more intensely committed to religious belief and practice than are the Han. Moreover, there has been a strong revival of religion everywhere in China since the end of the major persecutions against it that characterized the Cultural Revolution. However, there are very wide disparities and differences among the minorities themselves and, in some cases, within them.

There are several general types of religion among China's minorities, the three most important being Islam, Tibetan Buddhism and traditional folk religions especially widespread among the southwestern minorities. The Dai people of Yunnan are among the few ethnic groups in China to practise the Theravada Buddhism so prevalent in Thailand and Burma. Christian missions made some headway among some of the minorities, and there are still remnants of this success to this day among the Miao and other minorities. In addition, Christian missionaries have been active everywhere in China since the 1980s and have had some success, including in the minority areas.

Plate 2.11 A traditional Tibetan kitchen at the Drepung Monastery, outside Lhasa (June 2002)

In visiting ethnic areas in China, I have been struck by the persistence of religious traditions. In rural Hui and Uygur communities, the Islamic clergy is frequently as socially influential as the local CCP branch, and sometimes even more so. The great majority still appear to believe in Islam and many practise it quite strictly. Several other minorities retain commitment to Muslim faith.

Tibetan Buddhism is still very strong among the Tibetans, although it is not as universally accepted as in former times. A survey carried out by a Hong Kong-led team from June to September 1996 in various Tibetan areas found that the proportion of believers in Tibetan Buddhism among 2,758 people interviewed was 86 per cent, with 10.5 per cent professing no religious belief, and the remainder committed to other religions. In Lhasa, the percentage of those believing in Tibetan Buddhism was only about 76 per cent and of those not believing in any religion as high as about 22.5 per cent. Most of the non-believers were CCP members or cadres, that is administrative or professional personnel.[31] The other major ethnic group to espouse Tibetan Buddhism is the Mongolians, but their belief is nowadays incomparably weaker than the Tibetans'.

Upon travelling in ethnic areas in the south of China, I was struck by the fact that shrines appear more or less universal in rural homes. During a visit to Dai areas in September and October 2000 I saw a Buddhist temple in every village I passed, and learned from local officials that the number of functioning temples in Dehong Dai-Jingpo Autonomous Prefecture in southwestern Yunnan was 642. There has been a boom in temple construction in recent years in the Dai areas, and in many places a strengthening of the influence of monks and religious figures generally.

Where religion is a manifestation of traditional ethnic culture, the CCP tolerates it and allows it to flourish openly. However, if it enters the realm of politics the authorities tread on it very quickly and firmly. Both the Islam of the Uygurs and the Buddhism of the Tibetans have been accused of meddling in politics, and even of stirring up separatist feeling among their respective ethnic groups. In 1996 a campaign among the monasteries of Tibet showed amply that the government would 'no longer tolerate monasteries . . . functioning as centers of political and nationalistic opposition'[32] and there was similar action in Xinjiang. 'Strike hard' campaigns saw police entering temples and mosques they suspected of anti-government political activity, and suppressing it firmly where they did find it.

Religion may weaken in social power as globalization gathers momentum, especially in the cities. However, I do not expect Islam among the Uygurs and several other minorities or Tibetan Buddhism among the Tibetans to wither in the foreseeable future. Their clergies show no sign of shrinking influence among the people. Tibetan Buddhism can only gain from having become part of a 'new spirituality' in Western countries, since Western adherents are very active in their concern for the state of the religion in its home territory.

Family

There are strong differences not only among nationalities in terms of family life, but between the city and countryside. As in other respects, there are wide differences in the family patterns of China's minorities. Many are influenced by Confucianism, the Koreans being a prominent example, others by Islam, such as the Uygurs. The southwestern minorities, including the Tibetans, Zhuang, Miao and Yao, are by tradition generally more easy-going and less authoritarian in family matters than their Confucian and Islamic counterparts. Although the CCP advocates equality between the sexes, it has not given a high priority to implementing this policy among the minorities, so that results have been very uneven.

There is a major difference between the cities and the countryside, with reforms much more thoroughgoing in the former. Urban lifestyle in family and other matters has gone a fairly long way towards accepting modernizing and globalizing influences characterized by such phenomena as changing family relationships, pop music and Western-style dancing. Young Tibetans in Lhasa are much more likely to amuse themselves through disco clubs and television than in traditional ways. Women are entering the professions; young people are beginning to show greater independence of their elders and young women of their menfolk.

In the countryside, traditional patterns remain surprisingly strong. Old gender stereotypes still dictate what tasks individuals will carry out, what they will learn at home and how they will treat their relations. Although modernization is beginning to create an impact, it remains very uneven and generally weak. During a visit to Miao communities in Hainan Province early in 2000 I was surprised to find that hereditary headships, in which 'Miao kings' (*Miaowang*) marry several wives who aim to produce sons to succeed them in their rule, still exist.

Secessionist movements: Tibet and Xinjiang

With the major exception of Outer Mongolia, the PRC regards those territories that belonged to the Qing empire as part of China, including Manchuria (the northeast), Inner Mongolia, Xinjiang and Tibet. Other than in Tibet, secessionist problems have been fewer than in the Republican period. However, they have resurfaced since the 1990s and are currently among the major challenges the PRC faces.

The People's Liberation Army took over Tibet in 1950, with the Dalai Lama's government forced to sign an agreement with the central authorities in May 1951. Under this agreement Tibet would join the PRC but as an autonomous region where local elites would retain most of their previous power.

Conflict continued in the Tibetan areas through the 1950s, and a large-scale rebellion erupted in March 1959 in Lhasa, which was immediately put down with considerable brutality by Chinese troops. The Dalai Lama fled and set up a kind of government-in-exile in Dharamsala in India. He has remained there ever since as the leader of a Tibetan community that condemns Chinese behaviour in Tibet and opposes its rule there.

During the Cultural Revolution, only very sparse news came from Tibet and it seemed as though the situation was quiet. The reality, however, was different. This was a period when Mao Zedong attempted to suppress all religion and traditional culture, both in Tibet and the rest of China. Later reports revealed that monasteries were destroyed in Tibet and monks forced to return to lay life, with many physically harmed or killed. Social and political control was so tight that secessionist movements got nowhere.

The 1980s saw a major revival of religion and traditional culture in Tibet, with a much more liberal policy. Ironically, the relaxation of tension also saw a revival of separatist feelings and movements. In September and October 1987 there was a series of demonstrations in Lhasa in favour of independence for Tibet. These were led by monks and immediately suppressed by Chinese police and troops with casualties resulting, though in numbers which differ greatly according to the source. Demonstrations continued in 1988 and 1989, all of them suppressed. Those of 5–7 March 1989, commemorating the thirtieth anniversary of the March 1959 uprising, were large enough that, in Lhasa, the central government declared martial law for the first time in the PRC's history.

The 1990s saw far fewer separatist movements in Tibet. The Chinese authorities adopted a 'carrot and stick' approach. They pumped extensive funds into the region, undertook many infrastructural and other economic projects and encouraged richer regions further east to assist with the Tibetan economy and standard of living. They also tightened political control in Tibet and ran a series of 'patriotic' campaigns designed to encourage Tibetans, including the clergy, to support integration with the rest of China. In 1996, they 'launched a major campaign aimed at cleansing the monasteries of political dissidents'.[33]

In July 1996, the Dalai Lama gave a speech before the British Parliament in London. In it he attacked the Chinese on grounds of cultural genocide and human rights abuses, but also suggested that all he was demanding for Tibet was 'genuine autonomy', not full independence. He repeated the same formula of 'genuine autonomy' on many subsequent occasions, appearing to leave the door open for negotiations with the Chinese government. The Chinese authorities continued to attack him as a splittist, but the Dalai Lama's London concession certainly handed them a major victory in terms of the status of Tibet.

In September 2002, two representatives of the Dalai Lama actually visited Lhasa for discussions with the government there. They returned saying they noted a 'new sincerity' in China's attitude towards Tibet, and the Dalai Lama's government welcomed the visit as useful. Certainly, it appears to have made the atmosphere of relations between the Dalai Lama and Beijing less poisonous. Beijing appears to have been acting from strength in this tentative overture towards dialogue, but is unlikely to be forced to grant anything remotely resembling the Dalai Lama's formula of 'genuine autonomy'. The visit has strengthened the Chinese government's hand, rather than weakened it.

In Xinjiang, experience and Chinese reactions have been in some ways similar to Tibet, in other ways different. There was some armed opposition in the 1950s, which the Chinese crushed, but there was nothing corresponding to the 1959 Tibetan uprising and no leaders even remotely able to garner the international support enjoyed by the Dalai Lama. Just as in Tibet, the Cultural Revolution in Xinjiang was characterized by oppression and attempts to eradicate traditional culture, including religion. Mosques were closed and/or destroyed, with clergy forced into lay life, attacked or even killed.

Although the 1980s saw clashes between local people and Han immigrants, it did not experience much separatism. However, the 1990s were quite different. They began with a rebellion in Baren Township in Akto County not far from Kashgar in south Xinjiang in April 1990. The leader, Zahideen Yusuf, was a native of Baren and a religious student inspired by the 'holy war' concept the Afghan mujahideen were practising. The Chinese authorities suppressed the rebellion within a day and Yusuf and some of his supporters were killed. However, trouble has continued sporadically in Xinjiang since then.

In May 1996 the Xinjiang CCP held a work conference to discuss the autonomous region's problems, especially those relating to continuing separatist riots, terrorist activities and bombings. In a reaction somewhat similar to that adopted in Tibet, the meeting decided to try to stop any illegal import of arms, and to crack down on opposition of all kinds, including reorganizing CCP branches dominated by Muslims. On the other hand, the government also tried to improve the economy to give local minorities a real incentive to continue as part of the PRC.

These measures failed to have the desired effect, at least in the short term. Early in February 1997 there was a series of anti-government riots in Yining (known to the Uygurs as Gulja) in north Xinjiang, near the border with Kazakhstan. These were again crushed by Chinese authorities. On 25 February, dissident Muslims exploded bombs on buses in the Xinjiang capital Ürümqi. Leader Deng Xiaoping had died on 19 February, and the memorial service in his honour took place on the same day as the bombings. The message appeared to be that the dissidents had nothing but contempt for China's most important leader of the last quarter of the twentieth century.

Attempts to crush opposition by Uygur separatists have continued to the present time, as has the opposition itself. Reports continue of attempts to introduce arms into minority areas for the purpose of resisting Chinese rule. Early in 2001 the government was reported to have undertaken a major crackdown on the illegal but highly lucrative trade of guns in several parts of China, including both Tibet and Xinjiang. Under most circumstances, carrying a gun is illegal in China, but in minority areas like Tibet and Qinghai guns for hunting are tolerated. Source regions of this illegal gun trade include Kazakhstan, Kyrgyzstan and Tajikistan, which formerly belonged to the Soviet Union, South Korea, Vietnam, Burma and Hong Kong.[34] It is very well known to the authorities that illegal owners of guns include political separatists, especially those in Xinjiang where the doctrine of the 'holy war' still exerts influence among Muslims.

The incidents of 11 September 2001 could not fail to affect the situation in Xinjiang. In January 2002, the Chinese government released a long statement listing terrorist attacks by Muslim Uygur separatists, claiming there were close associations with the Al-Qaida network the United States blamed for the incidents. It appears to be using the 11 September incidents as a reason for increasing its attacks against separatist activities in Xinjiang.

Some foreign policy ramifications of the minorities

Since many members of the minorities live in areas near national boundaries, they sometimes affect China's relations with cross-border countries, especially since in some cases, members of the same ethnic group live on both sides of such national markers. From time to time the Mongolians of China have been involved in China's relations with Mongolia and, to a lesser extent, the Koreans in China's relationships with North and South Korea.

In some cases, what happens along boundaries may affect both China and the neighbouring country, but without impacting seriously on their relations. Since the 1990s, Dai areas bordering Burma have facilitated the smuggling of narcotics into China, despite overtly expressed opposition from both countries. It is not Dai people themselves who are the chief culprits in the illegal trade, but corrupt entrepreneurs and officials, and those in their pay, yet some Dai get caught up in this trade. There are Dai villages that actually straddle the border, being partly in China and partly in Burma. They are exceedingly difficult to control, because the Dai on the Chinese side of the village are identical in culture and language to the Shan on the Burmese side, and the locals move quite freely across the border. The narcotics trade may benefit from the good relations currently existing between Burma and China.

In addition, Chinese entrepreneurs have established gambling dens in areas of Burma very close to, or even on, the border with China, and many Chinese, some of them Dai, go to these dens. I actually saw an island gambling den in the middle of a river separating Burma from a Dai area of China. The island is no-man's land, in neither Burma nor China. Many Chinese go there to gamble and, although gambling is illegal in China, authorities do nothing about this, on the grounds that the area is outside their jurisdiction. Both the Chinese and Burmese entrepreneurs, and probably authorities too, make money from this gambling den.

The two minority areas most relevant to international relations are Tibet and Xinjiang. In the case of Tibet the country most involved is the United States and with Xinjiang it is Russia and its predecessor the Soviet Union. In both cases, especially the latter, there is a range of other states involved in a complex web of interrelationships. In particular, the 11 September incidents and the war against terrorism have made the United States much more involved in Central Asia and hence Xinjiang than it ever was before 2001.

From the mid-1950s to the early 1970s, the United States was actively involved in helping Tibetan separatist forces stir up trouble against Chinese rule.[35] Certainly the Chinese government accused the United States of aiding and abetting the traditional ruling elite, including the monasteries, especially in the 1959 rebellion. China's relations with India were very good indeed during most of the 1950s. However, the 1959 rebellion and the deteriorating situation in Tibet helped both to poison and exacerbate Sino-Indian relations from the late 1950s on.

The accusation of American meddling was also raised over the separatist movements of the late 1980s. Just a few days before independence demonstrations occurred in late September 1987, the Dalai Lama had been in Washington addressing congressional committees with denunciations of Chinese rule. By 1987, Sino-American relations were actually enjoying a post-1949 peak, and the Tibetan demonstrations were a major factor signalling a more bumpy road ahead, with a far greater emphasis on human rights as a divisive issue.

The 1980s witnessed the entrance of two related phenomena relevant to the Tibetan situation. One was that the Dalai Lama began to take up a much more active diplomacy, especially towards the Western countries. The other was that public opinion in these countries took a more active interest in the situation in Tibet, and overwhelmingly blamed China for suppressing Tibetan religion and culture and committing human rights abuses in Tibet. Although governments continued to recognize Tibet as part of China, public opinion in the Western countries and India was generally in support of an independent Tibet.

In 1995, a controversy arose over the selection of the Eleventh Panchen Lama, the Dalai Lama supporting one candidate, the Chinese another. The Chinese choice won the day and was enthroned on 8 December 1995. However,

Western government leaders and lobby groups condemned China for its involvement in such a matter, and for acting against the wishes of the Dalai Lama. Chinese authorities also suffered accusations of religious persecution for having placed the Dalai Lama's candidate under house arrest.

Tibet has thus been a significant factor in China's relations with the West and especially the United States. However, it is worth noting that several other factors and incidents have loomed somewhat larger than Tibet in affecting Sino-American relations. General issues encompass a host of trade and human rights matters, while specific incidents include the crackdown on the student movement, often known as the Beijing Massacre of June 1989 and the bombing of China's Belgrade Embassy in May 1999 by the forces of the North Atlantic Treaty Organization (NATO).

From the early 1960s to the 1980s, Chinese government leaders accused the Soviet Union of threatening China, including its western regions. However, when the Soviet Union collapsed at the end of 1991, China found itself with another threat to the west, namely that of Islamic radicalism. This gained support from Afghanistan and from the countries of Central Asia which had once been part of the Soviet Union, especially Tajikistan, Kyrgyzstan and Kazakhstan. The irony was that the governments of these countries were also very much afraid of Islamic radicalism, which meant that they shared common interests with China in opposing it. Despite the fall of the Marxist-Leninist Soviet Union, the ideologically similar PRC has generally enjoyed better relations with the post-Soviet states to its west than it did with the Soviet Union.

The best illustrative example relating to Xinjiang is the development of the 'Shanghai Five' consultations. In April 1996, the presidents of China, Russia, Tajikistan, Kyrgyzstan and Kazakhstan met in Shanghai to discuss mutual problems. These five presidents met each year down to 2000, successively in each of the five countries, and were joined in June 2001 by the president of Uzbekistan, the group being renamed Shanghai Cooperation Organization. One of the issues that has loomed large on their agenda is to prevent Islamic fundamentalism from destabilizing the region, including the cessation of illegal sales of weaponry, and terrorism.

The situation in Xinjiang has also involved other countries besides those included in the Shanghai Cooperation Organization. For instance, China frequently criticizes the United States for involvement in the Central Asia region. Pakistan has traditionally enjoyed very good relations with China, but at the turn of the century allowed its territory to be used for the training of Islamic militants wishing to fight in Xinjiang. When Chinese President Jiang Zemin visited Turkey in April 2000, he was keen to persuade the Turkish government to help stop illegal assistance by Turks to their Turkic Uygur brethren in Xinjiang.

China has attempted to portray its attacks on Uygur separatism as part of the United States' war against terrorism. The common interest in fighting terrorism played a role in improving the relations between the two countries and, in a report issued in May 2002 on counterterrorism in 2001, the United States was quite complimentary about China's efforts to suppress Islamic terrorism in Xinjiang. In August 2002, the United States government announced it had recognized the most important of the separatist groups, the East Turkestan Islamic Movement, as a terrorist organization. The pro-American leader of Afghanistan who replaced the Taliban, Hamid Karzai, visited China shortly after coming to power and expressed strong support for China's opposition to Uygur terrorist separatism. On the other hand, the United States continued to criticize China for human rights abuses in Xinjiang, including those aimed against Uygur separatism.

Conclusion

China's policy towards its minorities has been generally successful in integrating the various ethnic regions into China, at least in the sense that political control over these areas is generally firmer than at most periods in the past. There appears to be no doubt at all that in economic, social and cultural terms, as well as political, the minority areas are very much better integrated into China than ever before, with firmer communications and other infrastructure, much more trade and investment, and Han cultural and social influence and migration.

Among the various parts of China, only Tibet and Xinjiang show a real potential for achieving the status of a recognized nation-state. Yet there are reasons for thinking that even these are likely to remain part of China unless the central state collapses entirely. No foreign power, even the United States, is likely to want to get involved in any military struggle in favour of independence, and it seems that such support may be needed for success.

Ironically, the greater integration has also been accompanied by increased ethnic consciousness among many of China's minorities. It expresses itself in firmer attachment to traditional cultures and religions, and in resistance to being swept up in a Han uniformity. In part this rise has been driven by the state, but it would be unfair not to concede that minority elites have played a significant role as well.

Globalization has a way of homogenizing peoples according to patterns dictated by the richest and most powerful of the world's nations. On the other hand, some theorists have argued that globalization also spawns reactions and may even *intensify* feelings of identity. China joined the World Trade Organization in 2001, and that can only increase globalization pressures there. How this will affect the minorities remains to be seen. But to the present the trends are both towards homogenization and intensification of identities, in other words two contradictory processes are happening at the same time.

China has seen a considerable amount of ethnic conflict under the PRC, especially in Tibet and Xinjiang, as the foregoing account has made clear. Yet if we compare the PRC's record with that of many other contemporary states, or with China itself in the nineteenth and first half of the twentieth centuries, the CCP's stands out as relatively good. Moreover, if we consider that China is a continental country with sensitive borders susceptible to conflict and dispute, then the PRC does not appear to me to have been particularly derelict in coping with the problems it faces. The concern with national unity appears to me to be a legitimate one.

Scholars, journalists and others have argued over the most likely near-term future for China. Will China continue to grow strategically and economically, or is it more likely to split into several or numerous parts, with the country disintegrating into chaos? Of course nobody knows. But surely disintegration into violence and war would benefit very few people. If the PRC shows some sensitivity in handling border and minority issues, among many others, then the country has a good chance of remaining together as a more or less integrated unity. Would that suit the minorities? Certainly it would suit most of them, but not all. There may in time be a possibility of devising a form of autonomy that would suit the interests of the Tibetans, coming into the category of what the Dalai Lama has termed 'genuine autonomy'. Under the present circumstances of poisonous relations between the Chinese government and the Dalai Lama, this appears very difficult. However, it is not impossible that such relations might change over the coming decades, as new leaders emerge and China becomes more open and prosperous.

At the beginning of the twenty-first century, China exhibits two contrary trends, which parallel processes among the minorities. One is towards globalization, the other towards greater nationalism. China does not wish to be pushed around, but it does wish to join the world community as a recognized great power, especially in its own region. A more powerful China may mean less influence for individual nationalities like the Tibetans and Uygurs, but a more prosperous overall country. China may become more integrated into the world through globalization, but it is most unlikely that it will allow its future to be determined by anybody but its own people.

Notes

All China photos were taken by Colin Mackerras.

1 See Chih-yu Shih, 'Ethnicity as policy expedience: Clan Confucianism in ethnic Tujia-Miao Yongshun', *Asian Ethnicity*, March 2001, vol. 2, no. 1, pp. 73–88.
2 Chiang Kai-shek, with notes and commentary by Philip Jaffe, *China's Destiny and Chinese Economy Theory*, New York: Roy Publishers, 1947, p. 40.
3 David D. Wang, *Under the Soviet Shadow: The Yining Incident, Ethnic Conflicts and International Rivalry in Xinjiang, 1944–1949*, Hong Kong: The Chinese University Press, 1999, p. 407.
4 See a list of these autonomous areas, with dates of establishment, in Colin Mackerras, *The New Cambridge Handbook of Contemporary China*, Cambridge: Cambridge University Press, 2001, pp. 254–6.
5 See a translation of this law in Katherine Palmer Kaup, *Creating the Zhuang: Ethnic Politics in China*, Boulder, CO and London: Lynne Rienner, 2000, pp. 183–97.
6 This was published both in Chinese and English in *Zhonghua Renmin Gongheguo minzu quyu zizhi fa* (*Law of the People's Republic of China on Regional National Autonomy*), Beijing: Nationalities Press, 2001.
7 Ralph A. Litzinger, *Other Chinas: The Yao and the Politics of National Belonging*, Durham, NC and London: Duke University Press, 2000, p. xx.

8 Kaup, *Creating the Zhuang*, p. 180.

9 Lin Yaohua, Jin Tianming and Chen Kejin, *Minzuxue tonglun, xiuding ben* (*General Survey of Ethnology*, revised edn), Beijing: Central Nationalities University Press, 1997, p. 106.

10 Wu Shimin, Wang Ping, *et al.*, *Minzu wenti gailun* (*Summary of Nationalities Problems*), Chengdu: Sichuan People's Press, 1999, p. 7.

11 Dru C. Gladney, *Muslim Chinese: Ethnic Nationalism in the People's Republic*, Cambridge, MA: Harvard University Press, 1991, pp. 262–4.

12 For instance, Alatan, Sun Qing, Hua Xinzhi and Qi Xiaoping, *Lun minzu* (*On Nationalities*), Beijing: Nationalities Press, 1989, p. 68.

13 Yang Kun, *Minzuxue gailun* (*Summary of Ethnology*), Beijing: Social Sciences Press, 1984, p. 147.

14 See the figures, based on Chinese official sources, in Mackerras, *The New Cambridge Handbook*, pp. 211–12, 251. The figures do not include Taiwan, Hong Kong or Macau, even for the 2000 census.

15 Xu Xifa, *Zhongguo shaoshu minzu jihua shengyu gailun* (*Summary of Family Planning Among China's Minority Nationalities*), Ürümqi: Xinjiang People's Press, 1995, pp. 164–73.

16 Ibid., pp. 174–80.

17 It is also striking that the re-registration among the Manchus more or less stopped after the 1990 census; the 2000 census shows the Manchu population at 10,682,262, a growth of less than 1 per cent a year since 1990. See National Bureau of Statistics of China (comp.), *Zhongguo tongji nianjian* (*China Statistical Yearbook 2002*), Beijing: China Statistics Press, 2002, p. 97.

18 Sun Jingxin *et al.*, *Kua shiji de Zhongguo renkou, Xinjiang juan* (*The Population of China Towards the 21st Century, Xinjiang Volume*), Beijing: China Statistical Press, 1994, pp. 17, 25.

19 Justin Ben-Adam, 'China', in David Westerlund and Ingvar Svanberg (eds), *Islam Outside the Arab World*, Richmond, Surrey: Curzon, 1999, p. 206.

20 See these census figures in Liu Weixin *et al.* (comp.), *Xinjiang minzu cidian* (*Xinjiang Nationalities Dictionary*), Ürümqi: Xinjiang People's Press, 1995, p. 891 and those for 1997 in Xinjiang Uygur Autonomous Regional Gazetteer Compilation Committee (comp.), *Xinjiang nianjian* (*Xinjiang Yearbook*) *1998*, Ürümqi: Xinjiang Yearbook Press and Xinjiang People's Press, 1998, p. 9.

21 Bruce Gilley, '"Uighurs need not apply"', *Far Eastern Economic Review*, 23 August 2001, vol. 164, no. 33, p. 27.

22 The figure of 19.25 million comes from *Renmin ribao* (*People's Daily, Overseas Edition*), 3 April 2001, p. 1.

23 The 1990 figure, from the census of that year, is given in Population Census Office of Xizang Autonomous Region (comp.), *Xizang zizhiqu 1990 nian renkou pucha ziliao, dianzi jisuanji huizong* (*Tabulation on the 1990 Population Census of Xizang Autonomous Region, Computer Tabulation*), Lhasa: Xizang Publishing House, 1992, p. 38. The 2000 figure is from *Renmin ribao*, 3 April 2001, p. 1. It is true that the figures are open to contest. For instance, they do not include the army or the short-term floating population. Many people do not accept them at all, especially among the Tibetan government-in-exile and its supporters. However, what is important here is the comparisons with other regions and, if the census figures can be broadly accepted for Xinjiang and elsewhere, then they can also be for Tibet.

24 See Yan Hao, 'Tibetan population in China: Myths and facts re-examined', *Asian Ethnicity*, March 2000, vol. 1, no. 1, especially pp. 33–4.

25 See Colin Mackerras, *China's Minorities: Integration and Modernization in the Twentieth Century*, Hong Kong: Oxford University Press, 1994, p. 205.

26 Katherine Palmer, 'China's nationalities and nationality areas', in Christopher Hudson (ed.), *The China Handbook*, Chicago and London: Fitzroy Dearborn Publishers, 1997, p. 284.

27 See these and more detailed figures in Mackerras, *The New Cambridge Handbook*, p. 258.

28 See Chen Qiuping, 'Progress seen in minority population', *Beijing Review*, 19–25 July 1993, vol. 36, no. 29, p. 15.
29 Jacques Lamontagne, 'National minority education in China, a nationwide survey across counties', in Gerard A. Postiglione (ed.), *China's National Minority Education, Culture, Schooling, and Development*, New York and London: Falmer Press, 1999, pp. 167, 155.
30 Barry Sautman, 'Expanding access to higher education for China's national minorities, policies of preferential admission', in Postiglione (ed.), *China's National Minority Education*, p. 193.
31 Yu Zhen and Guo Zhenglin, 'Xizang, Sichuan Gansu Zangqu shehui fazhan diaocha baogao' ('Report of a social survey in the Tibetan areas of Tibet, Sichuan and Gansu'), in Yu Zhen and Guo Zhenglin (eds), *Zhongguo Zangqu xiandaihua, lilun, shijian, zhengce* (*The Modernization of China's Tibetan Regions: Theory, Practice, Policy*), Beijing: Central Nationalities University Press, 1999, pp. 46–7.
32 Melvyn C. Goldstein, 'The revival of monastic life in Drepung Monastery', in Melvyn C. Goldstein and Matthew T. Kapstein (eds), *Buddhism in Contemporary Tibet: Religious Revival and Cultural Identity*, Berkeley, Los Angeles, London: University of California Press, 1998, p. 51.
33 Melvyn C. Goldstein, 'Introduction', in Goldstein and Kapstein (eds), *Buddhism in Contemporary Tibet*, p. 14.
34 See Clara Li, 'Beijing alarmed over rise in illegal arms trading', *South China Morning Post* (Hong Kong), 10 February 2001.
35 See Chris Mullin, 'Tibetan conspiracy', *Far Eastern Economic Review*, 5 September 1975, vol. 89, no. 36, pp. 30–4.

Further reading

The study of China's minorities has grown exponentially in recent years. This is because field-workers have been allowed into minority areas in the period of reform to an enormously greater extent than was the case before, and facilities for travel there have vastly improved at the same time. Also, interest in ethnic affairs has grown greatly worldwide.

Not surprisingly, it is in China that the greatest amount of work has been done, the overwhelming majority in the Chinese language. Much of this work is at the level of propaganda, but a great deal of it is path-breaking and has provided one of the bases for the best work carried out in English. A well-known and commonly cited work in English published in China is Ma Yin (ed.), *China's Minority Nationalities* (Beijing: Foreign Languages Press, 1989). This contains a brief run-down on all the fifty-five state-recognized minorities. In the West a pioneering study for its time was June Teufel Dreyer, *China's Forty Millions, Minority Nationalities and National Integration in the People's Republic of China* (Cambridge, MA and London: Harvard University Press, 1976), which focused on policy towards the minorities in the first years of the PRC, but also included a good deal of recent historical background.

The following takes account only of the main books in the English language published since the 1980s. The content of the books listed here is strongly focused towards the period since the CCP came to power in 1949. It will be seen that the Tibetans and Tibet have attracted by far the greatest interest in the West among China's minorities. It should be added that the Tibetans and many others of China's minority nationalities have been the subject of article-length studies, which are not mentioned below.

General books on China's minorities

Harrell, Stevan (ed.), *Cultural Encounters on China's Ethnic Frontiers*, Seattle and London: University of Washington Press, 1995.

Heberer, Thomas, *China and its National Minorities, Autonomy or Assimilation?*, Armonk, NY and London: M.E. Sharpe, 1989.

Mackerras, Colin, *China's Minorities: Integration and Modernization in the Twentieth Century*, Hong Kong: Oxford University Press, 1994.

Mackerras, Colin, *China's Minority Cultures: Identities and Integration since 1912*, Melbourne: Longman Australia, New York: St Martin's Press, 1995.

Mackerras, Colin, *China's Ethnic Minorities and Globalisation*, London: RoutledgeCurzon, 2003.

Books on particular topics

Hansen, Mette Halskov, *Lessons in Being Chinese: Minority Education and Ethnic Identity in Southwest China*, Seattle: University of Washington Press, 1999.

Postiglione, Gerard (ed.), *China's National Minority Education, Culture, Schooling, and Development*, New York and London: Falmer Press, 1999.

Safran, William (ed.), *Nationalism and Ethnoregional Identities in China*, London, Portland, OR: Frank Cass, 1998.

Tibet, the Tibetans

Barnett, Robert (ed.), *Resistance and Reform in Tibet*, London: Hurst, 1994.

Goldstein, Melvyn C., *A History of Modern Tibet, 1913–1951: The Demise of the Lamaist State*, Berkeley: University of California Press, 1989.

Goldstein, Melvyn C., *The Struggle for Modern Tibet: The Autobiography of Tashi Tsering*, Armonk, NY: M.E. Sharpe, 1997.

Goldstein, Melvyn C. and Beall, Cynthia M., *Nomads of Western Tibet: The Survival of a Way of Life*, Berkeley, Los Angeles: University of California Press, 1990.

Goldstein, Melvyn C. and Kapstein, Matthew T. (eds), *Buddhism in Contemporary Tibet: Religious Revival and Cultural Identity*, Berkeley, Los Angeles, London: University of California Press, 1998.

Grunfeld, Tom A., *The Making of Modern Tibet*, London: Zed Books, 1987; 2nd revised edn, Armonk, NY: M.E. Sharpe, 1996.

Harrer, Heinrich, trans. Ewald Osers, *Return to Tibet*, Harmondsworth: Penguin, 1985.

Shakya, Tsering, *The Dragon in the Land of Snows: A History of Modern Tibet Since 1947*, London: Pimlico, Random House, 1999.

Xinjiang

Benson, Linda, and Svanberg, Ingvar, *China's Last Nomads: The History and Culture of China's Kazaks*, Armonk, NY and London: M.E. Sharpe, 1998.

Rudelson, Justin Jon, *Oasis Identities: Uyghur Nationalism Along China's Silk Road*, New York: Columbia University Press, 1997.

Other minorities

Bulag, Uradyn Erden, *The Mongols at China's Edge: History and the Politics of National Unity*, Lanham, MD and Oxford: Rowman & Littlefield, 2002.

Gladney, Dru C., *Muslim Chinese: Ethnic Nationalism in the People's Republic*, Cambridge, MA: Harvard University Press, 1991.

Gladney, Dru C., *Ethnic Identity in China: The Making of a Muslim Minority Nationality*, Stanford, CA: Harcourt Brace & Co., 1998.

Harrell, Stevan, *Ways of Being Ethnic in Southwest China*, Seattle and London: University of Washington Press, 2001.

Harrell, Stevan, Bamo Qubumo and Ma Erzi, photographs by Zhong Dakun, *Mountain Patterns: The Survival of Nuosu Culture in China*, Seattle and London: University of Washington Press, 2000.

Kaup, Katherine Palmer, *Creating the Zhuang: Ethnic Politics in China*, Boulder, CO and London: Lynne Rienner, 2000.

Litzinger, Ralph A., *Other Chinas: The Yao and the Politics of National Belonging*, Durham, NC and London: Duke University Press, 2000.

Schein, Louisa, *Minority Rules: The Miao and the Feminine in China's Cultural Politics*, Durham, NC and London: Duke University Press, 2000.

3   *In* Japan, but not *of* Japan

Kirsten Refsing

Since the Second World War, Japan's self-image has rested on the idea that it is both homogeneous and unique. According to this image, the nation consists of middle-class families with a hard-working father, a happy homemaker mother, and a gradually diminishing number of children. Grandparents living in the same house or nearby help to complement the picture. All these happy families are of the same blood, speak the same language, and are carriers of the same immutable and uniquely Japanese traditions. Together they endeavour to collaborate for the ultimate good of the whole country, thus forming the essential building blocks of the uniquely Japanese *communitas*[1] on which the Japanese state is supposedly based.

The image of uniqueness and homogeneity has its historical roots in pre-war Japan. American pressure in 1853 ended almost 200 years of isolation, in which travel abroad was forbidden and few Japanese ever saw or spoke to a foreigner, since foreigners were, with only a few exceptions, routinely turned away from its shores. The end of isolation created a strong desire to 'catch up' and emulate anything 'Western'.

This enthusiasm for the 'West' was initially driven by a feeling of having dropped behind the United States and the powerful European countries, and a need to protect Japan from a fate similar to China's, namely subjugation and division of their land by foreign powers. The Meiji government (1868–1912) wanted to create a homogeneous nation that felt like 'one people', and at the same time to conquer and assimilate other nations. It incorporated Hokkaido and the Ryukyu islands in the early decades of the Meiji period and took Taiwan and Korea as colonies, respectively in 1895 and 1910. Quite a few Japanese went abroad, coming back with ideas that helped state formation and assisted Japan to catch up to the West. The new additions to the Japanese state did not become Japanese without problems, however. On the one hand, some resolutely refused to accept the Japanese attempts at acculturation, and on the other the Japanese conquerors were not prepared to accord the conquered people equal status. Korea provides a good example: there was continuing resistance to becoming 'Japanese', with the Japanese state violently suppressing dissent. But the Meiji government did achieve some success in unifying its expanding empire and creating a centralized state of homogeneous citizens. In the process, traditional Japanese ideas and values were revisited and re-evaluated.

With the rise of the military in the 1930s, the traits that had driven feelings of being backward and behind had turned around to become the basis for a feeling of spiritual superiority, especially in comparison to the rest of Asia. Part of becoming a strong nation in those days was to expand and acquire colonies, and Japan saw itself as the carrier of a civilization and of special virtues that justified it in invading and annexing its neighbours. In 1931 Japan occupied the north-eastern provinces of China, setting up the puppet state of Manchukoku in 1932, and it later occupied much of the rest of China. Following its attack on Pearl Harbor at the end of 1941, Japan seized much of the rest of East and Southeast Asia. For the Japanese state of the day, the same ideology of its superior civiliza-tion and special virtues even justified Japan in taking on the Western powers in war when it seemed necessary to do so.

When Japan lost the war in 1945, these feelings of superiority suffered a harsh blow, and for a few decades, an inferiority complex vis-à-vis the West, and in particular the American victors, returned in full force. Nevertheless, with the rapid recovery and growth of the Japanese economy and infrastructure in the late 1950s and early 1960s, culminating in the Tokyo Olympics in 1964, the idea that Japan was unique and special gained strength again, although now that Japan had lost all its overseas possessions and its military ambitions, the imperi-alistic overtones of the pre-war period were absent.[2]

The refined and aesthetic, but also hard-working and efficient image of the Japanese was an attractive one, not only to the Japanese themselves, but also to many foreign researchers who were charmed by the Japanese hospitality and courtesy, and impressed – or by the late 1960s even alarmed – by the country's rapid progress. So Japanese and non-Japanese collaborated for a while in spreading ideas about 'Japanese uniqueness'. 'Unique' is, of course, a concept that requires a basis for comparison, and the Japanese basis for comparison was 'the West', primarily exemplified by the United States and Western Europe. Comparisons of the kind that claimed that the Japanese were peaceful because they ate rice and vegetables, while 'Westerners' were belligerent and aggressive, because they ate meat, abounded. Peter Dale's book carries several tables listing the major opposites between 'us' and 'them', which the author has culled from a number of mainly Japanese sources.[3] A genre of writing on such themes termed *Nihonjinron*, meaning literally 'theory of the Japanese', produced a variety of theories of Japanese uniqueness ranging from scholarly tomes to superficial writings for the general public, both in Japanese and in English.

By the late 1970s, however, the number of people from different disciplines engaging in research on Japan had become so large and diverse that cracks began to appear in the perfect façade. One scholar after another,[4] Japanese as well as Western, published critical articles and books debunking the myth, and soon the *Nihonjinron* style of writing about Japan fell into thorough discredit among scholars, even though it is still not unusual to see it in popular books and articles. Once the debunking began, it was actually very easy to punch holes in the homogeneity myth. In recent years, several books have appeared in English with titles that make the multi-faceted nature of Japan explicit, such as *Multicultural*

Japan, Multilingual Japan, Multiethnic Japan, Diversity in Japanese Language and Culture and *Japan's Minorities: The Illusion of Homogeneity*.[5]

In historical times, Japan has never been a homogeneous country.[6] Chinese and Korean scholars and scribes arrived before the sixth century, and many stayed. To the north and south of the main islands, in areas that only later became incorporated into the Japanese state, such as Okinawa and Hokkaido, there were indigenous peoples, who were not at all like the mainland Japanese. Inside mainstream Japanese society there was a rigid division into four classes: warriors, farmers, artisans and merchants, in descending order of respectability. Outside these four classes, which were really an ideological construct that hid the diversity of Japanese society, were the Buddhist clergy and the imperial family, and some people were seen as so marginal that they were labelled 'non-people'. This continued up until the mid-nineteenth century.

During the so-called 'closed country' period (1639–1853), there was a flourishing community of Chinese in Nagasaki city, and a small and isolated community of Dutch men on the artificial island of Dejima, off Nagasaki Harbour. No other foreigners were admitted, nor were the Japanese themselves permitted to leave their country. As soon as Japan opened up the first treaty ports to foreigners in 1853, there was an influx of Americans and Europeans, as well as Chinese traders and students. When Japan began to have imperialist aspirations in the twentieth century, the number of Koreans and Taiwanese who came to Japan, voluntarily or involuntarily, grew rapidly as well.

Apart from a few citizens of countries friendly to Japan, all foreigners of Western origin were forced to leave Japan during the Second World War. However, many people of Korean and Chinese descent stayed and were subsequently co-opted into the Japanese war effort both as draftees and as labour in an economy that experienced more and more serious labour shortages as the war proceeded. Others were forcibly imported at this time as labourers.

In the decades since the war, the influx of people from all over the world has resumed, with some staying for a shorter time while others settled more or less permanently. In recent years a variety of foreign migrants have come to Japan, such as construction workers from China, Southeast, South and Central Asia, entertainers – sometimes a euphemism for sex-workers – from the Philippines and Thailand, and refugees from Indochina during and after the Vietnam War (1965–73). Many Europeans and Americans come for business or study purposes, and some settle for many years. A small, but interesting, addition is the Filipina and Thai brides who have consented to marry Japanese farmers in remote areas. Some farming communities have deliberately chosen this way to alleviate the problem of *yomebusoku*, the lack of young Japanese brides who will consent to sharing the hard work on a farm under the watchful eyes of a traditional mother-in-law. Also, on a smaller scale, there are the part-Chinese descendants of Japanese women and children left behind when Japan left Manchuria in great haste on the eve of defeat in August 1945. They became part of Chinese families through adoption or marriage and are now beginning to return to Japan with their Chinese families and descendants.

As can be seen from the above, Japan is a society much like many others, with a great deal of variety among the population that lives within its borders and with constant new additions to the mix. If it is different from other heterogeneous societies, it is only in its reluctance to accept and deal with this reality – an attitude that is probably more easily maintained because many of those who are different are also geographically segregated from the mainstream. The Ainu are mostly in Hokkaido, the Okinawans in the Ryukyu Islands. *Burakumin* tend to live in special areas, and many of the poorer immigrants of Korean and Chinese origin choose to live there or in similar enclaves, too. Still, the Japanese are hardly exceptional, at least in Asia, in trying to gloss over differences and promoting an image of a unified population. In contrast to societies such as the United States, Canada and Australia, Japan does not aspire to multi-ethnic hybridity, but rather prides itself on homogeneity.

The *burakumin*

An estimated three million Japanese belong to the *burakumin* ('village people') category. The *burakumin* are not an ethnic minority in the sense of being physically different, but they are still non-'Japanese' inasmuch as they are not permitted to join the *communitas* of 'Japanese-ness', even though they are indigenous to Japan and indistinguishable in appearance and lifestyle from other Japanese. They are literally outcasts and identified, not by what they *are*, but by what they are *not* – namely ordinary 'Japanese'.

The name for this people has changed many times, from a host of derogatory terms to more politically correct and neutral terms. Even the term *burakumin* has come to be seen as having too many negative connotations, so in 1997 the Buraku Liberation League decided to replace it with *burakujuumin* (people who live in *buraku* communities). This term has yet to become widely used, which is why I have used the more common *burakumin* here.

In the minds of many Japanese mainstream people, *burakumin* are ritually impure because of traditional occupations to do with slaughtering of animals, leatherwork and night-soil collection, which required the people involved to live apart from other citizens. However, the historical background for the existence of this particular group is a great deal more complicated than simply the nature of the occupations of some of its members. In the Tokugawa era (1603–1868), a group of outcasts emerged with the establishment of the rigid class system, in which the four classes of warriors, farmers, artisans and merchants were set up. Outside the classes were groups of people who did not fit in, and some of these were relegated to a category of *hinin* or non-humans. Social upheavals, such as famines, dislocated many people and some of those ended up as permanent inhabitants of the areas set aside for the non-humans.[7] Apart from the 'impure' occupations held by some inhabitants of those areas, they were all poor, and the fact that they were gathered into their own communities and separate from the mainstream led to the persistence of discrimination against them and their descendants even after the class system was abolished.

Even today, *burakumin* are mainly identified by where they live (or have lived), namely in the so-called 'integration areas' or *doowa chiku*, where they are eligible for various kinds of community support. There are more of these areas in the Kansai area of central Japan than, for instance, in the Tokyo area, but in post-war Japan the areas in which they are segregated are nowhere conspicuous.

Since the early twentieth century, the *burakumin* have had strong liberation movements that have won many concessions for the group, but which have also, through their sometimes quite violent activism, further alienated many main-stream Japanese. In 1969, a Special Measures Law was introduced and large amounts of government money were directed at improving the conditions for *burakumin*. The first decades of the legislation coincided with Japan's rapid eco-nomic growth, and conditions for *burakumin* improved considerably in such areas as housing, education and employment. The rise in living standards and educa-tional attainment, however, has stalled, and *burakumin* still score lower than main-stream Japanese in areas such as progress to higher education and average income. According to McLauchlan, the dropout rate in high school is twice as high for *burakumin* youth than for Japanese; the number of *burakumin* in perman-ent stable employment is 12 per cent lower than that of Japanese; and the ratio of *burakumin* to Japanese relying on social welfare is 20:1 in the prefectures worst affected by the economic downturn.[8] Another disturbing factor is that the gov-ernment money spent on improving the situation for *burakumin* communities has become a source of resentment in the poorer segments of mainstream Japanese society who would like to see similar help coming their way.[9]

Despite both past and present Japanese views to the contrary, the *burakumin* are not in the least physically or ethnically different from the rest of the Japan-ese. Still, their position in society and the treatment they have suffered is com-parable to the way in which the Japanese have treated ethnic minorities, and thus they deserve mention in this context. The main areas of discrimination against *burakumin* are in matters of occupation, and marriage. Some employers make use of illegally compiled lists of people of *burakumin* origin in order to avoid employing one of them unwittingly.[10] Similarly, when two young people decide to marry, their respective families may carry out extensive background checks to ensure that the family line will not be tainted by 'impure' blood. The Liberation Movement has published countless reports of tragic incidents resulting from such discriminatory attitudes, and by ruthlessly pursuing all public figures suspected of discriminatory attitudes on the one hand, and promoting civic education on the other, the Liberation Movement aims eventually to remove all traces of unequal treatment of *burakumin*.[11]

The Ainu

The Ainu were originally a people of hunters, fishermen and gatherers, who, during the seventeenth and eighteenth centuries, supplemented their livelihood by extensive trade with neighbouring peoples.[12] They are physically distinct from the Japanese, with different facial features and, not least, by having abundant body hair and beards.[13] These differences, however, have been obscured to some extent by generations of intermarriage since the Japanese began to colonize Hokkaido in 1869. Another source of mixing was the not-infrequent cases in which Ainu couples adopted Japanese baby girls from their parents who, because of poverty, either abandoned them or gave them to Ainu families.

Ainu language is quite different from Japanese,[14] but there are no longer any mother-tongue speakers of Ainu alive. The language declined sharply from around the turn of the twentieth century with the introduction of Japanese schooling, and many Ainu discouraged their children from using the language in order to get them more easily accepted into Japanese society. Today, efforts are being made to keep the language alive by producing teaching materials and offering night-school classes; and a small newsletter and a weekly radio programme contribute to these efforts. Since the 1980s many tapes of Ainu oral literature have been collected, several new Ainu–Japanese dictionaries have been produced, and new museums have been created to display artifacts of traditional Ainu life and crafts. However, even at its highest, the Ainu population hardly exceeded 25,000 in number,[15] and very few of those who can claim Ainu descent are engaged in revival efforts.

During the Tokugawa era (1603–1868), the military government granted a small fief in Hokkaido to the Matsumae clan, and they were allowed a monopoly over trade between the whole of the island and the rest of Japan. The Matsumae clan gave concessions to Japanese merchants, who were eager to trade in the furs, sea products and goods such as Chinese silk uniforms, which the Ainu obtained through exchange with peoples on the mainland.[16] In return, the Ainu got rice, liquor, cotton textiles and lacquer ware, all of which quickly became integrated elements in the Ainu social system, creating a dependence on the Japanese trade. The merchants were soon exploiting the Ainu, and by the late seventeenth century, many Ainu had been forced into working, for very little pay, in the fishing industries run by Japanese merchants. The incorporation of the Ainu territory into the Japanese state became complete after the establishment of the Meiji government, and farmer-soldiers were sent to Hokkaido from 1869 to accomplish the acculturation of the Ainu. A colonial office[17] was set up to turn Hokkaido into an agricultural society.

With the drive to create a nation, Japan, like other nations, had no place for 'barbarians', and the Ainu were seen as a primitive race, destined to become extinct. Once this definition was in place, a 'Protection Law for the Natives' was promulgated in 1899 to alleviate conditions for the 'dying race', and the Ainu were given land for farming and encouraged to send their children to school. Schooling, however, was different for Japanese and Ainu children, and in many cases farming did not work out either. By the first decades of the twentieth century, the Ainu were thoroughly demoralized and often destitute. A few, who had managed to get an education and who allied themselves with Japanese and foreign supporters, started local organizations, and in 1930 the first Hokkaido-wide organization was formed[18] with the objective of having the inherently discriminatory Protection Law revised. This goal was reached in 1937, but because of the war, the Ainu organization was disrupted and did not regain momentum until the 1970s. At the beginning of the twenty-first century, the Ainu have formed ties with other indigenous communities around the world and have managed to gain visibility within Japan. Through their efforts in the United Nations and elsewhere, they have managed to catch international attention, thus creating pressure on the Japanese government to acknowledge their existence as a *bona fide* ethnic minority. In 1997, many years of fighting for a new law to replace the old protection law was crowned with success when the New Ainu Law (*Ainu Shinpō*) was passed.

One important factor in getting the new law though Parliament was the efforts of Shigeru Kayano, the first Ainu man to manage to get elected to the Japanese Diet or Parliament, from 1994 to 1997. Mr Kayano is still a tireless advocate of Ainu rights and at the same time makes great efforts to promote the Ainu language and culture through teaching and writing. The New Ainu Law aims to promote Ainu culture and to disseminate knowledge of Ainu tradition. It provides financial support for efforts in this direction, but does not touch upon the status or rights of the Ainu people as an indigenous people within Japan's borders.

The Okinawans

Okinawa is the name of the main island in the Ryukyu Archipelago.[19] Okinawa became a tributary state of China in the late fourteenth century, and this arrangement made Okinawa a prosperous centre for entrepôt trade with several East and Southeast Asian countries through the fifteenth and sixteenth centuries. In 1609 the Satsuma domain in southern Japan invaded the islands and forced a treaty on the Ryukyu kingdom in 1611. Satsuma thus became the overlords of the Ryukyu kingdom, and the islands had to pay taxes to Satsuma. This relationship was not disclosed to the Chinese who required tributary states to be independent states and, by keeping it secret, Ryukyu and Satsuma were able to keep the tributary relationship in place so that both could profit from it. During the seventeenth and eighteenth centuries, a succession of Chinese emperors supported the Ryukyu kingdom, which meant that its culture flourished in spite of the exploitation its Japanese masters inflicted.[20] In the late eighteenth century, however, a series of natural disasters, combined with demands for higher taxes to support Satsuma's failing finances, gradually put an end to prosperity.

In 1879, the kingdom of Ryukyu was abolished. Japan annexed Okinawa and turned it into a prefecture. Both Ryukyu and China tried to resist,[21] but to no avail, and after the Sino-Japanese War of 1894–5, all remaining ties with China were cut. Japan then began a process of trying to 'Japanize' the people in Okinawa, and it was in this process that the Japanese formed some of their enduring prejudices about the strangeness of the Okinawans. Another effect of the assimilation efforts was that large numbers emigrated overseas and, by 1935, 15 per cent of the Okinawan people were living outside Okinawa.[22]

In the spring of 1945, American troops landed on Okinawa, and the 'Battle of Okinawa' left lasting scars on the island. Between a quarter and a third of the population lost their lives, and most of the dead were civilians. American firepower killed many people, but large numbers lost their lives or were put in harm's way by the Japanese soldiers stationed on the island. Food and bomb shelters were in short supply, and many followed the command of the Japanese military to commit suicide rather than surrender to the Americans. The Japanese army shot some as 'spies' because they were overheard speaking in the local dialect. The end result was that many Okinawans blamed the tragedy on the Japanese army, who had sacrificed Okinawa to keep the Americans out of the Japanese home-lands for as long as possible.[23]

After the Second World War, Okinawa became a military colony and it remained American territory until 1972. The Americans seized much of the most valuable land on the main island, destroyed the possibilities of a viable Okinawan agriculture and kept many Okinawans interned for two years before releasing them to an economy that was a wasteland. Some Okinawans sub-sequently obtained jobs in and around the bases and the United States improved infrastructure and provided expanded educational opportunities. The United States invested money and effort to convince the people in Okinawa that they were not Japanese, but had their own identity as 'Ryukyuans'. To this end, they created museums and libraries and even tried to revive a dialect of Ryukyu as the standard language by creating a radio station broadcasting in that language. The American presence on the island was portrayed as liberation from Japanese oppression. Many Okinawans resisted this attitude as well as the continued pres-ence of the American military, and anti-American rallies were frequent, accom-panied by displays of the prohibited Japanese flag and a call for 'return to the motherland'.[24]

After May 1972, Okinawa again became a prefecture under Japanese rule, but in spite of efforts to boost the islands' economy, the prefecture remains as it has been since 1972, Japan's poorest, with average incomes well below the mainland, though it is true that it has a *per capita* income higher than that of most countries. The Japanese flag is no longer seen as an expression of protest against the Americans but rather as a symbol of Japanese imperialism,[25] and many schools in Okinawa have resisted the Ministry of Education's efforts to reintro-duce the national anthem and flag. Reversion to Japan in 1972 left the base structure intact and American bases still take up 20 per cent of the land of the main island. The rape of a 12-year-old girl by three American soldiers in 1995 precipitated the largest anti-American protests in the island's history.[26] At the same time, an Okinawan cultural boom during the 1990s, coupled with the loss of Japanese self-confidence, led to profound changes in the situation of Okinawans in Japan, including a growth in Okinawan nationalism. This has found expres-sion in numerous ways, including the establishment of Okinawan museums and memorial representations of the war.

The population of the islands is around 1.4 million. The indigenous languages of the Ryukyu Islands (called 'Ryukyuan' as a group) are related to Japanese, but the two are not mutually intelligible. After Japan's annexation of Ryukyu in 1879, the native languages began to decline, and vigorous efforts on the part of the islands' intellectual elite to assimilate helped push the native language into the background as 'backward'. Today, Japanese is the most common language in daily use. Speakers of a Ryukyu language are generally bilingual, and most are over 40 years of age.[27]

The Koreans

There are about 600,000 to 700,000 Koreans who live in Japan today, this number not including Koreans who have obtained Japanese citizenship. Fukuoka estimates the total number of people of Korean origin to be at least 1 per cent of Japan's population,[28] which makes it the largest non-'Japanese' ethnic group. They originate from different parts of Korea, and most of them arrived in Japan before the Korean War (1950–3) consolidated the division between North and South that began in 1945. Although there have always been people of Korean descent living in Japan, the vast majority of the present population are descendants of Koreans who were forcibly transported to Japan in the 1930s and 1940s to carry out badly paid manual labour.[29] Other groups to come during the thirty-five years of Japanese colonialism (1910–45) included those who came seeking education or better-paid work than was available at home, or for the lure of the metropolis as viewed from a poor colony, a situation similar to migrants in many other societies.

During the years when Korea was a colony of Japan, all Koreans were by definition Japanese citizens. When the war ended Korea became an independent state, and the Koreans in Japan lost their Japanese citizenship and became Koreans by definition, although in reality many remained stateless. If they wanted to become Japanese citizens, they had to apply for naturalization, and in the process were required to give up their Korean citizenship, take on Japanese names, and swear allegiance to the Japanese Constitution, something that many were not prepared to do. If they remained Korean citizens, however, they had few rights and were required to carry with them at all times their alien registration cards. Every time the card was renewed, they had to be fingerprinted,[30] and for many this was akin to being treated like a criminal. Like other aliens, they were barred from jobs in the government or civil service.

The division of Korea created a division between the Koreans living in Japan as well. This was not necessarily geographically based, since most had come from what is now South Korea, but an expression of a political choice that was made at the time of the partition when the majority supported the North.[31] In the 1960s the balance shifted, and the ratio between those who claim allegiance to South Korea and those who stick with North Korea is now estimated to be 7:2.[32]

There are two major organizations for Koreans in Japan, one that supports the South and one that supports the North. Each runs its own schools, four in the case of the South-affiliated organization, which teach in Japanese but have Korean as part of their curriculum,[33] and around 150 for the North-affiliated organization, which teach only in Korean.[34] Only two of the former and none of the latter are recognized by Japan's Ministry of Education, and therefore their graduates cannot seek admission to the Japanese elite national universities, but only to private or municipal universities. The great majority of second- or third-generation Koreans speak only Japanese and go to Japanese schools.

A large number of the Koreans who have lived in Japan for a long time have become naturalized Japanese citizens and have adopted Japanese names, but many of those who are still technically 'aliens' use a Japanese alias in Japanese contexts such as schools and workplaces. In some cases, the Japanese name is used to avoid discrimination, while in others it is more a matter of having become so used to the Japanese name that the Korean one seems strange. Those who are politically active in anti-discrimination movements and the movement to obtain reparations for the 'comfort women', that is those women whom the Japanese army kidnapped during the war and forced into prostitution for Japanese soldiers, tend to use their Korean names as a matter of pride.[35]

Even Koreans who have become Japanese citizens are in many cases still recognizable on the basis of their family name (which may include the character for the original Korean name) or because of their place of residence. Many famous entertainers and popular singers in Japan are reported to be of Korean origin. To the Japanese there is no difference between a Korean with a Japanese passport and one without, and in this respect there are striking similarities to the way the *burakumin* are viewed. Membership of the Japanese *communitas* can only be achieved through birth and maintained through appropriate behaviour.

Many Japanese employers demand a copy of a job applicant's family registration papers, and this immediately gives away the background of Korean applicants who are not registered in this way. Although recent legislation has opened up the possibility for people of Korean descent to be hired as teachers and other kinds of civil servants, many still experience rejection on the basis of their background.[36] Marriage is another area of discrimination. The number of marriages between Japanese and Koreans has increased in recent years and they are now more common than marriages between two Korean–Japanese partners. Fukuoka estimates that there are seven Korean–Japanese who marry a Japanese partner for every two that marry a partner of Korean descent.[37] There is, however, a marked imbalance between the sexes: Korean women marry Japanese men almost twice as often as Korean men marry Japanese women, which might imply that many Korean men in Japan have difficulty in finding a marriage partner.[38]

The Chinese

Overseas Chinese are found in almost all countries throughout the world, and Japan is no exception. The Chinese in Japan today number more than 330,000 people.[39] Some Chinese have resided in Japan for generations and become naturalized Japanese citizens, while others are more recent arrivals and may be sojourners. They are often excluded or just mentioned in passing when minorities in Japan are described,[40] perhaps because they have rarely been at the centre of conflict as a group and are relatively self-sufficient and often affluent. This image, however, is no longer a true one. More recent immigrants from Mainland

China are seen as a major problem. Although the majority are hard-working people struggling to survive under difficult circumstances, many cannot support themselves and demand government assistance, and a few have even resorted to crime.

The history of Chinese immigration to Japan stretches back over centuries. Some came to seek their fortunes in trade; others left China because of poverty or political unrest; and many, especially from Taiwan, came for higher education. The 1911 revolution in China, which put an end to imperial rule, was fomented in Japan where Sun Yatsen fled to escape persecution, and other famous Chinese figures, such as the writer Lu Xun, began their careers as foreign students in Japan. After the Second World War, some came from Taiwan to start businesses in Japan, and in recent years a large number of Mainland Chinese have come to Japan to study or work.

The Japanese view of China and the Chinese has undergone many ups and downs. Originally China was seen as a source of knowledge, and Buddhism and Confucianism were imported and incorporated into the Japanese worldview. The Japanese writing system is based on Chinese characters, and for a long time the Japanese saw the Chinese as a superior, or at least equal, power. When foreign encroachment on China grew in the nineteenth century this image gradually shifted to one of contempt, and the Japanese victory in the Sino-Japanese war of 1894–5, following which China ceded Taiwan to Japan, further confirmed the weakness of the Chinese in Japanese eyes. In 1932, Japan made Manchuria into a puppet-state and, during the Second World War, the Japanese set out to conquer the whole of China and make it part of their grand vision of a 'Greater Asia Co-Prosperity Sphere'.

The image of China took a turn for the better in the years around Japan's decision to recognize the People's Republic of China (PRC) in 1972. The peak was reached in 1970 when as many as 78 per cent declared that they had 'friendly feelings' towards China. After the Tiananmen massacre in 1989, however, the proportion fell to 51.6 per cent, and at the end of the twentieth century passed 50 per cent on its way downwards.[41] The central issue seems to be anxiety at the possibility of China's rise to the major regional power, displacing Japan – this at a time of Japanese stagnation and uncertainty. Furthermore, the persistent Chinese refusal to accept Japan's attempts at providing an apology for its war atrocities leaves some Japanese impatient and bewildered. This factor, combined with China's failure to publicize the receipt of generous Overseas Development Aid, has been widely criticized in the Japanese press.

The shifting images of China, however, do not seem to influence how the long-term Chinese residents in Japan are viewed. Chinese immigrants who are poor and do manual work have generally been badly treated and looked down upon, while the more established and wealthy Chinese are accepted, but often ignored and avoided. The internal support systems for Chinese in Japan, based on common geographical origin or on family ties, have always been strong, and, in spite of the split in the Chinese community caused by the division of China into the PRC and Taiwan, each group still manages to care for its existing members. Newer immigrant labourers from Mainland China, however, are generally excluded from this support system and tend to rely on official assistance from Japanese authorities and organizations.[42]

There are several Chinese schools in the big cities with large Chinese populations, and they strive to educate bilingual students with almost equal emphasis on Chinese and Japanese learning.[43] Nevertheless, quite a large percentage of the students in these schools are there because their Japanese is either non-existent or not good enough to get them into Japanese schools.[44]

A subgroup of Chinese immigrants are the relatives and descendants of Japanese children and women who became separated from their families and were left behind when the Japanese fled Manchuria and China after their defeat in 1945. The children were brought up by foster parents and in most cases speak only Chinese; the women often married Chinese men and tried to pass as Chinese. In 1974 some Japanese families began to look for their lost relatives in China, and since then around 20,000 returnees and family members from China have settled in Japan, together with 7,000 to 8,000 who are residing there while they await determination of their status. The original family member who was left behind is, of course, Japanese by blood, but the accompanying family is Chinese. But regardless of biological origin, all of them are strangers to Japanese society and culture and must struggle if they want to fit in. This group is quite politically active and demands compensation as war victims from the Japanese state. Some subsist on government assistance and the local government and support organizations provide schooling and legal aid.

In Japan, but not *of* Japan

This chapter has presented some groups, which are *in*, but not *of*, Japanese society. The groups presented above are marginalized because of imagined or real ethnic differences from mainstream Japanese. But they are not the only ones who find themselves marginalized by the hegemonic discourse. There are many others who fall short of the range of qualifications required to be fully 'Japanese' and to fit into the ideal image. People with physical or mental handicaps, and people who drop out of the mainstream through their lifestyle choices, such as despised occupations, substance abuse, crime and other kinds of aberrant behaviour, are all marginalized – overlooked if possible, and looked down upon if they cannot be ignored. In the late nineteenth and early twentieth centuries a large number of Japanese emigrated to the United States and to Brazil, and those of their descendants who choose to return to Japan also fall somewhat short of qualifying as 'proper Japanese', either because of linguistic shortcomings or because of 'un-Japanese' behaviour. Similarly, Japanese children whose fathers have been stationed abroad with the whole family are seen as lacking in Japanese-ness, and special programmes have been set up in schools to help them reintegrate.[45] It is even possible to claim, as Maher and McDonald do,[46] that Japanese women are also a marginalized group. Co-opted as they are into playing a supporting role in the male definition of what constitutes 'Japanese-ness', their freedom of movement and their individual choices are severely limited. Still, this social image is not unassailable. Korean, Ainu and *burakumin* activists have won many victories in recent decades, and lately, Japanese women's disenchantment with marriage and motherhood is causing a great deal of worry among bureaucrats. With one of the world's lowest birthrates and with more and more young women and men delaying marriage, the future for Japan looks bleak in terms of social solidarity. The financial crisis, of course, adds further to the bleakness. The image of a successful economic giant with a hard-working, uniform population is fading, and the so-called 'normal' elite is beginning to look like a minority in a mathematical sense, in terms of headcount.

This underscores the fact that, when we talk about minorities, we are talking about power relations more than about anything else. Who has the power and who has usurped the right to define what is 'ethnic' and what is 'mainstream'? Power structures tend to perpetuate themselves, not only by making decisions in the present and designing the future, but also by unceasingly creating and recreating the history and traditions that support them. Schöpflin puts it as follows: 'The purposiveness of all institutions is that they survive, that they ensure that whatever else happens, they remain intact and retain their basic elements untouched.'[47] The 'othering' of certain groups is a necessity for maintaining a sense of 'self' and for this 'self' to survive, and in this respect, Japan is no different from any other nation in the world. Awareness of 'face' vis-à-vis the rest of the world can be a powerful tool against the Japanese establishment's efforts to pretend that Japan is homogeneous, because Japan is always extremely preoccupied by how it is viewed by the rest of the world. However, when it comes to how diversity inside the nation is tackled, few countries, if any, can cast the first stone. 'Different but equal' remains a distant ideal in most, if not all, countries, as well as in the world at large.

Notes

1 Wim van Binsbergen defines *communitas* as 'an intersubjective sense of transcendence of individuality into sociable collectivity' – a definition that was not written with Japan in mind, but that fits the hegemonic ideology in Japan extremely well. See Wim van Binsbergen, 'In search of spirituality: Provisional conceptual and theoretical explorations from the cultural anthropology of religion and the history of ideas', paper presented at the Research Group on Spirituality, Dutch/Flemish Association for Intercultural Philosophy, 29 October 1999. Published on http://www.shikanda.net.

2 See also Harumi Befu, *Hegemony of Homogeneity*, Melbourne: Trans Pacific Press, 2001, pp. 123–41 for a brief overview, and Peter Dale, *The Myth of Japanese Uniqueness*, London: Croom Helm, 1986, pp. 201–23 for a more detailed analysis.

3 For example, Dale, *The Myth of Japanese Uniqueness*, pp. 42–51.

4 E.g. Befu, *Hegemony of Homogeneity*; R.A. Miller, *Japan's Modern Myth: The Language and Beyond*, New York: Weatherhill, 1982; Ross Mouer and Yoshio Sugimoto, *Images of Japanese Society*, London: Kegan Paul International, 1986; T. Aoki, '*Nihonbunkaron*' no henyō (*The Metamorphosis of 'Theories of Japaneseness'*), Tokyo: Chūkō Bunkō, 1990.

5 Donald Denoon, Mark Hudson, Gavan McCormack and Tessa Morris-Suzuki (eds), *Multicultural Japan: Paleolithic to Postmodern*, Cambridge: Cambridge University Press, 1996; J.C. Maher and G. Macdonald (eds), *Diversity in Japanese Culture and Languages*,

London and New York: Kegan Paul International, 1995; J.C. Maher and K. Yashiro (eds), *Multilingual Japan*, Clevedon, UK: Multilingual Matters Ltd, 1995; J. Lie, *Multiethnic Japan*, Cambridge, MA: Harvard University Press, 2001; M. Weiner (ed.), *Japan's Minorities: The Illusion of Homogeneity*, London: Routledge, 1997.

6 Lie, *Multiethnic Japan*, pp. 170–1 puts this even more strongly when he says: 'Japan has always been multiethnic. Ethnic diversity began neither with the coming of the new foreign workers in the 1980s, nor with the influx of colonial subjects in the early twentieth century, nor even with the arrival of *toraijin* from the Korean peninsula over a millennium ago. . . . One cannot speak of Japan without speaking of ethnic diversity'.

7 I. Neary, 'Burakumin in contemporary Japan' in Weiner (ed.), *Japan's Minorities*, pp. 54ff.

8 A. McLauchlan, 'The current circumstances of Japan's Burakumin: Are Japanese economic woes about to reverse 25 years of progress?', *New Zealand Journal of Asian Studies*, 2001, vol. 2, no. 1, pp. 123, 128, 131.

9 McLauchlan, 'The current circumstances of Japan's Burakumin', p. 130.

10 Kitaguchi Suehiro, trans. with introduction by Alastair McLauchlan, *An Introduction to the Buraku Issue: Question and Answers*, Japan Library, Richmond: Curzon Press, 1999, p. 66.

11 See also Kitaguchi, *An Introduction to the Buraku Issue*.

12 See Brett L. Walker, *The Conquest of Ainu Lands: Ecology and Culture in Japanese Expansions, 1590–1800*, Berkeley: University of California Press, 2001.

13 For descriptions of how Europeans saw the Ainu in the latter half of the nineteenth century, see Kirsten Refsing, *Early European Writings on Ainu Culture: Travelogues and Descriptions*, vols 1–5, *The Ainu Library 3*, Richmond: Curzon Press, 2000.

14 See Kirsten Refsing, *The Ainu Language*, Aarhus: Aarhus University Press, 1986.

15 There is no accurate way of knowing the size of the Ainu population before the Japanese began to exploit their land and register the population. Early Western sources, citing Japanese population counts, estimate the population in the late nineteenth century at between 8,000 and 16,000 people (see Refsing, *Early European Writings on Ainu Culture*, pp. 40, 52, 75); R. Siddle, 'Ainu: Japan's indigenous people', in Weiner (ed.), *Japan's Minorities*, p. 18, says 'perhaps forty thousand' at the time when the distinct Ainu culture appeared around the thirteenth century, but this remains an educated guess.

16 Walker, *The Conquest of Ainu Lands*, pp. 135ff.

17 The Japanese have persisted in defining this as an office for the *development* of Hokkaido, and the Japanese name means just that (see also Siddle, 'Ainu', p. 17).

18 R. Siddle, *Race, Resistance, and the Ainu of Japan*, London and New York: Routledge, 1996, pp. 133ff.

19 I owe thanks to Stanislaw Meyer, PhD student at the University of Hong Kong, for assisting me with background material and personal observations for this section.

20 K. Taira, 'Troubled national identity: The Ryukyuans/Okinawans', in Weiner (ed.), *Japan's Minorities*, pp. 151–2.

21 Taira, 'Troubled national identity', pp. 153ff.

22 Taira, 'Troubled national identity', p. 157. Some of these emigrés went to other places in Japan.

23 R. Siddle, 'Colonialism and identity in Okinawa before 1945', *Japanese Studies*, vol. 18, no. 2, 1998, 131–2.

24 S. Rabson, *Assimilation Policy in Okinawa: Promotion, Resistance, and 'Reconstruction'*. Cardiff, CA: JPRI (Japan Policy Research Institute) Occasional Paper No. 8, 1996, unpaginated web version.

25 Rabson, *Assimilation Policy in Okinawa*.

26 A.G. Mulgan, 'Managing the US base issue in Okinawa: A test for Japanese democracy', *Japanese Studies*, 2000, vol. 20, no. 2, 159.

27 A. Matsumori, 'Ryukyuan: Past, present, and future', in J.C. Maher, and K. Yashiro (eds), *Multilingual Japan*, Clevedon, UK: Multilingual Matters, 1995, p. 32.

28 Fukuoka Yasunori, trans. Tom Gill, *Lives of Young Koreans in Japan*, Melbourne: Trans Pacific Press, 2000, p. 39.

29 Michael Weiner, 'The representation of absence and the absence of representation: Korean victims of the atomic bomb', in Weiner (ed.), *Japan's Minorities*, p. 84.

30 Until 1992, not just Koreans but *all* foreigners staying over sixty days in Japan had to have their fingerprints registered, regardless of their country of origin.

31 Fukuoka, *Lives of Young Koreans in Japan*, pp. 21–2.

32 Fukuoka, *Lives of Young Koreans in Japan*, p. 22.

33 These schools are to a large extent attended by the children of South Koreans temporarily stationed in Japan. Fukuoka, *Lives of Young Koreans in Japan*, p. 25.

34 Fukuoka, *Lives of Young Koreans in Japan*, p. 25.

35 Fukuoka, *Lives of Young Koreans in Japan*, pp. 27–33.

36 See also George Hicks, *Japan's Hidden Apartheid: The Korean Minority and the Japanese*, Aldershot: Ashgate, 1997, pp. 120–6.

37 Fukuoka, *Lives of Young Koreans in Japan*, p. 36.

38 Fukuoka, *Lives of Young Koreans in Japan*, pp. 36–7.

39 Barry Turner (ed.), *The Statesman's Yearbook: The Politics, Cultures and Economies of the World 2003*, Houndmills, Hampshire and New York: Palgrave Macmillan, 2003, p. 960 gives a figure of 335,575 (registered Chinese foreigners, as of 31 December 2000). This is quite a lot higher than the *c.* 150,000 given in 1995 by J.C. Maher, 'The *kakyo*: Chinese in Japan', in Maher and Yashiro (eds), *Multilingual Japan*, p. 126.

40 There are two exceptions: Weiner (ed.), *Japan's Minorities*, pp. 108–39, has a chapter entitled 'A model community: The Chinese minority in Japan', by Andrea Vasishth; and Maher, 'The *kakyo*', pp. 125–38.

41 *Gaikoo ni kansuru yoronchoosa* (*Opinion Poll on Foreign Relations*), Japan: Ministry of Foreign Affairs, 2000.

42 Vasishht, 'A model community', pp. 135–6.

43 Maher, 'The *kakyo*', p. 132.

44 Maher, 'The *kakyo*', p. 137.

45 For example, see R. Goodman, *Japan's International Youth*, Oxford: Clarendon Press, 1990.

46 Maher and Macdonald, *Diversity in Japanese Culture and Language*.

47 G. Schöpflin, *Nations Identity Power: The New Politics of Europe*, London: Hurst & Co., 2000, p. 7.

Further reading

There are several anthologies dealing with different minorities within one volume, such as J.C. Maher and G. Macdonald (eds), *Diversity in Japanese Culture and Languages* (London and New York: Kegan Paul International, 1995); and Michael Weiner (ed.), *Japan's Minorities: The Illusion of Homogeneity* (London: Routledge, 1997). J.C. Maher and K. Yashiro (eds), *Multilingual Japan* (Clevedon, UK: Multilingual Matters, 1995) deals more specifically with the languages spoken by such groups.

Some monographs or articles treat one group in particular. An easily read overview of the Koreans in Japan can be found in George Hicks, *Japan's Hidden Apartheid: The Korean Minority and the Japanese* (Aldershot: Ashgate, 1997). Also recommendable is Fukuoka Yasunori, trans. Tom Gill, *Lives of Young Koreans in Japan*, (Melbourne: Trans Pacific Press, 2000).

A very thorough book about the Ainu is R. Siddle, *Race, Resistance, and the Ainu of Japan* (London and New York: Routledge, 1996). Honda Katsuichi, trans. Kyoko Selden (with a Foreword by David L. Howell), *Harukor: An Ainu Woman's Tale* (Berkeley, Los Angeles,

London: University of California Press, 2000), originally published in Japanese in 1993, is a charming story about how Ainu life might have been before the Japanese arrived in great numbers. Brett L. Walker, *The Conquest of Ainu Lands: Ecology and Culture in Japanese Expansions, 1590–1800* (Berkeley: University of California Press, 2001) is an excellent analysis of the Japanese encroachment on Ainu lands. K. Refsing's twenty-five volume work, *The Ainu Library* (Richmond: Curzon Press, 1996, 1998, 2000 and 2002) gives a thorough presentation of Western writings about the Ainu, from the very first ones up to the Second World War.

A. McLauchlan (2001) 'The current circumstances of Japan's Burakumin: Are Japanese economic woes about to reverse 25 years of progress?', *New Zealand Journal of Asian Studies*, 2001, vol. 2, no. 1, 120–44, gives a good overview of the situation through statistics, and Kitaguchi Suehiro, trans. with Introduction by Alastair McLauchlan, *An Introduction to the Buraku Issue: Question and Answers* (Japan Library, Richmond: Curzon Press, 1999), is informative, albeit rather partisan.

The self-perception of the Japanese and the myth of 'Japanese-ness' are excellently analysed in Befu Harumi, *Hegemony of Homogeneity* (Melbourne: Trans Pacific Press, 2001); Peter Dale, *The Myth of Japanese Uniqueness* (London: Croom Helm, 1986); and J. Lie, *Multiethnic Japan* (Cambridge, MA: Harvard University Press, 2001).

4 Ethnicity in Indonesia

Gerry van Klinken

Ethnicity is nowhere but everywhere in Indonesia. It is nowhere because for seventy years between 1930 and 2000 no census measured Indonesia's ethnic composition. The New Order government of President Suharto (1966–98) had few explicit policies on ethnic groups, though it had several veiled and indirect ones. With the widespread support of the media and intellectuals, it was keen to develop a modern, non-ethnic Indonesia and therefore avoided mentioning anything 'ethnic'. The literature on ethnicity in Indonesia is surprisingly meagre and distorted as a result.

Yet ethnicity is everywhere. The tourist industry of the booming 1980s and 1990s thrived on exotic images of dancing tribesmen. More darkly, most people interested in Indonesia saw television images of indigenous Dayaks expelling settler Madurese from Kalimantan in several waves between 1997 and 2001, or heard about ethnic Chinese women selected for rape during the Jakarta riots of May 1998. Secessionist movements in Aceh and Papua have an ethnic character.

The conflicting aspects of ethnic relations will concern us the most in this chapter. Until 1998, Indonesia was not among the nations that sprang to mind in studies of ethnic conflict. But when the authoritarian New Order regime collapsed in May 1998, ethnic conflict was the biggest unpleasant surprise for Indonesians aspiring to democracy.

What is the nature of ethnic conflict in Indonesia? Is it a 'one-off' problem of post-New Order transition, or a new and lasting feature of the social landscape? What is being done about it, and what more could be done? What are some of the international implications? These are among the questions we will address.

This chapter is structured in five parts. In the first, we take a look at the urgent contemporary reasons why ethnicity has suddenly become such a problem for Indonesia. In the second and third, we review some ways in which scholars and policy-makers have thought about ethnicity in Indonesia, focusing on an important shift that took place in the early 1970s. In the fourth and fifth parts we go back to some of the most pressing among Indonesia's ethnic questions with the aid of insights we have gained from this review. One of these parts, the heart of the chapter, takes a practical public policy approach, while the other briefly examines the implications of a more radical structural analysis.

Plate 4.1 'Let's reclaim culture' – a composite of 'ethnographic' images depicting Indonesia's ethnic diversity, created by Galam Zulkifli, a well-known artist from the Gelaran Budaya community in Yogyakarta, Indonesia (Courtesy of *Inside Indonesia* magazine.)

Urgent issues

When indigenous Dayak warriors in West Kalimantan took up their machetes against settlers from the far-away island of Madura in late 1996, Indonesians were shocked. Their country consists of many ethnic groups, yet ethnic conflict on this scale had not occurred before. Hundreds were killed and tens of thousands displaced, mostly Madurese. Another such wave of killing and expulsion followed in 1999, and then another in the neighbouring province of Central Kalimantan in 2001.

The event that really brought home how serious this all was happened in January 1999 in Ambon, an island in the Moluccas (Maluku). Initially, just as in Kalimantan, settlers from other islands bore the brunt of anger from local Ambonese. However, the conflict soon became a religious war, pitting Christian Ambonese against all Muslims, whether settlers or native Ambonese.

By the end of 1999 Christian–Muslim fighting also broke out in the northern Moluccan islands of Ternate, Tidore and Halmahera. There too it was at first about place of origin, but became religious over time. Another Christian–Muslim conflict broke out around Poso in Central Sulawesi late in 1998, flaring up again at various times in 2000 and 2001. The Christians were locals while many of the Muslims were recent arrivals from South Sulawesi. Thousands have died in the Moluccas and in Central Sulawesi, with hundreds of thousands displaced from their homes, not to mention the destruction of houses, food gardens and economic infrastructure.

In each of these five places, West and Central Kalimantan, Ambon and the northern Moluccas, and Central Sulawesi, the conflicts went on for several years. As of mid-2002 they were each at a delicate post-conflict stage of rebuilding. Ambon remains segregated into distinct Christian and Muslim areas. The settlers expelled from Kalimantan at the height of the conflict are still not allowed to return to the homes they once owned there.

These were not the only conflicts we could call 'ethnic'. Others erupted suddenly then passed in a few days. About twenty Christian churches in the overwhelmingly Muslim town of Situbondo in East Java were burned down on 10 October 1996. Church burnings have become more frequent during urban riots in Indonesia. Conversely, Muslim mosques were burned in the mainly Christian town of Kupang in West Timor in late November 1998.

Other incidents hardly made the news. Rival ethnic gangs in the mega-cities of Jakarta and Surabaya often fight it out on the streets. Since 1994 locals in Luwu, just next to Central Sulawesi, have repeatedly attacked new settlers growing cocoa. By now dozens have died and thousands have lost their homes in Luwu, but the national media rarely bother to report the attacks.

Whether long-running or short and sharp, most of these events were new and required fresh effort to understand them. They inspired a series of academic conferences around the world.[1] The present chapter is part of this learning effort.

Other ethnic problems in Indonesia have a much longer history. Anti-Chinese riots go back to the gruesome massacre of 1740 in Batavia, the colonial city that later became Jakarta.[2] Rioters sporadically targeted Chinese shop-owners even during the repressive New Order. When the New Order collapsed amidst a major economic crisis, demoralized police and military did little to stop anti-Chinese rioting right across Java.

Some regions on the outer periphery of this vast nation have been trying to break away almost since Indonesia became independent. The colonial Dutch only subdued Aceh, on the far western tip of the Indonesian archipelago, after a huge military effort in the late nineteenth century. The region revolted against the newly independent capital in 1953, again in 1976, 1989, and again since late 1998. The Acehnese know they have a glorious history of their own. Such pride inspires the revolt and allows us to call it 'ethnic'.

Ambon, in the Moluccas, was at the heart of a brief secessionist revolt in 1950. Not surprisingly, echoes of this revolt were heard again a half-century later in the Ambon conflict that started in January 1999.

Papua lies at the eastern extremity. It has been known at various times and places as West Papua, West Irian, Irian Jaya or (in colonial times) Netherlands

New Guinea. Papua was only incorporated into the Republic of Indonesia in 1963. Resistance against the incorporation has always been strong, and it has grown since 1998. It too employs notions of Papuan identity that are ethnic.

The Indonesian armed forces invaded East Timor, also at the eastern end, in late 1975. The occupation was so brutal that it undid all the more civil Indonesian efforts to win over the population. In 1999 the half-island gained its freedom after the population voted overwhelmingly against Indonesia in a United Nations-supervised ballot.

Indonesia is not in a state of generalized civil war. The incidents we have mentioned remain isolated. All over the archipelago millions of people of diverse origins still live together in peace. Nevertheless, like India, Indonesia now has an ethnic problem and it is unlikely to go away soon.

Before we return to these issues, we must ask how people have thought about ethnicity in Indonesia in the past. Each way of thinking has led to a different set of practical policies. Our discussion will move from early thinkers, who saw ethnicity as a rather fixed cultural inheritance, to recent scholars, who see it in more negotiated, political and 'constructed' ways. An important assumption throughout is that, politically, ethnicity works in Indonesia much the way religion has done for a long time. This assumption will allow us to see that, after all, the recent ethnic conflicts are not entirely new but rather new expressions of an old pattern.

Early observations

How can a multi-ethnic entity such as this be a viable country? The first major study to address this question was written in the late 1930s, as the Dutch colonial era was about to be brought to a close by the Japanese invasion. Furnivall described the Netherlands Indies with the phrase 'plural society'. It consisted, he wrote, 'of two or more elements or social orders which live side by side, yet without mingling, in one political unit'.[3] By 'social orders' he had in mind three groups: the Dutch colonialists, native Indonesians and immigrant Chinese. Each of these were then still called 'races'. Today we would say 'ethnic groups'.

Plural society was not a happy place, in Furnivall's mind. Democracy was virtually impossible, since such a society had 'no common will'. The obvious implication (which Furnivall strangely enough does not draw) is that only a repressive state could hold it together.

The key thought behind Furnivall's concept of the plural society was that ethnic groups have an original identity that comes from within. They 'live apart as separate social orders'. Another scholar with similar views described ethnicity as an instinctual bond which is 'ineffable', 'unaccountable' and thereby inaccessible to reason.[4]

Physical characteristics were important to anthropologists in the nineteenth and early twentieth centuries. They distinguished the black-skinned, frizzy-haired Papuans of the eastern end from the brown-skinned, lanky-haired Malays indigenous to most of the rest of the archipelago.

Table 4.1 Seven largest ethnic groups in Indonesia (1930)

Ethnic group	Numbers in 1930	Percentage
Java	27,808,623	47.06
Sunda	8,594,834	14.53
Madura	4,305,862	7.28
Minangkabau (Sumatra)	1,988,648	3.36
Bugis (Sulawesi)	1,533,035	2.59
Batak (Sumatra)	1,207,514	2.04
Bali	1,111,659	1.87
Others	12,585,962	21.27
Total	**59,138,067**	**100**

Source: Departement van Economische Zaken, *Volkstelling 1930*, Batavia: Landsdrukkerij, 1933–6, vol. 8, pp. 88–9.

By contrast, the 1930 population census, the first complete census in what fifteen years later was to become Indonesia, adopted 'social criteria' to distinguish peoples. Language spoken, customs and habits were the main ones.[5] We will call this the 'ethnicity is culture' school of thought. The 1930 census recorded no fewer than 137 ethnic groups. Most were found in the thinly populated eastern part of the archipelago, especially in Netherlands New Guinea (Papua). If the census-takers had not introduced certain simplifying assumptions, the number would have been even greater. For example, all animists or Christians living in the interior of Dutch-held Borneo (now Kalimantan) were classified as one group, Dayak, even though respondents called themselves by a great variety of names such as Kenyah, Kayan, Iban or Ot Danum.

Several recent atlases of spoken languages are available for Indonesia.[6] Many dialects with few speakers have become extinct in the modern era. Whereas the Outer Islands (beyond Java) were thinly populated but showed great ethnic diversity, the densely populated heartland island of Java was ethnically almost homogeneous. Java consisted of just three main groups, Javanese, Sundanese and Madurese (plus a couple of tiny other ones). Table 4.1 shows the seven largest groups of 'natives' in the archipelago in 1930.

Ethnic Javanese inhabit the central and eastern part of the volcanic island of Java. Like all the people of the archipelago they are predominantly rural, practising irrigated rice agriculture. Their cultural values are drawn from two sources. The values of the sultanates of Solo and Yogyakarta reproduce a refined courtly etiquette, which has become common among the Indonesian bureaucratic upper class more generally, who upholds it for the whole nation. The trading areas along the island's north coast, meanwhile, are proud of their more egalitarian Islamic values.

Bali, Indonesia's only remaining Hindu area, also has a fine courtly tradition. The Hindu heritage it once had in common with Java is here preserved in a living priestly caste. The Sundanese live in the mountainous western end of Java. Though their language is related to Javanese, many insist on the differences with their more numerous neighbours. Madura, off the east coast of Java, is in parts stony and dry, and this has led many impoverished Madurese to seek their fortunes abroad. The Minangkabau of West Sumatra, the Bataks of North Sumatra, and the Bugis of South Sulawesi are also great travellers. A disproportionate number of Minangkabau and Batak intellectuals are among the early Indonesian nationalists in Jakarta who led the nation to independence. Many Bugis are seafarers, their ships once sailing as far as Madagascar.

Ethnic identities are everywhere associated with pre-colonial political units. Java's large kingdoms have a long history of producing homogeneous ethnic identities. The rest of the archipelago had a great variety of smaller coastal kingdoms. 'Stateless' tribal societies inhabited inaccessible valleys in the interior, especially in Papua. Once these political units were incorporated into the Netherlands Indies, the identities that adhered to them were transformed in ways we shall investigate below.

Most Indonesians are Muslims. Christianity (both Protestant and Catholic) is found mainly among several smaller groups on the periphery of the archipelago who were reached by missionaries before Islam had gained many followers there. The largest concentration is in the east, from North Sulawesi, through Ambon, to Papua.

One ethnic minority about whom much has been written is the immigrant Chinese. Making up less than 3 per cent of the population, they today hold a disproportionate share of the private wealth as small-town shopkeepers all over the archipelago. Most came to the archipelago in colonial times as poor labourers. Their current identification with a particular economic sector has made them the target of discrimination.

In 2000, for the first time since 1930, a census again asked an ethnic question, and it again covered the entire population. (The intervening censuses were samples and did not ask about ethnicity.) Census-takers went out into the field armed with an even longer list of coded ethnic groups than in 1930, no fewer than 1,072, mostly in Papua. Indonesia's population has nearly quadrupled since 1930, but we do not see a major shift in the main ethnic categories. Javanese are still by far the largest group. What we do see is a significant increase in the number of people no longer living in their 'ethnic home'. The pace of movements of people picked up enormously especially during the New Order: 10 per cent of all Indonesians now live in a province they were not born in. In a third of provinces, the proportion exceeds 20 per cent.

When Indonesia claimed its independence in 1945 (it was internationally recognized in late 1949), the country's rich ethnic diversity became a constant reminder of Furnivall's dilemma: how can a democratic society be shaped out of such multiplicity? In the 1950s, Western policy literature for the newly decolonized countries of Africa and Asia gave a generally optimistic answer to this question. It was phrased in the language of a social science construct known as 'modernization theory'.[7] Bring people into contact with one another, teach them modern values and they will quickly develop into a homogeneous nation of 'Indonesians'.

Many anthropologists thought ethnic groups had acquired their unique cultural characteristics through isolation. It was therefore thought to be a straightforward matter to wear off the sharp edges of their uniqueness by reducing isolation. The process of bringing people into the mainstream of national culture was called assimilation, while that of shaping a 'national' culture was called nation-building. Modernization literature was rather confident that the state had the capacity to shape people's feelings, especially through education. One recent example drew on Indonesian census data to map areas where nation-building was going well and less well.[8] Watching national television had a high integrative value, as did literacy in the Indonesian language and adherence to world religions. Assimilationists assumed that involving people in communication networks that spanned the entire nation would help create new kinds of commonalities.

There were problem cases. Assimilating immigrant Chinese and remote tribal groups represented a special challenge.

A large body of literature written about the overseas Chinese in Southeast Asia during the 1950s and 1960s shared the basic assumption that they were distinctive because of something within their culture.[9] Their Confucianism in the midst of a sea of Islam, their exclusive marriage practices and their 'clannish' associations and festivals, set the Chinese apart.

In a time of nation-building, such exotic cultural practices raised political suspicions. Their supposed loyalty to China turned them into potential traitors. The Cold War had placed China and Indonesia in opposite blocs. The Indonesian government responded by introducing measures to pressure Chinese Indonesians into assimilating. Chinese language schools were closed, Chinese characters were not seen on the streets and festivals were banned.

Tribal minorities in the remote interior were quite different targets for government-sponsored assimilation. Without a role in the national economy, they were basically regarded as expendable. Subsistence farmers living in the hills of war-torn or tense border regions such as West Kalimantan, Papua and East Timor were forced to move closer to roads and encouraged to adopt government-supervised world religions. 'Security' was usually the reason given. But, even away from the borders, a similar policy applies, justified on civilizing and welfare grounds. It is the nearest thing to an 'ethnic' policy Indonesia has, and is administered by the Social Welfare Department.[10]

However, engineering human affections is not a simple matter. The anthropologist Clifford Geertz wrote a classic statement concerning the problems of 'integrating' traditional cultures into a modern state. He thought such cultures too conservative to permit change in a few short decades. He summed up his argument skilfully in this sentence:

> The unfamiliar civil state, born yesterday from the meager remains of an exhausted colonial regime, is superimposed upon this fine-spun and lovingly conserved texture of pride and suspicion and must somehow contrive to weave it into the fabric of modern politics.[11]

The nation-building project contained an authoritarian streak. It tended to blame the backwardness of the people for Indonesia's failure to catch up with the modern world. An Indonesian university textbook in anthropology, outdated but still read today, said it expected the traditional units to decline in importance as Indonesia became more urban and modern.[12] Traditional attitudes were 'wasteful', 'feudal' and obstacles to development. They needed to be reformed, for example by a good dose of modern Catholicism as in Flores.[13]

Beyond the indigenous peoples, assimiliationism's mildly repressive aspects involved a general ban on any political discussion of ethnicity. The rule banning discussion of ethnicity, religion, race and class went back to a Dutch colonial ban on publicly voicing 'feelings of hostility, hatred or contempt against one or more of the groups of the population in the Dutch Indies'.[14] In practice, the Dutch were more concerned about hostility towards their own rule. The same applies to New Order Indonesia which followed a policy similar to the Dutch, except that it sprinkled all its public pronouncements with references to the rather vague national philosophy known as Pancasila.

New questions

The basic view of ethnicity in the literature we have surveyed has been that 'ethnicity is culture'. Moreover, it was often believed that a distinctive culture was the product of isolation. An example of this view can be found in a major survey of ethnic groups around Southeast Asia in the early 1970s. It concluded the following about Indonesia's traditional cultures: 'Diversity of historical influences, together with isolation on often remote islands or in interior mountain valleys, have produced a complex mosaic of self-conscious ethnic groups and categories.'[15]

The 'ethnicity is culture' view frequently led to pessimistic conclusions about the future of Indonesia, especially where faith in the promises of modernization theory had begun to fade. Perhaps the bonds created by nation-building measures would be too weak to prevent these cultures from reasserting themselves. For example, Levinson concluded the Indonesian section of a worldwide survey of ethnic groups with the dark observation: 'There is no central unifying force across all the ethnic groups. . . . The natural forces that might create and maintain a national culture and identity are weak, and the government has supported policies designed to foster unity.'[16] Levinson's list of 'natural forces' was distinctly unsophisticated, including rice-eating, Islam, badminton, keeping dogs and cocks as pets, and the generally high status of women.

Certainly ethnicity has persisted in post-1998 Indonesia in ways modernization theorists had not foreseen. But the view that ethnicity is a cultural legacy of isolation does not provide much insight into why this might occur even where ethnic groups are no longer isolated. In 1969 the Norwegian anthropologist Fredrik Barth wrote the introduction to a book that changed the way scholars think about ethnicity. Barth's breakthrough was to give up the idea that ethnicity had to do with a culture developed in isolation. In reality, he said, ethnic groups define their identity by contrasting it with that of others. It is a product not of isolation but of interaction with outsiders. Ethnicity thrives in big cities as well as in isolated hill tribe cultures. People say 'I am black', meaning they are not white, or 'I am Dayak', meaning not Madurese. Their identity comes not from within themselves but from relating across the boundary of their group to others. The important point about ethnicity, Barth wrote, is 'the ethnic *boundary* that defines the group, not the cultural stuff that it encloses'.[17] Interaction is the key, not isolation.

This perspective opened up new research questions. These were no longer questions about 'the cultural stuff' inside the group boundary, like religious beliefs or marriage customs, but questions that made anthropologists more interested in the way groups within society interact. A fruitful conversation opened up with other scholars – sociologists, political scientists and historians.

A beautiful example of an anthropological study written in the Barthian spirit was Lowenhaupt Tsing's book on the Meratus Dayaks of South Kalimantan. Its key observation was not that these mountain dwellers were isolated, but that they had been marginalized. They interacted with the rapacious logging economy and with the militarized state, and that interaction defined their ethnicity for them. Sometimes that interaction consisted of evasion – by hiding in their forests – but at other times they used it to look for employment there.[18]

Even before Barth, some scholars had already said we should be studying ethnicity with the tools of sociology. Some of them, like Leach, had done their early work on Indonesia,[19] but been largely ignored. The biggest name among these pioneers was Max Weber, the father of sociology. In a passage written in 1922 that was subsequently forgotten, Weber said that ethnic groups have no fundamental reality of their own, but are created for quite political reasons: 'It is primarily the political community, no matter how artificially organized, that inspires the belief in common ethnicity.'[20]

Scholars around the world quickly took up these ideas. They began to notice that, while some ethnic phenomena were indeed disappearing as the process of modernization brought people into contact, new phenomena were appearing in even the most modern countries, like the movement among black Americans for equality with whites. Perhaps ethnicity, far from disappearing as the world grew modern, was part and parcel of being modern!

They began to see, as Weber had done long before, that ethnicity was a highly political phenomenon. Far from being ancient entities, they discovered whole ethnic groups that had been 'invented' only quite recently by various political actors as part of a political struggle. The process had to do with the need to obtain resources, and by implication power relations. The core of ethnicity may indeed comprise ideas of common ancestors, of a biological origin, a past, a culture and a piece of land. But who those ancestors were exactly, what type of culture they transmitted and where they lived, were all open to question. The opportunities for manipulating the symbols of ethnicity were virtually limitless. Ben Anderson's influential book *Imagined Communities*, which drew on Indonesian examples, was based on such ideas.[21]

Public policy problems

Now that we have begun to think about ethnicity in political ways, our discussion needs to take a practical turn. First, we have to look in more detail at what we mean by ethnicity. Second, we should distinguish between different kinds of ethnic conflict occurring in Indonesia. Finally, we want to know what the policy options are for some of the most important kinds.

The Introduction suggested features to be included in defining an 'ethnic group'. It put priority on a belief in common ancestry and memories of a shared historical past, and stressed the notion of kinship. People are comfortable in an ethnic group because to them it feels like family. It listed a range of other characteristics, including language and religion.

In non-Western countries religion is far less a matter of personal choice than of the community and its collective memory. In the Indonesian conflicts discussed at the beginning of this chapter, it is often not possible to draw a clear distinction between a 'tribal' dispute over place of origin and a religious one. The conflict in Ambon was initially between indigenous Ambonese and settler Buginese, but within a few days it had become one between Christians and Muslims from any place of origin. We should not treat the post-1998 'ethnic' conflicts about place of origin as if they were a totally separate phenomenon from religious conflict.

Religious differences have been one of the fundamentals of politics in Indonesia since colonial times, and much has been written about them. The most important dividing line between political parties has always been less about 'left versus right' ideology than about religion. Most of the violence Indonesia has experienced since 1945 has had a religious element.

The shift between religion and place of origin that occurred in Ambon has actually been common in the history of politics, particularly outside Java. In North Sumatra in 1955 the Protestant party Parkindo effectively represented the local ethnic interests of Bataks in North Tapanuli.[22] The religion-based Darul Islam revolt of the 1950s was in Aceh less about religion than about defending Acehnese interests.[23] The post-1998 conflict in Poso, Central Sulawesi, is about religion as well as about place of origin: the Christians are local Pamona whereas the Muslims are mostly settler Buginese. Recently, inflammatory pamphlets in Central Kalimantan have repeatedly attempted to shift the terms of the conflict from place of origin to religion (in a way that would give the Madurese many more friends).

Even more important than an inclusive definition of ethnicity is one that recognizes its political nature. We have already seen that Max Weber viewed ethnicity as something artificial. Ethnicity was derived from politics, and not politics from ethnicity. David Brown agreed with Weber but began his book on ethnic politics in Southeast Asia by defining ethnicity as an essentially *defensive* 'ideology': '[e]thnicity is interpreted here as an ideology which individuals employ to resolve the insecurities arising from the power structures within which they are located.'[24]

Ethnicity is a refuge in times of crisis. And 1998 was a time of such crisis in Indonesia. However, whether offensive or defensive, we need to keep a careful eye on political actors and ask: might this idealistic ethnic leader have perhaps a quite worldly agenda? What is that agenda?

Now we need to note the variety of ethnic conflicts. Commentators who conclude that ethnic conflict is causing Indonesia to 'break up', like Yugoslavia or the Soviet Union in the 1990s, tend to assume that all ethnic conflict is the same. Yet the long list of issues with which we began this chapter should have warned us that this is not the case. To create some conceptual order out of the confusion, let us now turn to a monumental study by Ted Gurr and his associates.[25] After examining 233 ethnic conflicts around the world in the four decades since the Second World War, they divided them into four main categories (and a minor fifth one). Each defined a different type of militant ethnic group, with its own history and political objectives. Examples of all these categories are found in Indonesia:

- *Ethnonationalists*: live in a defined territory and want separation from the state, often with a history of once being independent. The Acehnese are a good Indonesian example, perhaps the Papuans too.
- *Communal contenders*: live dispersed throughout the territory in a plural society, and compete with other such groups for a share of political power. Christians versus Muslims in Ambon or Poso are good examples.
- *Ethnoclasses*: live dispersed throughout the territory in a plural society, and want greater participation in the state to achieve equal rights and opportunities in order to overcome the effects of discrimination resulting from their immigrant and minority status. Indonesian Chinese are not the best example, since most are economically better off than the average, rather than worse off as the model suggests, but their ethnicity does function economically.
- *Indigenous peoples*: live in a defined territory and want greater autonomy from the state that rules it, being mainly concerned with protecting their traditional lands, resources and culture. The Papuans could be an example of this, as could the Dayaks of Kalimantan.
- *Militant (religious) sects*: usually small groups who struggle purely for a religious ideology. The militant Laskar Jihad sect that came to Ambon from Java to help defend their Islamic brethren in 2001 is a good example.

In practice not every conflict falls neatly into only one category. For example, Papua has elements of ethnonationalism as well as indigenous peoples. And ethnoclass could apply to some communal contender groups as well. Moreover, Gurr's scheme is open to criticism because he is not just describing but also explaining conflicts. But his remains a helpful aid so long as we do not take it too far.

Among Gurr's five categories, we discuss only the first two in this chapter. These involve the greatest number of people and the greatest challenge to Indonesia's future.

Communal contenders

Of Gurr's five categories of ethnic conflict, none emphasizes the constructed, political nature of ethnicity more clearly than the 'communal contender'. The focus when analysing this type of conflict is usually on elites who are experiencing a political crisis or opportunity. The aim of these powerful individuals is not to split the country, as ethnonationalists do. They benefit from the currently existing state, and want to stay inside it. But they are playing a competitive game with other state elites. They want a better deal for themselves and their followers, and especially jobs in the public service. At the very least, they want to stop others from walking over them. Unlike ethnonationalists such as the Acehnese, who are dominant in a certain area, communal contenders tend to be dispersed all over the country, for example Christians and Muslims around Indonesia.

At the national Indonesian level, religious politics have grown more tense since 1998. These are communal contender-type situations. Fortunately, they have so far been kept in check by a tacit agreement among the national elite not to raise the stakes to dangerous levels. A discussion of national religious politics is beyond the scope of this book.[26]

Similar checks on ethnic conflicts at local levels since 1998 have not been effective everywhere. All five new conflicts with which we began the chapter are of the communal contender type. The Ambon conflict, for example, was between Christians and Muslims, who are each spread over the whole province and thus do not control a distinctive territory. The conflict stayed strictly within the provincial boundaries.

The prize for which local elites strive is control over the resources of the local state. Increased local autonomy since 1999 has made that prize more attractive. For them the burning question is: who will be provincial governor, or district head, or district secretary? The bureaucracy dominates the economies of the outer islands. Whoever controls the civil service controls the major source of wealth, whether in the form of jobs, contracts or sheer corruption. These local elites do not enjoy much influence in the national capital, so they cannot bring national political parties into play. Instead, they try to build a large and enthusiastic following by building on informal local networks of religion or place of origin.

Career interests of local middle-class elites were the key element in triggering these five conflicts. These people had enjoyed a comfortable niche as functionaries of Suharto's New Order in the outer islands. Years of authoritarianism had been a blessing for them. But the democratizing changes brought about by the end of the New Order spooked them. The prospect of free elections, and the introduction of new local autonomy laws, exposed them to competition in which the rules were unclear. The five events all seem to correlate with such key transitional moments.

However, we cannot understand these conflicts only through the perspective of local elite careerism. They also exposed sharply felt divisions within the communities in which the elites lived. The sharpest of them all was the one between locals and new settlers. People have always moved around the Indonesian archipelago. But the pace of movements of people increased greatly within the Indonesian archipelago after independence and especially during the New Order.[27] Robert Cribb's maps show that Central Kalimantan and Central Sulawesi had by 1980 already experienced so much in-migration that 11–20 per cent of the population was born elsewhere. These areas also experienced very little out-migration. For those whose area this was, the wave of settlers came upon them like a foreign invasion. East Kalimantan and several provinces in Sumatra had even higher proportions of new arrivals. Since 1980 the pace has only increased, and the patterns have shifted somewhat. Some movements were part of an officially sponsored programme of transmigration, which aimed to open up 'empty' land for peasants from overcrowded Java and Bali. Many more moved of their own accord.

The government hoped that transmigration would bring different people into contact with one another, reduce isolation and thus help to create all-round Indonesian citizens even in the remotest parts of the archipelago. There has indeed been a lot of intermarriage, resulting in a new generation of 'Indonesians' of no particular ethnicity. (Ironically, the ethnic question in the 2000 census failed to count these model citizens because 'Indonesian' was not on the list of 1,072 ethnicities.) But the outbreak of Dayak–Madurese fighting in Kalimantan shows that the experiment was not a complete success.

How do people build their identities as Dayak, Madurese and so on, in the face of the government's nation-building efforts to the contrary? That is an interesting but little-researched question. Older-style anthropologists would say the answer is obvious: such identities are deeply rooted in the collective memory and are resistant to change. An answer that Max Weber would appreciate more is that people often have an interest in reproducing or even inventing an ethnic identity under circumstances where they are competing with others. The modern state, and the radically changed economy that it brings, has created such circumstances. Far from erasing people's ethnic identities, the modern state has in some ways encouraged them. Indonesia is a constructed country, with no real pre-colonial history of working together as a single political unit. The very process of constructing it, ironically, has created ethnic boundaries where they did not exist before.

Dayak-ness, for example, is an invented ethnicity. In the nineteenth century, the term was merely a convenient if somewhat fuzzy category in the minds of anthropologists.[28] It did not refer to a single community but to all those people who lived in the interior of Borneo and were not Muslim. Dayak college students turned it into a political reality in 1919 when they established a Dayak Union (Serikat Dayak). Its purpose was to build support for their own entry into the civil service. Their better-educated Banjar cousins in nearby Banjarmasin were snapping up all the good jobs. From that moment until the present day, Dayak ethnic associations have played the role of elite-driven political parties and lobbying organizations. In the process, they developed a local discourse about the rights of indigenous 'sons of the soil' (*putra daerah*) to control the local bureaucracy. It was a descendant of the 1919 Dayak Union that mobilized Dayaks to expel the Madurese in 2001.

Dayak ethnic associations also seem to play the role of employment agency. Poor people are dependent on their powerful patrons, who tend to be ethnic 'relations'. As in much of Indonesia, people of certain ethnicities tend to have certain jobs, especially at the lower end of the employment market. This can give rise to competition with an ethnic edge. In such a competitive environment, ethnic stereotypes flourish in the form of jokes and popular insults.

Ethnic feelings are real. Nevertheless, most analysts who write about ethnic conflict in Indonesia talk more about elite interests than about those of the majority of people. They do this for a good reason. The ethnic groups in conflict tend to be approximately equal in wealth and influence. They are, Horowitz wrote, part of an 'unranked' system.[29] This gives the conflict between them quite a different and more elitist character than that between a wealthy and a poor group.

Apart from the ethnic Chinese, who are comparatively wealthy but do not have any political power, Indonesia's ethnic groups are unranked. There is no marked difference in wealth between ethnic Dayaks and Madurese in Kalimantan. Each group has its small wealthy elite and its large poor majority. Similarly, the Christians and Muslims who fought one another in Ambon and in Central Sulawesi were approximately equal in material terms. Even the politically and numerically dominant Javanese are not vastly richer, on average, than other Indonesians.

The reason that Indonesia's ethnic system is unranked can be found in history. The different ethnic groups were each autonomous societies, more or less equal in wealth, before colonialism forced them to join what later became the Indonesian nation. Since then a lot of movement of people has taken place, amounting in some places to an invasion – for example of Madurese in Kalimantan. However, the invaders were often as poor and powerless as the indigenous inhabitants. We can at the most speak of an incomplete invasion, and not of the complete subjugation of an indigenous people by powerful newcomers.

Conflicts between rich and poor groups in a ranked system are a struggle for justice by a weak and oppressed group. They offer some hope of greater fairness in the outcome. But conflicts between equally poor groups in an unranked system offer no such hope. Instead, they are often struggles between local elites for influence, using any arguments that come to hand. Conflicts in an unranked ethnic system have a conservative character in which the only people who stand to gain are the elites struggling for power.

The ethnic conflicts that have occurred in Indonesia since the end of the New Order have this darkly conservative character. It is doubtful, for example, if Central Kalimantan became a better place after the immigrant Madurese were killed or expelled. Certainly there was little to choose morally between the Christians and the Muslims who fought each other to exhaustion in Ambon, North Maluku and Poso.

Some observers go further than this. They suspect that the conflicts were deliberately started to sabotage Indonesia's experiment in democracy. The greatest failures of democracy after the New Order have occurred in the areas we have discussed. These have been the places where the military have begun to restore their influence.[30]

Rather than a struggle between rich and poor, Indonesia's recent ethnic conflicts have tended to be between indigenous and settler populations. Certain sectors of the local population have felt outsiders were overwhelming them. In Ambon and Central Sulawesi, local Christians had always dominated provincial and district government. They feared that Muslims, both local and outsiders but with better Jakarta connections, might be 'catching up' at their expense. Dayaks in Kalimantan looked back nostalgically to 1957, when they won control over Central Kalimantan as a new Dayak province. In 2001 they made a strong claim that outsiders had eroded their indigenous privileges. However, in none of these cases was it clear that the indigenous population was substantially poorer than the settlers.

Indigenous leaders argued strongly that they were 'sons of the soil'. Indigenous people should have more rights than settlers, said Dayak spokespersons in Central Kalimantan. Christian Pamona in Central Sulawesi argued the same way. The timing of each of these conflicts coincided with major power shifts that affected the fortunes of district- and provincial-level business and political power brokers. The Ambon conflict broke out early in 1999 as preparations were intensifying ahead of the first free elections Indonesia had held for over four decades. In North Maluku, conflict broke out over the question of who would control a new province that had been created there in 1999. The Central Kalimantan conflict happened in early 2001, as the regional autonomy laws were about to bring significant changes to the administration. West Kalimantan had the worst of a series of communal conflicts around Indonesia in the run-up to the last elections of the Suharto era: elites were beginning to worry how safe their future was with the ageing dictator. In each of these areas, the local elites who led the fighting had a history of working with the authoritarian Suharto regime.

What do these observations tell us about practical solutions to Indonesia's recent ethnic conflict? The first thing that must strike an observer is how relatively unimportant the post-1998 conflicts seemed to be to Jakarta. All were allowed to rage for months or years with hardly any serious attempt to resolve them. One explanation is that everyone in Jakarta was too busy with their own post-Suharto power struggles to worry about the regions. But another can be found in the ethnographic map of Indonesia.

Ethnic (place of origin) competition does not have the same importance everywhere. Java, at the heart of the nation, is ethnically quite homogeneous. The outer islands are ethnically diverse, but they are marginal not only geographically but also politically. When place-of-origin ethnic conflict does take place, it tends to happen in pockets around the country, because the nation consists of many dispersed ethnic groups. Indonesia's large number of ethnic groups makes it impossible for any one group to organize enough backing to exercise a decisive influence on Jakarta. The one exception is the Javanese, and they do not need to play this game.

People in Java, therefore, have tended to think of politicized ethnicity as a marginal issue that belongs to the 'primitive' regions beyond Java. This makes place-of-origin ethnic conflict a localized, parochial issue for the outlying regions. Far from causing the break-up of the country, local leaders on both sides of such a local conflict tend to look to Jakarta to help them resolve their problems. Indeed, this tendency has confirmed the view in Jakarta's elite circles that only a 'strong hand' can hold Indonesia together.

A return to centralist rule seems to be the favoured option within the nation's deeply conservative political establishment, among whom the military retains a central place. They fear that giving greater powers to the regions might lead to ever-greater demands and eventually cause the country to fly apart. They also feel that the ethnic lobby in the regions remains weak. By contrast with, say, Malaysia, the level of (non-religious) ethnic organization in Indonesia is still low. Apart from a range of somewhat shadowy ethnic associations that lobby behind the scenes, there are almost no ethnic newspapers, political parties, labour unions or cooperatives.

However, Jakarta cannot afford to be complacent about place-of-origin mobilization in the outer islands. The economic and political crisis of 1998 robbed the national capital of much of its authority in this far-flung archipelago. By 2002, the economy had still not recovered to pre-crisis levels. Moreover, the growth worldwide of a free-market ideology, the end of the Cold War and a growing interest in human rights everywhere, all combined to weaken the ability of a big Third World state like Indonesia to exert its will from the centre. The customary New Order military brutality was also proving increasingly counter-productive in silencing dissent. The emergence, both of ethnic conflict in these five areas and of an open but peaceful ethnic discourse in many other places, suggests that a new level of political action has been born in the regions beyond Java (and in some cases even within Java) that will be difficult to suppress.

Moreover, there is the danger of escalation. What used to be a 'communal contender' problem in the peripheral areas outside Java could turn into an 'ethnonationalist' problem. In the late 1950s, Indonesia was beset with a range of ethnic regional revolts from West Java, Sumatra, through Kalimantan, Sulawesi and the Moluccas.[31] They were eventually put down with military action. This danger points to the need for new solutions that attempt to deal seriously with Furnivall's dilemma of the 'plural society'.

One practical solution could be to allocate greater economic benefits to certain ethnic groups over others. This is sometimes called affirmative action or reverse discrimination. Such distributive schemes have been attempted in Indonesia. As in Malaysia, they have tried to help indigenous Indonesians (*pribumi*) compete more effectively against immigrant Chinese. But they have not been effective. The Banteng scheme of the 1950s fell far short of the ambitious Malaysian New Economic Policy. The corruption it encouraged has not recommended it to the following generation, although it was discussed again during the anti-Chinese rioting of 1998.

A more political solution is to give the ethnic groups access to power in some way. An electoral arrangement is one possibility: allow ethnic groups to form political parties, or set ethnic quotas in legislative bodies. Another is a territorial arrangement of autonomy or even federalism. The strongest spokesperson for these ideas is Lijphart.[32] Contrary to pessimists such as Furnivall, who fear that democracy is impossible in deeply plural societies, Lijphart believes a certain limited kind of democracy can be made to work. His basic idea is that rival ethnic elites should be encouraged to work together closely in a grand coalition, rather than compete to see who wins. Malaysia is one example often regarded as successful. Others, such as Lebanon, worked for a time but then collapsed into warfare. Lijphart quoted Indonesia of the 1950s as a positive example because of its broad-based cabinets that included the various religious groups.[33] Post-Suharto cabinets have also been rather inclusive in this way.

Most thinking along these lines has been about religion, but place-of-origin ethnicity has some recognition as well. The special autonomy deals offered to Aceh and Papua in 2002 stipulated that locals should hold leadership. Elsewhere too, some parts of the regional autonomy laws introduced all over Indonesia in 1999 have been interpreted to mean that leadership at the district level should be held by native-born people. One of the provisions was that local leaders should 'know and be known among' the local population.

Indonesians remain cautious about officially acknowledging place-of-origin ethnicity. Nowhere, not even in Aceh and Papua, are the new ethnic associations openly included in political negotiations. It is not difficult to sympathize with this caution. Indonesian citizens who live in the regions but were not born there perceive the indigenous movement as a threat. Significant local ethnic cleansing has taken place in all the conflict areas of Indonesia, producing a serious problem of internally displaced people (IDPs). The prospect of having local government run by ethnic chauvinists is not a pleasant one for those who always hoped that Indonesia could rise above ethnicity.

However, there are also arguments for giving the ethnic associations a seat at the negotiating table, especially in conflict situations. By having them share responsibility for coming up with solutions that work, they gain a stake in the process. It is also inherently healthier to talk openly about deeply felt issues than to repress them only to have them burst out unexpectedly later. Moreover, opening up political competition to local groups does not have to lead to chauvinism. Non-ethnic, non-religious parties could also emerge, in which indigenous people work together with settlers on local issues.

Ethnonationalists

With the term 'ethnonationalism', our intellectual journey that began with anthropology has taken us into hard-core political science. Connor introduced his book on ethnonationalism by saying he used the terms nationalism and ethnonationalism interchangeably.[34] A fundamental ideal of twentieth-century statecraft has been that of national self-determination. One of the doctrine's main architects was US President Woodrow Wilson during the First World War. He argued that national borders should follow the demographic dispersion of a people as closely as possible. Although an unobtainable ideal in most cases, including Indonesia's, its appeal has only been strengthened by the collapse of the essentially non-ethnic Soviet Union into many ethnic nations in 1989.

The strongest ethnonationalist movement seen within Indonesia so far was in a territory that did not belong there. The movement in East Timor pre-dated its incorporation into Indonesia. East Timor already had a young but vigorous anti-colonial movement against the Portuguese, who were in the process of decolonizing it when the Indonesian army invaded in October 1975. The Indonesian estab-lishment feared that a successful national liberation movement might result in a socialist regime on its doorstep. The subsequent occupation was marked by such brutality that it only strengthened the resistance movement. Averting their eyes from the bloodshed, most Western governments went along with it pragmatically in order to maintain relations with Jakarta.[35]

However, the United Nations (UN) never recognized the annexation. The East Timorese resistance kept up an effective global campaign. Its ideology was modern and secular rather than ethnic. In January 1999, Indonesia's president was facing a severe economic and political crisis. Hoping to restore Western confidence in his government, he announced that the East Timorese would be allowed an almost immediate vote on their future association with Indonesia. The UN swung into action and, despite serious intimidation by military-backed militias, the East Timorese voted overwhelmingly for independence on 30 August that year.

The destruction of East Timor by Indonesian forces in the aftermath of the vote seriously tarnished Indonesia's reputation overseas. Today, international assurances of support for Jakarta against separatism in Aceh and West Papua are always prefaced with conditions as to human rights.

After 1999, Indonesia still had two ethnonationalist movements in Aceh and West Papua, the country's two remotest extremities. Independence activists there, too, put forward historical arguments that they had been illegally annexed. In each case rich mineral resources are being exploited by Jakarta without giving much back to the locals living around the project sites. Each area has a history of resistance going back decades, making Indonesia look uncomfortably like its imperialist predecessor, the Netherlands East Indies. The movements in Aceh and Papua closely resemble the Indonesian anti-colonial movement against the Dutch, except that this time they are directed against the Indonesians them-selves. Ethnonationalists say the nation-state is practising 'internal colonialism'.

Aceh was the strongest political unit still holding out against the Dutch by the end of the nineteenth century. It took the Dutch nearly three decades and thousands of lives – their own and Aceh's – to annex it. Though Aceh initially supported the Republic of Indonesia, armed revolt broke out in 1953 and has done several times since then, whenever Jakarta weakened. Each time severe military action followed.[36]

West Papua, then known as Netherlands New Guinea and part of the Nether-lands East Indies, was not made part of the Republic of Indonesia when the Dutch gave up the rest of their colonial possessions in December 1949. The

Dutch said it was ethnically too dissimilar to be considered Indonesian, and the Indonesians lacked the bargaining power to force the point. When at last it was formally handed over to Indonesia in 1969, it was after an Indonesian military and propaganda campaign that alienated much of the Papuan population. The UN irresponsibly approved a 'vote' by 1,000 Papuan leaders who had been selected and massaged by the Indonesian military. The UN Undersecretary-General who handled the procedure, Chakravarthy Narasimhan, said belatedly (November 2001) that it had been a 'whitewash'. An anti-Indonesian guerrilla movement began almost immediately and persists to the present day, though at a lower level than in Aceh.[37]

Fears that Indonesia is about to break up are probably exaggerated. No new ethnonationalist movement has emerged since the end of the New Order in 1998. However, continued insensitivity in Jakarta might succeed in turning other ethnic conflicts into ethnonationalist movements as well. The Moluccas are particularly vulnerable to this shift.

Ambon was in 1950 the site of an embryonic ethnonationalist revolt led by Christian soldiers who had been in the employ of the Dutch colonial army.[38] This revolt was known as RMS (Republik Maluku Selatan). When Christian–Muslim strife broke out in 1999, the Muslim side immediately claimed the Christians were trying to revive the RMS. The Muslim argument was based on weak evidence and seemed motivated by the need to win backing from Jakarta. The prospects of success for secessionism were in any case bleak indeed. Ambon lies in the middle of the Indonesian archipelago, half its population is Muslim, and there is no international support for its secession. Yet an increasing (and increasingly politicized) turn to the majority Muslim religion in Jakarta will alienate the Christian population, which dominates eastern Indonesia from North Sulawesi, through parts of Maluku, to Flores, Timor and Papua.

In Kalimantan meanwhile, for some years there has been talk of a Greater Borneo, based on Dayak ethnicity and embracing the giant island's northern parts, now part of Malaysia. This romantic idea, too, received more of an airing than ever before during the ethnic violence after 1997. Even though it finds little resonance with most of the population, and cannot be called a secessionist movement by any stretch of the imagination, ethnic tensions will increase if Jakarta deals with Kalimantan insensitively.

Secession is an attractive option for people who feel their rights have been trampled. But how effective is it as a policy option? Ethnonationalist movements believe that achieving national sovereignty will help them shut out evils from outside. In reality, secession is far from a perfect answer to these evils. East Timor had a sturdy case under international law for the independence it eventually won. Yet its economic health and its physical security still depend on good relations with its former colonizer. The Indonesian military, embarrassed by its loss of prestige, has shown few signs it is prepared to be a supportive neighbour. The behaviour of its giant former colonizer next door will continue to limit East Timor's sovereignty. Economic globalization, meanwhile, will continue to make deep inroads into the lives of the poor, whether the country is independent or not. Similar considerations would apply to any other territory that manages to secede.

A more fundamental approach

The public policy approach we have discussed tends to assume that the state stands above ethnicity and can act as a neutral referee in conflict situations. The New Order rule outlawing public discussion of ethnic issues, and the similar colonial ban on 'spreading hatred', suggest that this is indeed the case. But a closer look reveals that the assumption is problematic.

We have already seen that political arguments about religion and about place of origin are so similar that they are practically two sides of the same ethnic coin. Open conflict about place of origin is new in Indonesia, but conflict about religion is not. Religion has been at the heart of Indonesian politics since the nationalist movement began in the 1920s. Even the New Order, which most people think was all about modernization, gave religion a central public role. Suharto always stressed how the Indonesian people's devotion to religion had kept them away from 'godless' communism. The practical importance of religion, in other words, was to prevent the poor from rising up in revolt.

With religion so important, religious people sometimes argued among themselves about the privileges of access to power. Religion and place of origin have been important ways of winning friends and influencing people within the ruling establishment. Cliques form based not on political ideology but on a common place of origin, or a shared religious orientation. Particularly as Suharto began to age and the New Order began to look shaky, the old conservative alliance between religion and power was rejuvenated. Money for one's friends was part of the deal. The webs connecting corruption, patronage and authoritarianism made up a shadowy reality that stood behind the formalities of the law. Shadowy it may be, but this informal state is every bit as real as the formal one, if not more so. Writing about the 1960s, Gunnar Myrdal called this a 'soft state'.[39] But his belief that it could be made tougher by the intervention of a small technocratic elite overlooked the entrenched interests of those who preferred it 'soft'.

Authoritarianism in Indonesia has taken two rather distinct forms. Religion and place-of-origin ethnicity play conservative, anti-democratic roles in each. Mahmood Mamdani wrote about the state in Africa using the phrases 'centralized despotism' and 'decentralized despotism'.[40] The terms are appropriate in Indonesia as well. Centralized despotism was a feature of the New Order of General Suharto. The military was its central institution and the money came from big capital projects such as oil, large-scale mining and manufactures.[41]

Decentralized despotism is a much older phenomenon, but it was largely forgotten during the centralizing years of the New Order. It re-emerged in the aftermath of Suharto's resignation in 1998. The ethnic conflict with which this chapter is concerned is the result of a revived decentralized despotism. New laws introduced in 1999 guaranteed greater regional autonomy. As they began to be implemented in 2001, conflicts in the regions intensified. The Central Kalimantan outbreak, in particular, was associated with the power shifts these new laws brought about.[42]

The key players promoting this decentralized form of rule are (aspiring to be) part of the local bureaucracy. Often they are, or claim to be, descendants of the traditional rulers of the area. Although most of them remain supporters of the New Order state party, Golkar, they tend to conduct their politics by constructing 'sons of the soil' arguments rather than spouting standard Golkar rhetoric about economic development. Their support comes from decentralized businesses like logging and small-scale mining (much of it illegal), as well as from the lower rungs of the military and the police who are involved in these lines of business.

The history of decentralized despotism goes back to colonial times. The Dutch put a lot of effort into constructing what they called indirect rule. Furnivall portrayed the Netherlands Indies as a model of the benefits of indirect rule.[43] The system worked by appointing traditional rulers (in Java called *bupati*) to colonial positions. The enormous power of the modern state that stood behind them quickly made them look quite untraditional. They became genuine local despots, who repressed and impoverished their own people with impunity. Their authority relied on traditional symbols tied to their place of origin. The language with which they ruled, therefore, was the language of ethnicity.

Decentralized and centralized modes of rule offer advantages to different elites. They have coexisted throughout Indonesia's history. Mamdani said the typical African state is 'bifurcated', or divided between these two modes of rule, one urban (centralized), the other rural (decentralized).[44] The phrase is applicable to Indonesia as well. Whenever Jakarta has been weak, the emphasis shifted to decentralized despotism. This happened in the 1950s, and again after 1998. If permitted to grow, it could lead to a form of federalism. Indeed, there is a neglected history of federalizing attempts in Indonesia. When the central state strengthens, however, it speaks of 'revolt' in the regions and wields the iron fist to restore control.

Both kinds of rule have been met with distinct forms of protest. Urban students have usually led the opposition to centralized despotism. They wrote the democratizing 'reformation' agenda to which post-Suharto governments have been forced to respond, in areas like freedom of the press and combating corruption.

Opposition to decentralized despotism, by contrast, has historically taken the form of the peasant revolt. The so-called 'social revolutions' that broke out in several places around Indonesia just after the Japanese Occupation in 1946 were directed against the traditional elites that had formed the backbone of the Dutch system of indirect rule. In the post-1998 period, they have taken the form of peaceful land seizures in many places around the country. Elements of the Free Aceh Movement and the Free Papua Movement can be seen as grassroots revolts against local forms of authority as well as against Jakarta. The urban student agenda of 1998 had no contact with these more rural forms of opposition.

In the euphoria of 'reformation' after the end of the New Order, the regional autonomy laws were seen as part of the democratization process. However, their democratic impulse has been weak. For various reasons, the empowerment of provincial and district-level elected assemblies has often failed to translate to popular control. Golkar has continued to dominate them, and their agendas are determined by 'money politics' rather than the popular will. Regional autonomy has revived decentralized despotism. Ethnic conflict is not a phenomenon of democratization but of despotism in the outer islands.[45]

This more fundamental analysis leads to a different kind of political action. In this view, political tinkering will not resolve the problem of ethnic conflict so long as the state itself is not fundamentally transformed. One could even argue that a federalistic programme in Indonesia might make things worse by encouraging local ethnic cleansing in myriad small units. What is needed is nothing less than a democratic transformation to make the state responsive to popular wishes at every level. This implies that urban democratic movements must reach out to popular movements in rural areas ruled despotically by ethnic elites. Together they need to build alliances for change. This is a long-term programme, and takes nothing away from the need for more piecemeal measures. But ultimately only popular empowerment can produce the kind of secure state where ethnic conflict withers.

Notes

1 See the Further reading section at the end of this chapter.
2 M.C. Ricklefs, *A History of Modern Indonesia since c. 1300*, London: Macmillan, 1993, 2nd edn, p. 90.
3 J.S. Furnivall, *Netherlands India: A Study of Plural Economy*, Cambridge: Cambridge University Press, 1944, p. 446.
4 D. Brown, *The State and Ethnic Politics in Southeast Asia*, London and New York: Routledge, 1994, p. xiii, quoting Geertz.
5 Departement van Economische Zaken, *Volkstelling 1930*, Batavia: Landsdrukkerij, 1933–6, vol. 8, pp. 44–6, a bilingual publication.
6 S.A. Wurm and S. Hattori (eds), *Language Atlas of the Pacific Area*, Canberra: ANU, 1983; C. Mosely, and R.E. Asher (eds), *Atlas of the World's Languages*, London: Routledge, 1994, summarized by R. Cribb in *Historical Atlas of Indonesia*, Surrey, UK: Curzon, 2000, pp. 31–7. See also the online linguistic maps of the Summer Institute of Linguistics at Ethnologue.com (http://www.sil.org/ethnologue/).
7 J. Finkle and R. Gablen (eds), *Political Development and Social Change*, New York: Wiley, 1970.
8 C. Drake, *National Integration in Indonesia: Patterns and Policies*, Honolulu: University of Hawaii Press, 1989.
9 L. Williams, *Overseas Chinese Nationalism: The Genesis of the Pan-Chinese Movement in Indonesia*, Glencoe, IL: Free Press, 1960; D.E. Willmott, *The Chinese of Semarang: A Changing Minority Community in Indonesia*, Ithaca, NY: Cornell University Press, 1960; G.W. Skinner, 'The Chinese minority', in R.T. McVey (ed.), *Indonesia*, New Haven, CT: Human Relations Area Files, 1963, pp. 97–117; V. Purcell, *The Chinese in Southeast Asia*, London: Oxford University Press, 1965.
10 L. Lenhart (1994) 'Ethnic minority policy and national development in Indonesia', in I. Wessel (ed.), *Nationalism and Ethnicity in Southeast Asia*, Munster/Hamburg: Lit Verlag, 1994, vol. 1, pp. 87–105.

11 C. Geertz, 'The integrative revolution: Primordial sentiments and civil politics in the new states', in C. Geertz (ed.), *Old Societies and New States*, New York: Free Press, 1963, p. 119.

12 R.M. Koentjaraningrat (ed.), *Manusia dan Kebudayaan di Indonesia*, Jakarta: Djambatan, 1971 (15th imprint 1995), p. 31.

13 Koentjaraningrat (ed.), *Manusia dan Kebudayaan*, p. 203.

14 C. van Dijk, 'Towards Indonesian harmony instead of Dutch contract: Haatzaai and Sara', in I. Wessel (ed.), *Nationalism and Ethnicity in Southeast Asia*, vol. 1, p. 77.

15 F.M. LeBar and G.N. Appell (eds), *Ethnic Groups of Insular Southeast Asia*, New Haven, CT: Human Relations Area Files Press, 1972–5, vol. 1, p. 12.

16 D. Levinson, *Ethnic Groups Worldwide: A Ready Reference Handbook*, Phoenix, AZ: Oryx Press, 1998, p. 229. See also the Further reading section at the end of this chapter.

17 F. Barth (ed.), *Ethnic Groups and Boundaries: The Social Organization of Cultural Difference*, London: Allen & Unwin, 1969, p. 15.

18 A. Lowenhaupt Tsing, *In the Realm of the Diamond Queen*, Princeton, NJ: Princeton University Press, 1993.

19 An example is E.R. Leach, *Political Systems of Highland Burma*, Boston, MA: Beacon, 1954.

20 M. Weber, *Economy and Society*, New York: Bedminster Press, 1968, p. 389.

21 B.R.O.G. Anderson, *Imagined Communities: Reflections on the Origin and Spread of Nationalism*, London/New York: Verso, 1991.

22 R.W. Liddle, *Ethnicity, Party, and National Integration*, New Haven, CT/London: Yale University Press, 1970.

23 N. Sjamsuddin, *The Republican Revolt: A Study of the Acehnese Revolution*, Singapore: ISEAS, 1985.

24 Brown, *The State and Ethnic Politics in Southeast Asia*, p. 1.

25 T.R. Gurr, *Minorities at Risk: A Global View of Ethnopolitical Conflicts*, Washington DC: US Institute of Peace Press, 1993.

26 See Further reading section at the end of this chapter.

27 Cribb, *Historical Atlas of Indonesia*, pp. 52–62.

28 J. Rousseau, *Central Borneo: Ethnic Identity and Social Life in a Stratified Society*, Oxford/New York: Clarendon Press/Oxford University Press, 1990; D.M. Tillotson, 'Who invented the Dayaks? Historical case studies in art, material culture and ethnic identity from Borneo', unpublished PhD dissertation, Canberra: Australian National University, 1994.

29 D.L. Horowitz, *Ethnic Groups in Conflict*, Berkeley: University of California Press, 2nd edn 2000, pp. 21–36.

30 The dynamics of such sabotage are described in general terms by J. Snyder in *From Voting to Violence: Democratization and Nationalist Conflict*, New York: Norton, 2000.

31 B.S. Harvey, *Permesta: Half a Rebellion*, Ithaca, NY: Cornell University Modern Indonesia Project, 1977; C. van Dijk, *Rebellion under the Banner of Islam: The Darul Islam in Indonesia*, The Hague: Martinus Nijhoff, 1981; A.R. Kahin and G.M. Kahin, *Subversion as Foreign Policy: The Secret Eisenhower and Dulles Debacle in Indonesia*, New York: New Press, 1995; A. Kahin, *Rebellion to Integration: West Sumatra and the Indonesian Polity*, Amsterdam: Amsterdam University Press, 1999.

32 A. Lijphart, *Democracy in Plural Societies: A Contemporary Exploration*, London/New Haven, CT: Yale University Press, 1977; A. Lijphart, *Patterns of Democracy: Government Forms and Performance in 36 Countries*, New Haven, CT and London: Yale University Press, 1999.

33 Lijphart, *Democracy in Plural Societies*, pp. 198–201.

34 W. Connor, *Ethnonationalism: The Quest for Understanding*, Princeton, NJ: Princeton University Press, 1994, Preface.

35 J. Dunn, *Timor: A People Betrayed*, Sydney: ABC Books, 1996.

36 T. Kell, *The Roots of Acehnese Rebellion 1989–1992*, Ithaca, NY: Cornell Modern Indonesia Project, 1995.

37 R. Osborne, *Indonesia's Secret War: The Guerilla Struggle in Irian Jaya*, Sydney, Allan & Unwin, 1985.
38 R. Chauvel, *Nationalists, Soldiers and Separatists*, Leiden: KILTV Press, 1990.
39 G. Myrdal, *Asian Drama: An Inquiry into the Poverty of Nations*, Harmondsworth: Penguin, 1968; abridged edn 1971, pp. 895–900.
40 M. Mamdani, *Citizen and Subject: Contemporary Africa and the Legacy of Late Colonialism*, Princeton, NJ: Princeton University Press, 1996, pp.17, 37–61.
41 See Further reading section at the end of this chapter.
42 G. van Klinken, 'Indonesia's new ethnic elites', in Henk Schulte Nordholt and I. Abdullah (eds), *Indonesia: In Search of Transition*, Yogyakarta: Pustaka Pelajar, 2002, pp. 67–105.
43 J.S. Furnivall, *Colonial Policy and Practice: A Comparative Study of Burma and the Netherlands India*, New York: New York University Press, 1956; C.A. Trocki, 'Political structures in the nineteenth and twentieth centuries', in N. Tarling (ed.), *The Cambridge History of Southeast Asia*, Cambridge: Cambridge University Press, 1992, vol. 3, pp. 75–126.
44 Mamdani, *Citizen and Subject*, pp. 16–23.
45 In a similar spirit to Mamdani, several studies have looked at the connections in Southeast Asia between money, gangsterism and local politics. Among them: R. McVey (ed.), *Money and Power in Provincial Thailand*, Copenhagen: Nordic Institute of Asian Studies, 2000; J.T. Sidel, *Capital, Coercion, and Crime: Bossism in the Philippines*, Stanford, CA: Stanford University Press, 1999; C.A. Trocki (ed.), *Gangsters, Democracy, and the State in Southeast Asia*, Ithaca, NY: Cornell University Press, 1998.

Further reading

Standard overviews of New Order statecraft, including the role of religion in it, include: H. McDonald, *Suharto's Indonesia* (Blackburn, Vic.: Fontana, 1980); D. Jenkins, *Suharto and his Generals: Indonesian Military Politics 1975–1983* (Ithaca, NY: Cornell University Press, 1984); M. Vatikiotis, *Indonesian Politics under Suharto: Order, Development and Pressure for Change* (London/New York: Routledge, 1993); R.E. Elson, *Suharto: A Political Biography* (Cambridge: Cambridge University Press, 2001); D.E. Ramage, *Politics in Indonesia: Democracy, Islam and the Ideology of Tolerance* (London: Routledge, 1995); R.W. Hefner, *Civil Islam* (Princeton, NJ: Princeton University Press, 2000).

Among extensive literature on the ethnic Chinese in Southeast Asia (including Indonesia), see C.A. Coppel, *Studying the Ethnic Chinese in Indonesia* (Singapore: Singapore Society of Asian Studies, 2002) and A. Reid, *Sojourners and Settlers: Histories of Southeast Asia and the Chinese* (Sydney: Allen & Unwin, 1996).

Studies adopting the 'ethnicity is culture' approach to Indonesia (in this chapter considered unhelpful) include: Lee Khoon Choy, *A Fragile Nation: The Indonesian Crisis* (Singapore: World Scientific Publishing, 1999), by a former Singaporean ambassador to Indonesia who fears a Yugoslav-style break-up; James L. Peacock, *Indonesia: An Anthropological Perspective* (Pacific Palisades, CA: Goodyear, 1973); Zulyani Hidayah, *Ensiklopedi Suku Bangsa di Indonesia* (Jakarta: LP3ES, 1997), which contains entries for 656 ethnic groups. One of the few studies to adopt a more helpful 'constructionist' view of ethnicity is Joel S. Kahn, *Constituting the Minangkabau: Peasants, Culture and Modernity in Modern Indonesia* (Providence/Oxford: Berg, 1993).

Studies on post-New Order violence, including ethnic violence, include O. Törnquist (ed.), *Political Violence: Indonesia and India in Comparative Perspective* (Oslo: SUM, 2000); B.R.O.G. Anderson (ed.), *Violence and the State in Suharto's Indonesia* (Ithaca, NY: Cornell University Southeast Asia Program, 2001); I. Wessel and G. Wimhöfer (eds), *Violence in Indonesia* (Hamburg: Abera-Verl, 2001); F. Colombijn and J.T. Lindblad (eds), *Roots of Violence in Indonesia* (Leiden: KITLV Press, 2002); C. Coppel (ed.), *Violent Conflicts in Indonesia: Analysis, Representation, Resolution* (London: RoutledgeCurzon, forthcoming 2004).

5 Ethnicity and class in Malaysia

Leong H. Liew

This chapter aims to explain the role of ethnicity in Malaysia, with some focus on the interplay of ethnicity and class in nation-building. Malaysia is a multi-ethnic country, in which the descendants of Chinese and South Asian immigrants brought in under British colonialism are a significant proportion of the population. In 1997, Malaysia's total population was 21,665,500.[1] Of these, about 60 per cent were Malays, 32 per cent Chinese, 7 per cent Indians, Pakistanis or Tamils, and 1 per cent aboriginal peoples. The overwhelming majority of Malays are Muslims, who numbered about 12.3 million in 2000. Other religions include Buddhism (4.02 million adherents in 2000), Chinese traditional religions (2.7 million), Hinduism (1.63 million) and Christianity (1.49 million).[2]

History

The British East India Company came to the region late in the eighteenth century in search of trade and military bases to conduct their valuable China trade. Due to the reluctance of the Malays to work outside their village communities for low pay in harsh working conditions, the British allowed free immigration, first from China and later from India. The Chinese were mainly absorbed in tin mining and the Indians in plantations. The racial division of labour was due to the fact that tin mining had Chinese capital invested and Chinese labourers preferred to work in culturally familiar surroundings, while British planters, from their Ceylonese and Indian experience, preferred the more familiar and submissive Tamil labourer. Colonial policy viewed the Malay peasants as producers of cheap rice for workers in the non-agricultural sector. One of the most unfortunate results of this policy was that, other than the aristocratic elite, the local Malays were generally much poorer than their immigrant counterparts, a fact that inevitably gave rise to racial tensions.

The Second World War

The war was significant for Malayan politics, as it was everywhere in Asia. First, Japanese defeat of the British in Malaya shattered the myth of white supremacy, and gave the Malayans greater self-confidence in their post-war anti-colonial struggle. Second, Japanese policies towards Malaya reinforced ethnic divisions there.

The Japanese exploited the communal differences among the Malayans. The Chinese were singled out for severe treatment because Japan and China were at war. The Japanese saw the advantages of preserving the formal authority of the sultans (Malay rulers) and maintaining the strategy of communalism that sustained them as a means of undermining any lingering loyalty to the British. The Indians fared only a little better than the Chinese. Many were conscripted as coolies and sent to the 'Death Railway' on the Thai-Burma border. However, the Japanese, keen to take advantage of the rise of Indian nationalism against British rule in India, promoted the establishment of the Indian Independence League (IIL) and Indian National Army (INA) in Malaya. Meanwhile, the Japanese enjoyed a good deal of support among the Malays.

It was the mainly Chinese- and communist-dominated Malayan People's Anti-Japanese Army (MPAJA) that led resistance against Japanese occupation. When Japan surrendered, for a few months, the Malayan Communist Party (MCP) and MPAJA were in control of the country and took revenge against those who had collaborated with the Japanese, many of them Malays. The events of this period left a lasting impression on the overwhelmingly Muslim Malays. For instance, a group of MPAJA guerillas is said to have slaughtered some pigs in a village mosque, after which Malays were forced to join them in a feast.[3]

Post-war struggle for independence

When the British returned to Malaya after the war, the MCP was legalized in recognition of its contribution to the British war effort.[4] The British also felt that they should reward the Chinese population for their contribution to resistance against the Japanese. Simultaneously, there was hostility in Britain towards the Malays because of the perception that they and their sultans had collaborated with the Japanese. The result was that the Colonial Office in London tried to institute constitutional reform in Malaya.

The reforms consisted of two main parts. First, the Straits settlements of Penang and Malacca and the nine Malay states were to be brought under one centralized government, the Malayan Union. Sovereignty was to be transferred from the nine Malay rulers to the Malayan Union under the British Crown. Singapore, where the population was largely Chinese (see Chapter 6) was excluded from the Union and established as a separate crown colony to ensure that the proposed Malayan Union would have a majority Malay population. Second, the reforms proposed to abolish the special position the Malays enjoyed with regard to citizenship rights. Non-Malays claiming Malaya as their home (based on birth or domicile) were to enjoy equal citizenship rights with the Malays.

The sultans and Malay population opposed the proposed reforms. It was thought by many Malays that the Malayan Union would destroy the Malay states and their sultans' sovereignty, which were the symbols of their community's special political status, and an affirmation of the fact that Malaya was a Malay country. Moreover, the Malayan Union would enable large numbers of non-Malays to acquire citizenship, and thus any advance towards self-government would inevitably result in a sharing of political power between the Malays and non-Malays. The first all-Malayan Malay organization was the United Malays National Organization (UMNO), set up in 1946, and the task of mobilizing and organizing Malay opposition to the Malayan Union fell to this body.

Malay opposition forced the British to abandon the Malayan Union. However, they were unwilling to abandon their two main objectives of establishing a strong central government and creating a common citizenship to promote Malayan-ness among the different ethnic groups resident in Malaya. The British decided to effect change through consultation with the Malays. The result was the Federation of Malaya Agreement of 1948, by which the British set up a Federation consisting of the nine Malay states and the settlements of Penang and Malacca, though not Singapore. The Agreement also accorded non-Malays the right to vote through acquiring citizenship. Thus the two main objectives of the British were met. The Agreement is significant for the Malays in recognizing their special position. Furthermore, instead of just five years residence, as proposed by the Malayan Union, the Federation required that non-Malays must reside in Malaya for fifteen years before acquiring citizenship, and applicants must have an adequate knowledge of either the Malay or the English language.

Non-Malays opposed the Federation Agreement largely because it accorded special rights to Malays. The Chinese Chambers of Commerce felt that the exclusion of Singapore would weaken the Chinese position in the Federation. The Malayan Indian Congress (MIC), formed in August 1946 by the Indian bourgeoisie, also opposed the Federation. Another opponent was the trade unions controlled by the MCP, which were growing increasingly militant as opposition coalesced against the Federation. The result was that the British responded with repression. They banned the MCP and militant trade unions and imprisoned many of their members without trial.

The Emergency, 1948–60

The MCP reacted by launching an armed struggle against the British at a time when many anti-colonial movements flared in Asia and Africa. The uprising was doomed to fail from the outset, because the MCP was pursuing conflicting objectives. By aggressively pushing workers' interests in the cities it alienated Malayan Chinese, Indian and British capitalists, and ultimately the British government. By aggressively pursuing the interests of non-Malays, it alienated the Malay intellectual left and, more importantly, the Malay peasantry. British counter-insurgency operations against MCP supporters in urban centres and plantations were particularly effective in using the contradictions in the MCP's objectives to their own advantage, gaining victory by 1960.

The communist insurrection speeded up British plans to grant independence to Malaya. The granting of independence to Malaya would deny the MCP and Malay left their anti-colonial platform and, in the long run, protect British economic interests. With the MCP threatening British economic interests, the British government cultivated the Malay sultans and other conservative Malays, supported by Chinese and Indian business elites, as protectors of British economic interests in an independent Malaya.

The British encouraged the formation of non-communist Chinese political organizations as a counterweight to the MCP. In February 1949, sixteen prominent Chinese businessmen formed the Malayan Chinese Association (MCA). Throughout the emergency period the MCA helped the British to relocate Chinese squatters into 'new villages' to deny support to the communists. The MCA also helped to recruit Chinese members into the police and armed forces, and carried out the government's anti-communist propaganda. The hallmark of the MCA, which has continued today, is its use of patronage to create a social base in the Chinese community. In the 1950s, the government allowed it to sponsor multi-million dollar 'social welfare' lotteries to raise funds for charity and social work and so increase its influence among the Chinese community. In addition, the Chinese business class used its economic muscle to bestow patronage on employment and cultural services in the Chinese community. With the MCP suppressed, the MCA was unchallenged as the dominant party representing Chinese interests.

In its search for Malay political allies, the MCA was attracted to UMNO not only because UMNO was the dominant party within the Malay community, but also because the national leaderships of the two shared a common English-language schooling experience and a fear of communism, both having an affinity for Western liberal political beliefs and capitalist practices. UMNO, MCA and MIC formed an Alliance to emerge as the undisputed victor in the country's first general election in 1955.

In February 1956 the representatives of the Alliance went to London to discuss terms of independence for Malaya. In 1957 the British government granted independence to Malaya and power was transferred to the Alliance of UMNO, MCA and MIC. The most significant terms of independence negotiated were:

- the Constitution would enshrine special privileges for Malays;
- Islam would be the official state religion;
- the privileged positions of the sultans would be guaranteed;
- Malay and English would be the only official languages; and
- citizenship would apply to all those born after 1957.

Post-Independence Malayan politics, 1957–63

The successful governance of Malaya since independence largely depended on the ability of the Alliance coalition leaders, particularly those of UMNO, to persuade their constituents to comply with the bargain their leaders had struck with the British in negotiating for independence, embedded in the country's Constitution: the granting of citizenship rights to non-Malays in exchange for recognition of the special position of the Malays. The new government provided effective governance, but its position soon eroded. The Malays felt that the special rights provided in the Constitution did not come quickly enough, while the Chinese made strident demands for equal rights, especially in terms of language and education.

Non-communist left-wing parties, like the non-Malay-dominated Labor Party of Malaya (LPM) and the Malay-dominated Partai Rakyat Malaya, or People's Party of Malaya (PRM), dominated opposition to the Alliance. Despite their common left-wing orientation, LPM and PRM were divided by their different stands toward the sensitive issue of special rights for the Malays. The Malay left embraced the special historical position of the Malays but LPM, like MCP, insisted on equality of rights among all ethnic groups. And although they came together as the Socialist Front in an alliance, they were never an electoral threat to the Alliance. Communal politics dominated the politics of independent Malaya, class being relegated to the background.

The formation of Malaysia

At the beginning of the 1960s, Britain was faced with the question of independence for Singapore and the North Borneo states of Brunei, Sabah and Sarawak. The British felt that independence for Singapore on its own would make it susceptible to communist subversion because of the strength of left-wing organizations there. The inclusion of Singapore in Malaya was one possibility but, in numerical terms, this would tilt the communal equation in favour of the non-Malays. In 1957, the population of Malaya was 49.3 per cent Malay and only 38.4 per cent Chinese, but with Singapore added the balance was 43.5 per cent Malay but 44.7 per cent Chinese. The British also believed that Brunei, Sabah and Sarawak on their own would be susceptible to communist subversion because of the power and influence of the Indonesian Communist Party (PKI) in neighbouring Indonesia. The British therefore came up with the idea of combining the North Borneo states, as well as Singapore, with Malaya to form the Federation of Malaysia.

In the end, oil-rich Brunei did not join because its sultan, one of the richest men in the world, feared loss of control of the state's oil revenues and subservience to a central government located in Malaya. Singapore joined the Federation of Malaysia but left in 1965. This was largely because of Prime Minister Lee Kuan Yew's concept of 'Malaysian Malaysia', with its implicit claim of equal rights for Malays and non-Malays. UMNO rightly saw this as a challenge to Malay authority, while MCA and MIC interpreted it as a move to replace them as representatives of the non-Malays in Malaya.

Assertion of Malay nationalism

The departure of Singapore from Malaysia did not end attempts to abolish special Malay rights and win equal rights for non-Malays. In the 1969 general elections, Malaysia witnessed the most aggressive campaign ever staged by dominant

Chinese opposition parties on non-Malay rights and they succeeded in making unprecedented electoral gains. The Alliance vote fell by 10 per cent and it lost the two-thirds majority it had previously commanded in the Lower House of the Federal Parliament, thus forfeiting its ability to amend the Constitution at will.

The electoral gains of the non-Malay opposition posed a threat to Malay political dominance and aroused a level of outrage and fear not experienced since the end of the Second World War. Moreover, the Malays had become increasingly impatient with the lack of progress in Malay economic welfare and the slow pace of implementation of Malay as the national language. The result was that serious inter-racial rioting erupted on 13 May 1969.[5] The worst-hit area was the capital Kuala Lumpur, which recorded 200 deaths. A group of young men led by Dr Mahathir Mohamad tried to replace the then prime minister Tunku Abdul Rahman, whom they considered to be too sympathetic to non-Malays. In the event, Mahathir was to become Malaysia's Prime Minister in July 1981.

The New Economic Policy

The May 1969 riots revealed to the non-Malays the indisputable fact of Malay superior political power, backed up by overwhelming Malay military power. The riots and their aftermath marked the onset of a steady process of monopolization of power by UMNO. In September 1970, Tunku Abdul Rahman resigned as Prime Minister and was succeeded by his deputy, Tun Abdul Razak.

In 1971 the government introduced a National Culture Policy. Its main point was that the national culture must take indigenous culture as the basis, although it was possible to accept suitable elements from other cultures. Emphasis in the moulding of the national culture must go to Islam. The policy was clearly Malay-centric and underplayed the cultural and religious traditions of the other races.

The most significant policy introduced by the new administration was the New Economic Policy (NEP), with its emphasis on improving the economic status of the Malays. The NEP was an ambitious twenty-year plan (1971–90),[6] with the following main objectives:

- to restructure Malaysian society to correct economic imbalance so as to reduce and eventually eliminate the identification of race with economic function; and
- to eradicate poverty by raising income levels and increasing employment opportunities for all Malaysians, irrespective of race.[7]

The most salient aspect of the plan was the restructuring of wealth ownership. Malays were targeted to own to at least 30 per cent of the share capital of the corporate sector by 1990, starting from a base of less than 2 per cent in 1970.[8] Between 1970 and 1984 most Malay households enjoyed real increases in income. According to government figures, incidence of poverty fell from 49.3 per cent in 1970 to 18.4 per cent in 1984 and 6.8 per cent in 1997. Inequality between ethnic groups also declined. In 1970 the mean income for Malay households in peninsular Malaysia was 44 per cent that of Chinese and 56 per cent that of Indians, but by 1987 the respective percentages were 61 and 80.[9]

In response to the 1969 riots, the Alliance government tightened political control.[10] It changed the Constitution to limit the type of issues that could be aired in public, and questioning the special position of the Malays and sultans became a seditious act, even inside Parliament. In 1974, Abdul Razak embarked on a strategy of incorporating a number of opposition parties into the Alliance, leading to an expanded alliance (*Barisan Nasional*) in which leaders of the minor parties follow the UMNO line in exchange for some minor ministerial positions.

In the bureaucracy, the influence of the Economic Planning Unit (EPU) in the Prime Minister's department was strengthened at the expense of Treasury, signalling a more interventionist approach in the economy. The government introduced new regulations to strengthen its control over the private sector, with the aim of increasing Malay participation in business. One of the most contentious policies was to introduce the requirement that existing large non-Malay businesses needed to restructure to assure at least 30 per cent Malay ownership, which often required non-Malays to sell shares to Malays at below market prices.[11]

The restructuring of asset ownership

The government set up state corporations like Permodalan Nasional Berhad (National Equity Corporation or PNB) and state economic development corporations (SEDCs) to accumulate corporate assets directly. Other bodies such as MARA (Majlis Amanah Rakyat, or Council of Trust for Indigenous People) were to focus on promoting private Malay entrepreneurship. Through takeovers and other forms of share acquisitions targeted both at foreign and non-Malay corporations, bodies like PNB succeeded in building up Malay ownership.

A major strategy for promoting Malay capitalists was through easy credit. Bank Negara set targets for bank lending to Malays. Failure to comply resulted in punitive charges imposed on commercial banks. New financial institutions were also established to promote Malay entrepreneurship. Loans were channelled to small businesses at below market interest rates. As a result, bank lending to the Malay community increased from 4 per cent of total loans approved in 1968 to 20.6 per cent in 1980 and to 28 per cent in 1985.[12]

The government regulated the amount of competition that Malay businesses had to face to improve their chances of success. For example, 30 per cent of public construction projects were reserved for Malay firms. The telecommunications department also reserved 30 per cent of its projects for Malay firms. Some ministries also ensured that Malay firms would make profits by guaranteeing them a cost-plus plan. In 1983, the Ministry of Trade and Industry announced a protection programme to improve the competitiveness of Malay businesses. Under this programme, only Malays would be allowed to enter eighty-seven low-technology industries, such as wood and rattan products, light engineering and construction materials.

While the NEP produced successful Malay entrepreneurs, many corporations set up with government assistance were poorly managed. Chief ministers and local politicians who sat on the SEDC boards often pushed for projects that would extend their patronage and enhance their political fortunes, paying little attention to economic sense. Managers sometimes conspired with non-executive members of the boards. They implemented projects because they could get remuneration from sitting on the boards of the new companies, some having as many as twenty-eight directorships in the subsidiaries of the SEDCs. It was common for SEDC officers to award contracts to companies they or their relatives had started. SEDC officers were therefore highly reluctant to close down companies that were making huge losses until central authorities forced them to do so. Despite efforts at reform in the 1980s, losses continued. According to a 1984 report, the aggregate losses of $360.6 million for 125 firms exceeded the aggregate profits of $346.8 million for 103 firms.[13]

In 1983, the Minister of Rural Development pointed out that only 6,000 of 55,000 loans MARA had granted Malay businesses had been repaid. Most of the defaulters had either gone bankrupt or saw no need to repay MARA's loans. In 1980, the Minister of Works and Public Utilities announced that only 20 per cent of the 5,000 Malay contractors registered with the Ministry could be regarded as successful. Only about 15–20 per cent of Malay businesses were on a sound footing.

Development of a Malay middle class

The most tangible benefit of the NEP was the creation of a larger Malay middle class and the shift of the Malay population from predominantly agricultural occupations to more diversified occupations. The size of the Malay elite and middle-class strata increased both absolutely and relatively. Between 1970 and 1980 the Malay share of the professional and technical strata increased from 47 to 50 per cent, while their share of the administrative and professional strata increased from 24.1 to 31.6 per cent.[14] Malays continued to be under-represented in the managerial/administrative stratum, but their share increased relative to other ethnic groups, while their absolute numbers doubled.

Education was another benefit that the NEP conferred on the Malays. Six new tertiary institutions were established after 1970, and the three existing ones vastly expanded in order to boost the intake of Malay students into local tertiary institutions. Both the Chinese and Indian enrolment fell in percentage terms and many Chinese and Indians had to go overseas to secure an education. Entry requirements were lowered and scholarships given to many Malays, rich or poor, entering university.

Education and the growth of the Malay middle class shifted the composition of the Malay elite. The Malay elite of the 1960s and 1970s was closely identified with the bureaucratic elite and aristocrats. By the early 1980s the elite Malays had shifted to the top political and commercial groups.

NEP and the non-Malays

Non-Malays have continued to prosper, despite the NEP.[15] Many have become indirect beneficiaries of the NEP through political access, patron–client linkages and Ali-Baba relationships whereby Malays who are willing to trade in their legal preferential treatment for immediate benefits act as a front for non-Malay enterprises. But among the majority of non-Malays, the NEP is viewed as an open and blatant form of racial discrimination. Many live with a persistent anxiety over the direction of ethnic preferential policies, and wonder whether their children will ever be treated equally in public policy and in access to public goods and services.

The 1990s and Vision 2020

The official end of the NEP in 1990 tapered into a new policy on development, that was best summed up through Vision 2020. This concept began in 1991 and envisaged that by 2020 Malaysia would attain 'full' socio-economic development. The criteria for this development would include industrialization, a high standard of living for everybody, a 'mature' democracy and ethnic harmony.

Mahathir's government relaxed the quotas the NEP had imposed to raise the Malay population in society and the economy. He did his best to encourage ethnic cooperation in the interests of Malaysia as a united nation, not just the Malay population. As one authority has written:

> Workforces were thus steadily convened across ethnic lines in tall office towers and industrial estates. Local Chinese business people were hailed by government officials as a welcoming incentive for investors from Taiwan, while opening conduits too for Malaysian investors in China. And Chinese professionals who had migrated overseas were invited by the government to return in order to work on the Multimedia Super Corridor project, the country's own Silicon Valley.[16]

There was a hope that the new policies, together with the long period of economic prosperity from the late 1980s to the 1990s, would bring Malays and non-Malays together. It is true that income inequalities widened during the 1990s, so that by 1997 Chinese household incomes were rising twice as fast as Malay households. Yet by and large the ethnic groups were never closer together than in the mid-1990s. Then came the Asian financial crisis beginning in mid-1997, which saw the Malaysian currency devalue by 40 per cent in 1998, and the economy contract by 7.5 per cent. In the same year, a dramatic political split erupted between Mahathir and his deputy Anwar Ibrahim, leading to the latter's trial and conviction on charges of corruption and sodomy.

Mahathir may have won this political battle, but Anwar had a good deal of support, especially among Malays. The Islamic Party of Malaysia (PAS) brought together a coalition based on resentment over the treatment of Anwar and it included the Democratic Action Party (DAP), a Chinese ethnic party. In the general election of 1999, the opposition succeeded in taking some votes from traditional supporters of UMNO, especially among Malays. However, most of the Chinese and other non-Malay feared PAS because of its perceived Islamic radicalism and turned their backs on the DAP, who they believed had 'gone to bed' with PAS. As a result their vote went to Mahathir and his UMNO, which won the election comfortably. There is great irony in the fact that this Malay nationalist should get such support from the non-Malay population. His relatively moderate ethnic policies, in a climate of fear of Islamic fundamentalism among the non-Malays, had clearly paid off.

Mahathir's last years as Prime Minister

In the last years before his retirement in October 2003, Mahathir showed himself more resilient than most observers had expected, and more able to cope with the wound the quarrel with Anwar had inflicted. He continued his policy of trying to promote ethnic harmony, despite the deep divisions within Malaysian society.

The 11 September 2001 incidents in New York and Washington only added to the divisions in society. Even before this crucial event, PAS has declared its intention to create an Islamic state in Malaysia, whereas Mahathir stood firmly for a secular state. Shortly after 11 September the opposition split. The DAP withdrew from the coalition, DAP veteran Chen Man Hin declaring that his party was 'alarmed by the calls of those who preach martyrdom and those who are prepared to die for an Islamic state'.[17]

Mahathir's stand against extremism certainly won him support, especially among non-Malays. The bombing of two night-clubs in Bali on 12 October 2002 by Islamic fundamentalists only served to intensify social divisions. Most Muslims rejected extremism, but PAS policy suggested there were some who did not. Malaysia's non-Muslim population supported Mahathir with increasing firmness.

During his last months as Prime Minister, Mahathir began several schemes aimed at reducing racial polarization and combating extremism, especially among the youth. The main part of his plan is to strengthen the national education system at the expense of private Islamic schools and those especially for Chinese or Tamils, so that young people of all ethnic groups should be educated together to a far greater extent than before. According to Mahathir in November 2002, 'National schools should be the preferred choice. . . . Besides, mixing with children from other races would help in national unity.'[18] The plan also includes regulating the content of the curriculum in the private Islamic schools, which Mahathir considers breed Islamic extremism.

The fact that Islamic extremism became a more serious and more obvious problem after the 11 September and Bali incidents did not mean that racial tensions, related also to the economic situation, disappeared. Urban poverty was the main reason behind riots between Indians and Malays in March 2001 in a poor suburb of Kuala Lumpur. Six Indians were killed in the disturbance, the highest death toll since the race riots of 1969.

The aboriginal peoples – the Dayaks

We turn next to a completely different side of ethnicity in Malaysia, namely to the 'aboriginal people' or *orang asli*. These people are the 1 per cent of Malaysians who are not Malay, Chinese or Indian, and they have a population of just over 200,000. All generally share a strong spiritual tie to the rain forest. Most aboriginal people live in Sarawak and Sabah on Kalimantan, the large island Malaysia shares with Indonesia and Brunei.

Among these peoples the most important are possibly the Dayaks, a term generally taken to refer to the indigenous, non-Muslim peoples of southern and western Kalimantan. At the end of the twentieth century there were over 2.2 million Dayaks in the whole island, including the non-Malaysian sections. There is brief discussion of the Dayaks in Chapter 4 on Indonesia.

The Dayaks traditionally lived along rivers. Their economies were based on the shifting cultivation of hill rice, with fishing and hunting subsidiary pursuits. They had a highly complex system of religious beliefs, which were generally animistic and polytheistic. Their communities were small and lived in longhouses, with several families and generations together. People married outside their own villages, the men generally going to join their wives' communities. Intertribal warfare was once common, with the custom of headhunting practised.

The traditional Dayak hinterland riverine culture is fast disappearing under the impact of modernization. Headhunting belongs to the distant past. The traditional villages still exist, but young adults are increasingly migrating to the cities, abandoning the old longhouses. A modern Dayak urban culture is emerging, with serious implications for the long-term survival of the old Dayak way of life.

Many urban Dayaks regret the passing of the old culture, even if they no longer know much about it. Policy in Malaysia, 'would seem to be directed at reducing ethnicity to a "guided culture", consisting of such superficial elements as costume and cuisine, perhaps only to be publicly evident on specially designated holidays'.[19] At the same time, Dayaks by and large appear quite amenable to modernity, and many are even developing vested interests in being modern through their urban life and work. There are advantages in modernity in terms of standard of living and the technologies that it brings. Many Dayaks recognize that modernity is here to stay and there is nothing they can do about it, so they had better accept the new realities and make the best of them.

Conclusion

The most difficult ethnic problems Malaysia has had to face are a legacy of British colonialism. It was the British who brought in immigrants from China and South Asia. The fact that the immigrants' economic level was, in general, higher than that of the local Malays has over time made for serious ethnic tensions, especially between Malays and non-Malays. The serious race riots of May 1969 both reflected and exacerbated the deep-seated ethnic divisions within society.

There is no doubt that communal or ethnic politics dominate class politics in Malaysia. While the NEP improved the absolute economic levels of poor Malays, the method of achievement has been the adoption of state policies with the primary purpose of creating a Malay entrepreneurial elite. The use of affirmative action policies based solely on ethnicity and not on class has led to a high level of alienation and low levels of social and political trust between Malays and non-Malays. Instead of creating a collective national consciousness or identity among all Malaysians, the NEP reinforced ethnic divisions in the country.

These were precisely the problems the nationalists of the 1990s tried to solve, but the economic crisis beginning in 1997 undermined their efforts. The change of emphasis towards combating Islamic extremism that has resulted from the 11 September and Bali bombing incidents is likely to ensure continuing racial polarization, despite government efforts to ameliorate it. We can be fairly confident in predicting that ethnic problems will pose a challenge to Malaysian governments for the indefinite future.

Notes

1 Barry Turner (ed.), *The Statesman's Yearbook: The Politics, Cultures and Economies of the World 2003*, Houndmills, Basingstoke and New York: Palgrave Macmillan, 2002, p. 1084.
2 Turner (ed.), *The Statesman's Yearbook 2003*, p. 1090.
3 Cheah Boon Kheng, *Red Star Over Malaya*, Singapore: Singapore University Press, 1983, p. 197.
4 Material in this section and the next are drawn largely from Michael Stenson, *Class, Race and Colonialism in West Malaysia*, St Lucia: University of Queensland Press, 1980.
5 John Butcher, 'May 13: A review of some controversies in accounts of the riots', in Kwame Sundaram Jomo (ed.), *Reinventing Malaysia: Reflections on its Past and Future*, Bangi: Penerbit Universiti Kebangsaan Malaysia, 2001, pp. 35–56.
6 E.T. Gomez and Kwame Sundaram Jomo, *Malaysia's Political Economy: Politics, Patronage and Profits*, Cambridge: Cambridge University Press, 1997, p. 24.
7 James V. Jesudason, *Ethnicity and the Economy: The State, Chinese Business, and Multinationals in Malaysia*, Singapore: Oxford University Press, 1989, p. 71.
8 Jesudason, *Ethnicity and the Economy*, p. 71.
9 Jesudason, *Ethnicity and the Economy*, pp. 114–15.
10 Ozay Mehmet, *Development in Malaysia: Poverty, Wealth and Trusteeship*, Kuala Lumpur: INSAN, 1988, p. 9.
11 Just Faaland, J. Parkinson and R. Saniman, *Growth and Ethnic Inequality: Malaysia's New Economic Policy*, New York: St Martin's Press, 1990, pp. 77–8.
12 Jesudason, *Ethnicity and the Economy*, p. 101.
13 Jesudason, *Ethnicity and the Economy*, p. 100.
14 Jesudason, *Ethnicity and the Economy*, p. 112.
15 William Case, *Politics in Southeast Asia*, Richmond: Curzon, 2002, p. 107.
16 William Case, 'The new Malaysian nationalism: Infirm beginnings, crashing finale', *Asian Ethnicity*, September 2000, vol. 1, no. 2, pp. 141–2.
17 Quoted in Michael Westlake (ed.), *Far Eastern Economic Review Asia 2002 Yearbook*, Hong Kong: Review Publishing Company, 2001, p. 154.

18 S. Jayasankaran, 'A plan to end extremism', *Far Eastern Economic Review*, 26 December 2002–2 January 2003, vol. 165, no. 51, p. 12.
19 Clare L. Boulanger, 'Inventing tradition, inventing modernity: Dayak identity in urban Sarawak', *Asian Ethnicity*, September 2002, vol. 3, no. 2, p. 231.

Further reading

Political economy

Faaland, Just, J. Parkinson and R. Saniman, *Growth and Ethnic Inequality: Malaysia's New Economic Policy*, New York: St Martin's Press, 1990.

Gomez, E.T., 'Political business in Malaysia: Party factionalism, corporate development, and economic crisis', in E.T. Gomez (ed.), *Political Business in East Asia*, London: Routledge, 2002. This book contains an excellent treatment of contemporary Malaysia's political economy, which is supported by rich empirical evidence.

Gomez, E.T. and K.S. Jomo, *Malaysia's Political Economy: Politics, Patronage and Profits*, Cambridge: Cambridge University Press, 1997. This excellent book analyses the political economy of Malaysia's NEP before the Asian crisis.

Jesudason, James V., *Ethnicity and the Economy: The State, Chinese Business, and Multinationals in Malaysia*, Singapore: Oxford University Press, 1989. Gives a comprehensive analysis of the operation of the first two decades of the NEP.

Jomo, Kwame Sundaram, *A Question of Class: Capital, the State, and Uneven Development in Malaya*, Singapore: Oxford University Press, 1988.

Jomo, Kwame Sundaram (ed.), *Industrialising Malaysia: Policy, Performance, Prospects*, London and New York: Routledge, 1993.

Jomo, Kwame Sundaram (ed.), *Mahathir's Economic Policies*, 2nd edn, Kuala Lumpur: INSAN, 1989.

Mehmet, Ozay, *Development in Malaysia: Poverty, Wealth and Trusteeship*, Kuala Lumpur: INSAN, 1988.

Searle, Peter, *The Riddle of Malaysian Capitalism*, St Leonards, NSW: Allen & Unwin, 1999. This book provides a comprehensive coverage of the complex relationship between the Malaysian state and Malay and Chinese business groups prior to the Asian crisis.

Politics

Case, William, *Politics in Southeast Asia*, Richmond: Curzon, 2002. The chapter on Malaysia provides a sophisticated elite-level analysis of Malaysian politics.

Cheah, Boon Kheng, *Red Star Over Malaya*, Singapore: Singapore University Press, 1983. This book provides an interesting account of Malayan resistance against the Japanese occupation during the Second World War and race relations in Malaya during and after the occupation. It explains in great detail the origins of the deep mutual distrust that the races in Malaysia have for one another.

Jomo, Kwame Sundaram (ed.), *Reinventing Malaysia: Reflections on its Past and Future*, Bangi: Penerbit Universiti Kebangsaan Malaysia, 2001.

Stenson, Michael, *Class, Race and Colonialism in West Malaysia*, St Lucia: University of Queensland Press, 1980. This book is a classic study on class and race in Malaysia.

Verma, Vidhu, *Malaysia: State and Civil Society in Transition*, Boulder, CO: Lynne Rienner, 2002.

6 Singapore

Multiracial harmony as public good

Chua Beng Huat

When it became politically independent in 1965, Singapore declared itself a constitutionally 'multiracial' country.[1] Singapore had to embrace multiracialism as a matter of geopolitical necessity, being demographically mainly Chinese, but carved out of the 'Malay' world of archipelagic Southeast Asia, constituted by a population increasingly 'homogenized' through the religion of Islam but divided by national identities of Malaysian, Indonesian, Moro Filipinos and Patani Thais. Unlike the other postcolonial countries that can identify their own 'indigenous' populations, delineate their 'national' boundaries and declare themselves 'owners' of the nation, Singapore had to turn a necessity into a virtue, transforming its demographic multiracial reality into a constitutional 'multiracial' country.

Multiracialism has become a constant ideological foundation in the nation-building project of the People's Action Party (PAP), which has consistently governed Singapore since 1959. This chapter is concerned with the logic of 'multiracialism' as a fundamental component of the state's ideological structure.

Chinese, Malays, Indians, Others

Immediately after the British established Singapore in 1819, the island attracted immigrants from China, India and its immediate neighbours for its commercial enterprises. A Chinese immigrant majority emerged quickly. The proportions of the residential population in Singapore, according to the 2000 census, were 76.8 per cent ethnic 'Chinese', 13.9 per cent 'Malays', 7.9 per cent 'Indians' and a small generic category of 'Others',[2] which includes everybody else; a composition that is locally abbreviated as CMIO.

Each of these general racial categories reduces and 'homogenizes' ethnic, linguistic and religious differences within each category. Among the 'Malays' were Javanese, Minangkabau, Baewanese, Achinese and Malays from peninsular Malaya; and the 'Chinese' included different linguistic groups of Hokkiens, Cantonese, Hakkas and Teochews, with perhaps even more diversity among the Indians. The elected government intensified this colonial 'flattening' policy: Modern Standard Chinese (Mandarin) is the sole Chinese language and all other Chinese languages and dialects are banned in official transactions, educational institutions and broadcast media. Of the 'Malays', in addition to 'standardizing' Malay as the common language, the state considers 'all Malays are Muslims', leaving no space for non-Muslim Malays. As for Indians, the defining element is geography, including anyone whose ancestors are from South Asia. Obviously, the homogenization process does not operate on a single criterion but on a set of convenient elements enabling the state to organize its administrative units into 'groups'.[3]

Under the CMIO scheme, every Singaporean is officially racially typed at birth. A child is automatically assigned the father's 'race', all possible ambiguities of racial identities being denied. Each Singaporean is presumed to be embedded in race-culture: For example, an assigned Chinese is assumed to be 'Confucianist' even though few Singapore-born Chinese under the age of 35 have ever read a Confucian text; while Malays are supposed to be steeped in Islam.

Racial equality rather than equality of individuals

The substance of multiracialism as administrative practice is based on the formal equality of the racial groups in several areas of policy and public interest. The most immediate areas are language, religion and festivals. All the major religious festivals are national holidays and the state supports race-cultural festivals with funds and other administrative resources.

Since the mid-1970s, with the introduction of a national education system, English has become the primary medium of instruction at all levels of schooling. However, all students must also learn their own 'mother-tongue' languages, such as Mandarin for Chinese, and Malay for the Malays. This demand is supposed to be a means of instilling in students traditional Asian values that will supposedly provide the 'cultural ballast' to combat 'Westernization'. In reality, however, as English becomes increasingly the language spoken in homes and on the streets, the survival of the 'mother-tongue' languages has to be boosted by annual one-month public campaigns dedicated to their use.

Within the general framework of racial equality, certain privileges are granted to the Malays through the constitutional recognition that they are the indigenous population of Singapore. First, Malay was made the 'national' language, with Mandarin, Tamil and English as the other three 'official' languages. However, this has become an empty symbol; with the effective adoption of English as *lingua franca*, very few non-Malays learn Malay. Second, Malays were to be given free education at all levels. However, with an emerging, visible Malay middle class, it is inequitable that their children get free tertiary education while students from poor Chinese and Indian families do not. Since the early 1990s, children of Malay middle-class parents pay tuition fees for tertiary education but the fees are channelled into a Malay community fund, while the government compensates the universities with equivalent monies. Consequently, tertiary education remains free for the community as a whole. Third, a prominent site is reserved in every public housing estate for the construction of a mosque, while churches and

Chinese temples compete by tender for sites made available anywhere in the estates, where 85 per cent of Singaporeans reside. Finally, Islam receives special administrative attention under the purview of a Minister for Malay and Muslim Affairs.

'Race' is thus maintained at a very highly visible level in the public sphere. It creates the political space to rationalize, enable, even require the ruling government to monitor and police the racial boundaries. The government thus sets itself up structurally as 'above' the particularistic interests of the racial groups, as the neutral umpire that allocates resources and adjudicates disputes among the races. The state is thus able to achieve and retain a very high level of autonomy relative to the racial groups within the society.

Costs of multiracialism

Multiracialism as a governmental regime has exacted costs from the groups, especially the Chinese and Malays. For the Chinese, as the overwhelming majority, it is the denial of their language as the national language and its reduction to the same status as 'merely' a mother-tongue. Whether relatively well educated and Mandarin-speaking or poorly educated and exclusively Chinese-dialect-speaking, all non-English-speaking Chinese individuals are highly disadvantaged in the political economy of contemporary Singapore. Attempts to raise the problem this disadvantage poses have led to the protestors being labelled as 'Chinese chauvinists' and, in a few cases, to political detention and self-imposed exile.

For the Malays, their weak economic position relative to the Chinese and Indians has been a persistent source of friction between the Malays and the government. The thorniest problem is the conscription of Malay men into the armed forces. Since 1969, every young male Singaporean has had to do at least two years of military service on completing secondary education. However, for the first two decades, Malay youths were not conscripted. Not till the mid-1980s did Malays in the armed forces increase in number or become a noticeable group among officers.[4] The government has never denied the discrimination but points to the imagined and imaginable potential 'moral' conflict that a Malay military man may face if Singapore were at war with its neighbours, Malaysia and Indonesia: he could be placed in a dilemma of having to shoot his own 'kin' and 'ethnic brethren' or his fellow Singaporeans.

An accumulation of issues has led to a persistent questioning by some Malays of whether the Malay Members of Parliament in the ruling regime are the best representatives of the interests of the 'community'. In its 2001 national conference, the Association of Muslim Professionals proposed the establishment of a 'collective leadership' of non-partisan Malay-Muslim organizations. The government summarily dismissed the suggestion as potentially racially divisive, with the potential to lead to similar organizations among the two other groups. Obviously, negotiated adjustments will continue to be the mode of operation between the Malays and the government.

Racial harmony as public good

The costs and anguish of multiracialism necessitate its underwriting by an idea of 'racial harmony', a public good that few could deny. As the 'risk' of disruption of racial harmony inheres logically within every discussion of race relations, the entire domain of 'race' is considered 'sensitive', best not raised publicly. Drawing on past instances of race riots, the government constantly warns the population of the 'tenuousness' of existing racial harmony, justifying the need for constant policing of racial boundaries. Public voicing of racial grievances has been quickly suppressed and the individuals publicly chastised, even criminalized as allegedly 'racial chauvinists' who threaten racial harmony.

The fact is that there has been no racial violence in Singapore since 1969. Could this be the result of suppressing discussion of race? Or is it because people are better educated, which would make suppression no longer necessary? Or perhaps the 'danger' of riots was exaggerated by mythologizing the past events, and if so, suppression was unnecessary in the first place. Unfortunately, the logic of deterrence continues to govern discourse on race in Singapore, which means that 'racial harmony' has continued to act as a repressive device for pre-empting public debate on issues and difficulties that all multiracial countries face, such as discrimination in the job market. Without public debate, 'racial harmony' is minimalist, maintained by passive tolerance of visible and recognizable differences without substantial cultural exchanges or understanding, and even less cultural boundary crossings.

This minimalist racial harmony has been reinforced by an ideology of 'meritocracy', facilitated by the promotion of English as a 'neutral' language for all Asians. Ever since independence, English has remained the language of government, public administration and commerce; subsequently it has become the primary language of education. 'Neutralization' thus enables the government to reduce everyone and every group to 'cultural equality', contributing to the development and maintenance of Singapore as a country where only 'merit' counts.

An emerging national identity

The ideological success of official 'multiracialism' is reflected in the ease, even self-congratulation, with which Singaporeans readily describe the nation as a multiracial nation, by citing all the religious, cultural and linguistic guarantees and practices of the state. Furthermore, there are constant worries about the 'disappearance' of the racially defined 'cultures' by the respective self-identified racial groups, not through the assimilation of each other but in the face of 'Westernization'.

However, the insistence on racial divisions as a means of generating demand for the state as an agent of harmony encourages the three racial groups to reconnect with their respective 'homelands'. Indeed, remittances to kin in China and India have always been significant to the local economies in these two countries; furthermore, Singaporean investors have capitalized on their respective racial ties in their transactions, as the economies in China and India liberalize. Of the three possible reconnections, the Malay one is the nearest, most immediate and perhaps most troublesome. Geographically Singapore is contiguous with peninsular Malaya, which accounted for its membership in Malaysia in 1963. Membership was brief, however. Singapore separated and became an independent city-state in 1965. Given this history, Malaysian Malays, apparently unable to sever all their real and imagined kin ties, often take it upon themselves to 'look after' the interests of Malays in Singapore.

A sense of nationalism, of 'this is our domestic affair', of 'we Singaporeans', has certainly taken hold. This is disclosed, ironically, by the position of the 'guest workers' in Singapore, who have been arriving since the mid-1970s.[5] The un-employed in the neighbouring countries of Southeast Asia, South Asia and the People's Republic of China, constitute a reserved labour force which continues to supply Singapore's labour demand. The national origins and ethnicities of a large segment of these guest workers are the same as the native Singaporeans: South Asians, generalized locally as 'Indians', Malays and Indonesians, general-ized as 'Malays' and ethnic Chinese. As such, these guest workers can be absorbed into local racial communities with relative ease. Yet they remain temporary and marginal because the state keeps them on temporary work permits, without any opportunity to obtain permanent residency or citizenship. Singaporean citizen-ship and status is privileged over possible racial connections, affinities and identities. Economic development and its consumer cultural implications have placed 'Singaporeans' as 'superior' to potential racial kin from 'underdeveloped' Indonesia, South Asia and the People's Republic of China. A sense of nationalist belonging, of being 'Singaporean', has apparently taken hold with economic success as a marker.

Looking ahead

The spectre of 'race riots', along with much of Singapore's past struggles to survive as a viable nation, has begun to recede in social memory. The proportion of Singaporeans who are locally born, with no interest in the imaginary home-lands of their respective races see themselves in 'nationalist' rather than racial terms, with many surveys finding that young people identify themselves first not according to race but the nation of Singapore. Overt discrimination or privileging of particular group(s) finds less and less resonance in the public sphere, as the presumed racial cultures become far less important in the daily life of Singaporeans.

In line with better education and rising expectations, Malays/Muslims have objected more and more to instances and areas of actual and perceived inequal-ities and voiced their dissatisfaction with existing society. With the international-ization of Islam since the 1970s, religion has become more relevant to the daily lives of the Malays. This became a focus of public debate after the 11 September 2001 destruction of the World Trade Center in New York. Singapore, being in a region where Muslims are the majority population, was unavoidably caught up in the global and regional vigilance against terrorism, placing the Malays in a defensive position.

In December 2001, a cell of fifteen alleged members of al-Qaida, the organization allegedly responsible for the destruction, was uncovered in Singapore. They were allegedly planning acts of terror against Americans in Singapore; thirteen were detained without trial under the Internal Security Act. Subsequent official statements linked them to a network of Muslim radicals working throughout the Philippines, Indonesia, Malaysia and Singapore.

Then, the president of an organization of young Muslims, the *Fateha*, went public on its Internet website with a claim that al-Qaida head Osama bin Laden was a better Muslim than the Malay members of Parliament in the ruling regime. Government ministers, Members of Parliament, Malay community leaders and other citizens immediately attacked him roundly in the mass media and he resigned from his organization within a few days.

Soon after, four Muslim parents sent their daughters to school with Islamic headdress, challenging the school uniform rule set by the Ministry of Education. The Ministry suspended the students after one week of failed negotiations. The students left the school, though their obedience to the Ministry put them in contravention of the compulsory education law. The issue of Islamic headdress had been simmering for over a decade, repeatedly raised with the government by Muslim leaders, but hitherto always away from public view. This instance of civil disobedience has exposed it to public debate but by no means solved it.

This series of events exposed the weakness of the prevailing minimal-tolerance multiracialism by revealing the absence of any deep cultural exchanges and understanding between the 'racial' groups. In response, a call has developed to encourage the crossing of racial and cultural boundaries. The government suggested that grassroots organizations, schools and other institutions organize 'inter-racial confidence circles' to break down racial group boundaries. Non-Muslims were invited to the performance, at different mosques, of the sacrificial ritual marking the end of the Haj period.

In a statement, Prime Minister Goh Chok Tong declared himself hostile to race-based politics. 'I want to reiterate that our national objective remains the integration of the different ethnic communities', he said.[6] Columnists of the pro-government national newspaper immediately penned pieces on a 'Singaporean Singapore',[7] a position long held by Singaporeans, who are against official insistence on racializing everyone. This changed government position may give rise to a new 'nationalist' discourse, the ground for which has already been prepared by the emerging Singaporean identity mentioned above. As for the government, the 'nationalist' discourse is as usual premised on the need for the people to pull together in the continuing struggle for the survival of the island-nation amid the intense competition of global capitalism.

Notes

1 The term 'race' is the preferred word of the Singaporean government, and by now Singaporeans in general, and it is therefore used throughout this chapter.

2 See Barry Turner (ed.), *The Statesman's Yearbook: The Politics, Cultures and Economies of the World 2002*, Basingstoke: Palgrave, 2001, p. 1405.

3 See details in Nirmala Purushotam, 'Disciplining difference: "Race" in Singapore', in Joel S. Kahn (ed.), *Southeast Asian Identities: Culture and Politics of Representation in Indonesia, Malaysia, Singapore and Thailand*, Singapore: Institute of Southeast Asian Studies, 1998, pp. 51–94.

4 Tan, Tai Yong, 'Singapore: Civil–military fusion', in M. Alagappa (ed.), *Coercion and Government: The Declining Political Role of the Military in Asia*, Stanford, CA: Stanford University Press, 2001, p. 287.

5 'Guest workers' are to be distinguished from 'foreign talents', the latter refers to highly educated, highly trained professionals who will add value to the labour force and are much welcomed by the government.

6 *Straits Times*, 26 February 2001.

7 *Straits Times*, 28 February 2001.

Further reading

The history of Singapore is covered in the autobiography of Lee Kuan Yew, Prime Minister from 1959 to 1990, and for many the main icon of Singapore's economic successes and political woes: *The Singapore Story: Memoirs of Lee Kuan Yew*, 2 vols (Singapore: Times Editions, 1998, 2000). Christopher Tremewan, *The Political Economy of Social Control in Singapore* (London: St Martin's Press, 1994) is a 'critical' analysis of the same story.

There is an extensive literature on multiracialism in Singapore by local academics. The following are examples: Geoffrey Benjamin, 'The cultural logic of Singapore's "multi-racialism"', in Riaz Hasan (ed.), *Singapore: Society in Transition* (Kuala Lumpur: Oxford University Press, 1976), pp. 115–33; Chua Beng Huat, 'Racial Singaporeans: Absence after the hyphen', in Joel S. Kahn (ed.), *Southeast Asian Identities: Cultures and the Politics of Representation in Indonesia, Malaysia, Singapore and Thailand* (Singapore: Institute of Southeast Asian Studies, 1998), pp. 28–50; Chua Beng Huat, 'Culture, multiracialism and national identity in Singapore', in Kuan-Hsing Chen (ed.), *Trajectories: Inter-Asia Cultural Studies* (London: Routledge, 1998), pp. 186–205; Nirmala Purushotam, *Negotiating Language, Constructing Race: Disciplining Difference in Singapore* (Berlin, New York: Mouton de Gruyter, 1997); Sharon Siddique, 'The phenomenology of ethnicity: A Singapore case study', *Sojourn: Social Issues in Southeast Asia*, 1990, vol. 5, pp. 35–62.

For an 'official' conceptualization of the economic 'backwardness' and 'marginalization' of Malays in Singapore see, respectively, Tania Li, *Malays in Singapore: Culture, Economy and Ideology* (Singapore: Oxford University Press, 1989) and Lily Zuraida Rahim, *The Singapore Dilemma: The Politics and Economics of Marginality of the Malay Community* (Kuala Lumpur: Oxford University Press, 1988).

7 Vietnam

A. Terry Rambo[1]

Vietnam is a multi-ethnic state composed of fifty-four officially recognized ethnic groups. It is unique among Southeast Asian countries, but similar to China, in that its ethnic minorities constitute only a relatively small fraction of the national population but occupy a vast part of the national territory, giving them a strategic importance greatly disproportionate to their numbers. The Vietnamese minorities, even those in the Central Highlands, also primarily occupy sensitive borders. The minorities are thus an extremely important component of Vietnamese society and ethnic relations are a matter of intense concern to the ruling Communist Party and the state.

Vietnam's ethnic minorities make up only 14 per cent of the national population. The lowland Vietnamese, who are officially designated as Kinh, form the vast majority of the population. According to the 1999 census, they number almost 66 million and constitute 86 per cent of the total population.[2] The fifty-three minority groups range in population from more than one million (Tay, Thai, Muong and Khmer) down to a few hundred people (Si La, Pu Peo, Brau, Ro Mam and O Du).

All of Vietnam's ethnic groups live in the uplands with the exception of the Kinh, Hoa (ethnic Chinese), Khmer (Cambodians) and Cham.[3] Most Kinh are wet-rice farmers in the Red River and Mekong deltas and the central coastal plains. About one-fifth live in urban centres, especially Hanoi and Ho Chi Minh City. Several million Kinh were resettled in the mountains during the last half of the twentieth century and are now the majority population in several upland provinces. The Hoa mostly live in urban centres, with the heaviest concentration in Ho Chi Minh City and the towns of the Mekong Delta. The Khmer are wet-rice farmers living in parts of the Mekong Delta while the Cham are farmers and fishermen, living in Phan Rang and Phan Thiet on the coast and in Chau Doc in the Mekong Delta. The remaining fifty groups are all found in the uplands, but otherwise share few common characteristics. Some groups, such as the Thai, Tay (Tho), and Nung, are wet-rice farmers whose villages have been in the same locations for generations, even centuries. Other groups, such as the E-De (Rhade) and Gia-Rai (Djarai, Jarai, Jorai), practice rotational shifting cultivation but live in relatively fixed settlements. Some groups of H'Mong (Hmong, Meo, Miao) in Lai Chau, Thanh Hoa and Nghe An are still shifting cultivators, but other

Plate 7.1 Thai woman cooking sticky rice, Lai Chau Province. Many minorities prefer sticky rice to the non-glutinous rice eaten by the Kinh (November 1995)

Plate 7.2 Tay and Hmong at weekly market in Ha Giang Province (January 1999)

Plate 7.3 White Hmong girl with pack basket, Ha Giang Province (January 1999)

Plate 7.4 White Hmong man transporting water 10 km from well to house, Ha Giang Province (January 1999)

Plate 7.5 Montagnard members of South Vietnamese local self-defence force, Phu Yen Province (1966)

groups of H'Mong in Lao Cai and Lang Son have constructed elaborately terraced wet-rice fields on steep hillsides and have lived in the same locations for many generations. A few very small groups, such as the Ruc of Quang Binh, followed an essentially hunter-gatherer mode of life but have recently been resettled into fixed villages.

In the northern mountains, the diverse minority groups generally lack large, clearly defined territories. Villages inhabited by different groups are interspersed together depending on specific local ecological conditions. The wet-rice farming groups (e.g. Thai, Muong) reside in valleys and intermontane basins, the rotational shifting cultivators (e.g. Kho Mu) live on the lower slopes of the mountains, while H'Mong settlements are generally found on high mountains above 1,000 metres elevation. Thus, ethnolinguistic maps of the region resemble the skin of a leopard with a bad case of measles. In the Central Highlands, however, prior to massive Kinh settlement after 1975, each tribal group occupied a clearly defined territory although they lacked any strong sense of group identity.

Vietnam's ethnic groups speak languages belonging to five major language families. The largest number, including the Kinh, Muong, Khmer and Ba-Na (Bahnar), speak languages belonging to the Austroasiatic family. The Cham, and several groups in the Central Highlands, including the E-De, Gia-Rai and Ra-Glai (Raglai, Roglai), speak Austronesian (Malayo-Polynesian) languages. Speakers of Thai-Kadai languages include the Tay, Thai and Nung. Sino-Tibetan speaking groups include the Hoa and several relatively small populations found along the border with China, including the Ha Nhi, Lo Lo and La Hu. The H'Mong and Dao (Dzao) belong to their own unique family.[4]

Detailed ethnological descriptions have been published for most of the mountain minorities but no fully satisfactory typology for grouping these diverse individual ethnic groups into larger categories has been proposed. From a political standpoint, perhaps the most significant distinction between groups is whether they have tribal or peasant forms of social organization. Shifting cultivators, such as the E-De, Gia-Rai and Ba-Na of the Central Highlands, who are often collectively referred to by the French term '*montagnards*', and the H'Mong and Dao of the northern mountains, display a tribal form of organization. Tribal society is relatively egalitarian and highly individualistic with leadership based on personal achievement rather than holding of a formal status. The Muong, Tay and Thai of the northern uplands were formerly organized as rank-stratified chiefdoms with people divided into nobles and commoners. Today, like the Cham and Khmer of the south they are peasant societies, as are the Kinh. Their social organization is hierarchical with centralized and institutionalized leadership. Of course, since 1954, all of these groups have been integrated into the Vietnamese nation-state and their traditional forms of socio-political organization largely supplanted by state administrative organs. But, at the local level, behaviour is still strongly shaped by traditional cultural institutions and values. These patterns have strongly influenced the extent to which different ethnic groups have been successfully integrated into the socialist nation-state. Peasant societies were readily integrated into the nation-state by a simple substitution of administrative elites in which communist cadre took the place of traditional mandarins or local nobility. Integration of tribally organized groups has proved to be more difficult, reflecting the fact that leadership of such societies is charismatic rather than based on ascribed status or bureaucratic position, making it difficult for the state to either co-opt tribal leaders or replace them with its own cadre. Pan-tribal associations such as clans also provide ready-made channels of communication among different communities within the ethnic group and facilitate organization of separatist movements that are very difficult for state security organs to penetrate. Thus it is among tribal societies that separatist tendencies remain most evident.

History

Ethnic relations in modern Vietnam have been strongly shaped by the prolonged struggle against foreign domination and for national independence. Consequently, issues of ethnic identity and the place of minority groups within the national society are highly politically charged. The official line is that all of the different groups residing within the present territory of Vietnam have always been unified into a single nation and have always fought together against foreign invaders. The historical reality that Vietnam's territorial boundaries were only established in relatively recent times as the result of continuous Kinh expansion into areas formerly occupied by autonomous societies, such as the Cham and Khmer empires, is ignored. In fact, the emergence of contemporary ethnic groups, including the dominant Kinh, is the outcome of a long and complex historical process. Some groups, such as the Muong and the Kinh, and many of the tribal groups in the Central Highlands, essentially evolved their current territories out of an earlier, relatively undifferentiated Southeast Asian cultural stratum. The Thai migrated into the northwest before the start of the current era, while the H'Mong and Dao migrated into Vietnam during the past two or three centuries, with some arriving from China and Laos as recently as the 1950s.

The Nguyen Dynasty (set up in 1802) claimed sovereignty over most of the mountain areas now incorporated within Vietnam's national borders, but frontiers were not clearly delineated and the state's effective control was limited to the Kinh-inhabited lowlands. Kinh mandarins were assigned to especially strategic areas in the northeastern mountains where they intermarried with the Tay elite, their descendants forming a hereditary nobility called the *Tho Ty*. Tribal groups in the Central Highlands were largely left to govern themselves. With the decline of state power during the nineteenth-century political turbulence, large parts of the northern mountains fell into a state of anarchy with Chinese paramilitary forces assuming *de facto* control until their defeat by the French in the late 1800s.

The French quickly took steps to delineate the borders of their new colony and to bring the upland minority groups under administrative control. In the northern mountains, the French ruled through the native nobles who were responsible for collecting taxes and maintaining order within their territories. In the tribal areas of the Central Highlands, the French relied on direct military presence to maintain a limited control. Some tribal groups, notably the Katu, were never fully 'pacified' and continued practising intertribal warfare until the 1960s. The Chinese, who began immigrating to the south in large numbers in the late 1800s, were organized into self-governing congregations (*bang*) based on dialects, with the head of each *bang* being held responsible by the colonial rulers for the behaviour of its members.

Ethnic relations prior to the August Revolution of 1945 were based on the spatial and occupational separation of different groups, and interactions between their members were infrequent and highly structured. The Kinh took the superiority of their culture for granted and considered the mountain minorities to be uncivilized savages. However, during the anti-French Resistance War (1946–54), relations between the Kinh and the minorities greatly intensified. Young Tay and Nung volunteers formed the first platoon of the Viet Minh liberation army organized by General Vo Nguyen Giap in 1944. Mountain minorities provided much of the military manpower of the revolutionary forces and tens of thousands of minority men and women served as porters carrying heavy loads of supplies across the mountains to support the fighting units. It has been plausibly argued that, without the strong support of the minorities, the Viet Minh would not been able to defeat the French.[5] The resistance bases of the Viet Minh were mainly located in the mountains and its Kinh leadership (including President Ho Chi Minh) lived for long periods in close contact with ethnic minorities, developing in the process a deep sympathy for their difficult situation, accompanied by a strong desire to improve their living conditions.

After winning independence in 1954, 'developing the uplands simultaneously with the lowlands' became a key policy of the Democratic Republic of (North) Vietnam. The Vietnamese state has expended a considerable share of its limited financial and human resources on attempts to develop the uplands and improve the minorities' living conditions, although the results of this investment have not been fully commensurate with their magnitude. Several million Kinh have been resettled in the uplands, resulting in much more frequent face-to-face contact between Kinh and the minorities but also increasing competition for scarce resources and jobs. For example, a community of Kinh migrants was implanted in the centre of the Dien Bien basin in the early 1960s. The pretty young women wearing Black Thai dresses who greet tourists arriving at the Dien Bien airport are actually Kinh who jokingly refer to themselves as members of the third Thai sub-group – Thai Den (Black Thai), Thai Trang (White Thai) and Thai Binh (Kinh descended from parents who migrated to Dien Bien from Thai Binh Province in the Red River Delta). Intermarriage between Kinh and members of minority groups such as the Muong, Thai and Tay is common, although rare with the H'Mong and other groups who are viewed as culturally backward.

Enhancing national integration is a constant preoccupation of the Party and great emphasis is placed on strengthening unity among the nation's different ethnic groups. The metaphor of the Vietnamese nation as a single 'great family' is frequently invoked and Kinh ethnic chauvinism officially discouraged. As in any multi-ethnic polity, however, there are unavoidable tensions between the desire to strengthen national integration and the recognition of the rights of minority cultures. The mass media, while overtly treating minority cultures sympathetically, all too often displays a condescending attitude in discussions of their cultural traits and beliefs that are presented as 'backward' and 'superstitious'.[6] Unfortunately, many minorities themselves have internalized these negative stereotypes. A recent study of ethnic stereotypes held by members of five communities in the northern mountains found that 78 per cent of H'Mong respondents, 65 per cent of Dan Lai, 29 per cent of Tay, and 7 per cent of Cao Lan, but no Kinh respondents, perceived their own cultural group as being 'backward'; 60 per cent of H'Mong, 55 per cent of Dan Lai, 33 per cent of Tay, 22 per cent of Cao Lan, but only 5 per cent of Kinh saw their own group as 'ignorant'.[7]

Ethnic identification

The Vietnamese term used for minorities is *dan toc thieu so*, which can be translated as either 'ethnic minority' or 'minority nationality' since *dan toc* is used interchangeably with both meanings depending on context. This usage reflects the influence of Soviet concepts about the place of ethnic minorities in socialist societies. The term *dan toc it nguoi* ('nationalities with small populations') was also commonly employed by Vietnamese ethnologists in the past but is no longer widely used.

Ethnic classification has always been a highly politicized activity. The French devoted considerable effort to identifying and describing different ethnic groups, with military officers or missionaries, rather than ethnologists, carrying out most of the work. A major distinction was drawn between the 'civilized' lowland peoples (Annamites [Kinh], Cambodians [Khmer], Cham and Chinese) and the 'savage' mountain peoples, who were collectively labelled as *moi* (a Vietnamese term meaning savage or inferior subject people). Assignment of names to groups was haphazard. After Vietnam won independence, determining the ethnic identity of its citizens became an important state priority. The initial directive to make a scientific ethnic classification came from President Ho Chi Minh himself. During a visit to a province in the northern mountains in 1958, he asked the local authorities how many ethnic groups lived there. The Provincial Chairman responded that there were sixteen groups while the Party Secretary replied that there were ten. Frustrated by the lack of a clear answer, President Ho ordered Vietnamese ethnologists to conduct research to determine precisely how many ethnic groups lived in Vietnam. They immediately began research to answer his question, but a comprehensive classification was not completed until 1979, ten years after Ho's death.[8]

Vietnamese ethnologists employ three criteria to identify ethnic groups:

* common language,
* common set of cultural traits, and
* a self-conscious identification as belonging to that specific group.

Only the third criterion is considered critical in defining ethnic groups. For example, the San Chay includes some local communities that speak a language belonging to the T'ai family and others that speak a Chinese dialect. In another example, all speakers of Thai languages are classified together as belonging to the 'Thai' ethnic group although these languages are not all mutually intelligible and the different local subgroups display considerable cultural differentiation. Vietnamese ethnologists justify this 'lumping' of different groups into a single ethnic category on the grounds that representatives of the various Thai communities themselves had decided that they were a single ethnic group at a national conference held in the early 1960s.[9]

Vietnamese have an essentialist concept of ethnicity. Ethnic groups are seen as natural phenomena rather than social constructs. Every citizen must belong to one of the fifty-four recognized groups with this affiliation shown on the identity card everyone carries. No ambiguity in classification is permitted. An individual having mixed ancestry must be assigned to only one group, normally the father's. The transactional approach to ethnic identity, in which ethnic groups are seen as being continuously reshaped by their interactions with other groups, has had little influence on the thinking of Vietnamese ethnologists. Discussion of the possibility that there may be more than fifty-four groups has not been encouraged, although recently a few Vietnamese ethnologists have cautiously begun to raise this issue. It is likely that if the three criteria for defining ethnic groups were fully and uniformly applied, many additional groups would be recognized and some now-separate groups might be merged. But, as in China, ethnic classification is a political issue, not a scientific one. Moreover, once a decision is reached, it rarely changes, unless original classifications were very unclear. And, in contrast to China, altering one's classification yields no benefits, such as exemption from restrictive family planning policy, which means there is little incentive to change.

Policy

The Vietnamese Constitution grants equal rights and duties to all citizens, regardless of ethnic affiliation, and prohibits ethnic discrimination. Minorities are guaranteed the right to speak their own languages and to preserve and develop the 'positive' elements of their cultures, although 'negative' cultural traits must be eradicated. It is the Kinh-led state, however, and not the minorities, that decides which traits are positive and which are negative. Traits are evaluated against the criteria of Marxist social evolutionary theory. Customs believed to be associated with a primitive evolutionary stage, such as matrilineal kinship or shamanism, are suspect. In the years immediately after reunification in 1975, doctrinaire cadres sometimes took extreme measures to eradicate such traits in the Central Highlands.[10] Heavy-handed measures to suppress traditional shamanism among the H'Mong have also been reported.[11] Recently, pressures to eradicate negative traits have relaxed somewhat although the authorities remain wary of any signs of the re-emergence of such practices. In March 2002 a decree was issued outlawing many traditional marriage customs of the minorities including 'bride capture', and the requirement that a woman must marry the widower of her deceased sister.[12]

The state actively encourages minority participation in national institutions. Minorities are represented at every government level from hamlet leader to the General Secretary of the Communist Party. Indeed, in April 2001, a member of the Tay minority Nong Duc Manh (born in 1940) was elected to this position, the most powerful in the whole country. Unusual in any country, the possibility of someone from an ethnic minority ascending so high is a credit to the level of ethnic tolerance in Vietnam. Individuals of minority origin hold over 17 per cent of seats in the National Assembly, although they make up only 14 per cent of the national population. Many senior local government leaders in minority areas are themselves members of minorities. If, however, the Chairman of the Provincial People's Committee is a minority, then the Party Secretary is likely to be a Kinh. The logic of this arrangement was vividly explained to me by a Kinh security official in a mountain province who held up his left arm saying that it represented the minority leader. The arm wobbled wildly around until he firmly grasped it at the wrist with his right hand, which he said represented the Kinh Party Secretary.

Specific policies toward the place of the minorities in the nation have changed over the years. In its earliest proclamations in the 1930s, the Party, following the then current Leninist line on nationalities, stated that minority nationalities could freely choose whether or not to belong to the Vietnamese state. Subsequently, in the 1950s, again showing the influence of Soviet and Chinese policies, autonomous zones were created for ethnic minorities in North Vietnam. Two zones were established, the Viet Bac zone in northeastern Vietnam, largely inhabited by Tay and Nung minorities, and the Thai-Meo autonomous zone in the northwestern mountains, later renamed the Tay Bac zone because it was inhabited by more than twenty minority groups in addition to the Thai and H'Mong (Meo). Minority groups in the Central Highlands were also promised by the National Liberation Front that they would be granted autonomous status but this promise was forgotten after 1975. Shortly after reunification, the autonomous zones in the north were dismantled and replaced with conventional provincial administrations. Today, the autonomous zones are rarely mentioned and no explanations are offered regarding their suppression.

Vietnam is now a unitary state with a standardized administrative model applied uniformly in all areas of the country. Every village, regardless of ethnic composition or location, displays the same administrative structure. It has its People's Committee, its Party cell, its Fatherland Front with its associated mass organizations (e.g. Women's Association), it has its agricultural cooperative and its militia unit. Depending on the community, these may have many members or only a handful, be highly active or relatively moribund, but all of them are linked into a hierarchical organizational structure that extends upward through the district, to the province, to Hanoi. This complex system transmits instructions from the central government to the villagers, and, to a lesser extent, information and criticisms from the villagers to the central authorities. Although seemingly cumbersome, this system can sometimes function with quite amazing efficiency, especially when security concerns are involved. Once, in a quite remote minority hamlet in the northern mountains, a Vietnamese colleague and I randomly interviewed an old man who, unknown to us, had been classified as a 'feudal element'. The hamlet leader reported our transgression and it was passed on to the province. Less than two weeks later security authorities contacted my host institution in Hanoi asking why I had been allowed to interview this suspect individual.

Economy

Although it is often claimed that the mountain minorities have wholly subsistence-oriented economies, in fact they have been deeply involved in trade and markets for many centuries. Although the poorly developed transportation system made it essential for every household to produce its own food, people relied on trade to obtain key necessities such as iron tools and salt, and prestige objects

Plate 7.6 Da Bac Tay women carrying firewood from forest to houses. Women of all ethnic groups work longer hours than men, Hoa Binh Province (February 1993)

Plate 7.7 Da Bac Tay family carrying new TV to house, Hoa Binh Province (April 1994)

Plate 7.8 Da Bac Tay women working on steeply sloping swidden field, Hoa Binh Province. Agricultural land is scarce in the mountains (February 1993)

Plate 7.9 Da Bac Tay woman weeding swidden field, Hoa Binh Province (1998)

such as bronze gongs and ceramic jars. Mountain-produced trade commodities must either have a high value to weight ratio (opium representing the ideal crop from the standpoint of value and ease of transport) or be self-propelled (live-stock). Although the transportation system has greatly expanded since the early 1990s, and the volume of trade greatly increased, the fundamental economic realities faced by the mountain minorities have not greatly altered. Ensuring food security is still the primary objective, and the range of commodities that can be profitably traded remains quite restricted, especially in remote areas. Opium production has declined in the face of intensive suppression efforts but an illegal trade in wild plant and animal species with very high value on the Chinese market has arisen to take its place.[13] Cash earned from this trade is used to purchase rice to make good local shortfalls in production and to buy consumer goods such as television sets and motorbikes.

The government has actively promoted production of cash crops in the uplands. Fruit, sugarcane, maize for livestock feed and timber for construction and paper pulp, are now widely grown. In the Central Highlands, many members of ethnic minority groups have become heavily involved in growing coffee. The recent collapse of coffee prices, itself largely the result of Vietnam's rapid expansion of production that glutted the world market, has had severe negative impact on their livelihoods.

During the French colonial period, the ethnic Chinese occupied a command-ing position in many sectors of the national economy, notably wholesale and retail merchandising and the rice trade, especially in the south. Chinese domi-nance of marketing was greatly reduced by the nationalization of commercial enterprises after 1975, the resettlement of hundreds of thousands of urban dwel-lers into New Economic Zones in the countryside, and the mass exodus of boat people (a large percentage of whom were Sino-Vietnamese).

Some social issues

Important social issues affecting the minorities include education, language policy, poverty, rights to land, and exploitation of natural resources and environmental degradation.

Education

Even during the Resistance War against the French, the Viet Minh mobilized soldiers and students to teach literacy classes in the most remote mountain settlements. After 1954, great efforts were made to establish schools and train teachers. Minority literacy rates dramatically increased, although they never achieved the almost universal level of the lowlands. These gains, which represent one of the socialist period's proudest achievements, have been threatened by the post-reform shifting of educational costs from the cooperatives to individual households. Poor households lack the means to pay school fees and cannot afford to lose the labour services of their children, so that even those enrolled in

Plate 7.10 Dan Lai children in village primary school, Nghe An Province (December 1987)

school are often absent to help their parents in the fields. Many parents, lacking the resources to provide schooling for all of their children, favour boys over girls. Consequently, literacy rates have declined in many communities.[14] In the more remote H'Mong villages, female literacy rates are often in single digits.

The physical state of schools is often shockingly bad. Teachers are poorly trained, badly paid and often absent from their classrooms while they carry on sideline activities to supplement their inadequate salaries. The situation of young Kinh women sent to teach in remote schools is particularly difficult. Not only must they live under difficult conditions, but their chances of finding suitable husbands are also very low. Few teachers can speak minority languages so that children from groups such as the H'Mong, where few people are able to speak the national language fluently, experience great difficulty in learning. Given the deficiencies of the primary education system, only a small percentage of minority children enter secondary school, while only a handful continue on to tertiary levels. In 1997/98 93 per cent of Kinh compared to 82 per cent of minorities had attended primary school, 32 per cent of Kinh and 8 per cent of minorities had attended upper secondary school, and 11 per cent of Kinh but only slightly more than 1 per cent of minorities had post-secondary education.[15] Thus, there is a persisting shortage of minority candidates with the qualifications to fill technical positions in the government services. Most extension workers, teachers and doctors in the uplands are still, of necessity, recruited from among the better-educated Kinh.

Language policy

Vietnam's language policies, although admirable in principle, have suffered from serious internal contradictions and problems of implementation. Successive decrees have affirmed that Vietnamese is the national language, which all citizens are expected to learn to speak, read and write. At the same time, the right of minorities to use their native languages is protected by the Constitution. Considerable effort has been devoted to developing standardized systems of writing for minority languages and to promoting their use in primary education and anti-illiteracy campaigns, but the results have been disappointing, reflecting flaws in the overall strategy. Rather than using existing local writing systems, wholly new systems were developed. For example, each of the Thai groups (Black Thai, White Thai, etc.) had its own traditional Pali-based script but these were consolidated into a new 'reformed' Thai alphabet that was alien to all of the groups so that Thai students could not read old texts that contained their cultural heritage. Not surprisingly, after an initial burst of enthusiasm, Thai students lost interest in studying the modern system. Similar problems beset efforts to introduce an alphabet for the Tay and Nung who had traditionally used Chinese characters. Adoption of the Roman alphabet as the vehicle for literacy effectively cut students off from their past.[16] In any case, after 1975, use of minority languages in primary schools was abandoned and all teaching was supposed to take place in the national language. It was not until the early 1990s that local authorities were allowed to reintroduce minority languages for primary-level teaching. In Cham and Thai areas, the new policy has been enthusiastically accepted but this time using the traditional scripts.

However laudable in principle, the educational use of minority languages faces many practical difficulties in such an ethnically diverse country. Few settlements are ethnically homogeneous so that only some children will be native speakers of whatever minority language is adopted for teaching purposes. Many minority languages are spoken by only a few hundred or thousand people, making it prohibitively expensive to produce literacy materials and train teachers in their use. In any case, the parents of many minority children are worried that teaching in the local languages will keep their children from becoming proficient in the national language and thus limit their opportunities for upward mobility.

Poverty

Many of the mountain minorities, as well as the Khmer living in the Mekong Delta, suffer from severe poverty. Minorities are 14 per cent of the national population, but in 1998 they accounted for 29 per cent of the poor.[17] In many remote villages the situation is much worse than national statistics suggest. A 1999 survey of five communities in the northern mountains found that the percentage of households falling under the food poverty line was 100 per cent in a Dan Lai hamlet in Nghe An Province, 93 per cent in a H'Mong village in Ha

Plate 7.11 Dan Lai woman fishing in river with basket, Nghe An Province (December 1998)

Plate 7.12 Dan Lai woman winnowing rice, Nghe An Province (December 1997)

Giang, 43 per cent in a Tay hamlet in Hoa Binh, and 22 per cent in a Cao Lan hamlet in Phu Tho. The sole Kinh community in the sample, in Phu Tho Province, had a poverty rate of 15 per cent. In the Dan Lai hamlet the annual average *per capita* cash and in-kind income was only US$22.[18]

The incidence of hunger is probably the most reliable measure of poverty levels in the mountains. In one Dan Lai hamlet studied by the author, only a single household had enough to eat in every month of the year! Fifty-five per cent of the households reported that they suffered from hunger for three or more months each year, with 35 per cent going hungry for five or more months. The food situation was somewhat better for a H'Mong village in Ha Giang Province, where 18 per cent reported being hungry for three or more months during the year; a Tay hamlet in Hoa Binh Province, where 9 per cent suffered hunger during three or more months; and Cao Lan and Kinh hamlets in Phu Tho Province, where only 5 per cent suffered hunger for three or more months.[19]

The Vietnamese government has launched a massive effort to reduce poverty with special attention being paid to minority communities. Notable progress has been achieved in a very short time. Nationally, the percentage of poor people declined from 58 per cent in 1993 to 37 per cent in 1998, while in the same period the incidence of poor people, mostly minorities, in the northern uplands declined from 79 to 59 per cent.[20] Unfortunately, despite this success in reducing absolute poverty, the relative gap in living standards between the mountains and the lowlands is growing rather than narrowing.

The main institutional vehicles for reducing poverty are the 133 Program for eradication of hunger and reduction of poverty and the 135 Program for socio-economic development, which target the 1,715 poorest communes in the country, a large share of which are minority communities, for special development assist-ance. The 135 Program provides funds to the People's Committees of every commune to use for locally initiated development efforts such as building roads and constructing irrigation systems. The communities benefit both through long-term improvement of infrastructure and immediate gains in income from em-ployment as labourers on these public works projects. In 1999 alone, the state committed the equivalent of nearly US$500 million to the 133 Program.[21]

The state provides direct assistance to households in poor communities by exempting them from payment of school fees and charges for medical services at village clinics, and it subsidizes transportation costs of essential commodities (kerosene, fertilizer, school notebooks) so that they can be sold at the same price in remote mountain communities as in the lowlands. The state also makes mas-sive transfer payments from the central budget to cover the administrative costs of local governments in minority provinces in the uplands. In the case of Bac Can, one of the poorest provinces in Vietnam, some 90 per cent of the provin-cial budget is provided by Hanoi, while 80 per cent of Cao Bang Province's budget is funded by the centre.[22] The economies of many minority households are now heavily dependent on government transfer payments that include sala-ries paid to cadre, pensions paid to retired cadre and soldiers, and monetary assistance given to households by development projects.

Rights to land

Under Vietnamese law, all land belongs to the state, with no recognition of traditional minority claims to land rights. In the north in the early 1960s and the south after 1975, cooperatives took over agricultural land and farmed it on a communal basis. Vast tracts of land in the Central Highlands, much of it formerly used by minorities for shifting cultivation, came under the control of state farms and state forest enterprises that were largely staffed by Kinh migrants.

Under reforms initiated in the late 1980s, wet-rice land formerly managed by the agricultural cooperatives was allocated to households, but allocation of hill lands has been much slower and encountered many obstacles, particularly in minority communities. In one Tay community I studied in Hoa Binh Province, the cadre from the district land office made many errors when preparing the land map, so that rights to plots actually being managed by one household were allocated to a different household. This has created a complex maze of overlapping rights that causes many difficulties for the farmers, including generating conflicts between households with competing claims.

Allocation of hill land has also suffered from other serious problems. Much of the land involved is officially classified as 'unused land' (*dat chua su dung*). In reality, as one Vietnamese researcher has observed, there is no land in the mountains that is not already being used by someone for some purpose or other.[23] Much of the land officially classified as 'unused' is actually fallow fields used for shifting cultivation where minority farmers are allowing the forest to regenerate before clearing and burning their plots again. Large areas are also used for grazing livestock and collection of bamboo and other non-timber forest products. Allocation of lands formerly treated as an open-access community resource to the control of individual households threatens to reduce the already inadequate resource base of many poor minority households.

Exploitation of natural resources and environmental degradation

The livelihoods of the mountain minorities are heavily dependent on natural resources and are being adversely affected by environmental degradation. The state has often displayed a rather schizophrenic approach to the management of natural resources and the environment, on the one hand encouraging reckless overexploitation of resources for short-term economic benefits while on the other hand promulgating policies aimed at protecting and conserving the environment.

The state sees the mountains as a vast treasure house of natural resources that must be exploited to support national economic development. The northern mountains contain at least thirty kinds of minerals and have 270 mines.[24] Mining makes a large contribution to national income but the local environmental consequences are often severe. Unregulated and illegal mining for gems and gold has badly disturbed many watercourses. Miners in the Truong Son mountain chain employ mercury to extract gold from river sediments with residues of this highly toxic chemical contaminating downstream water supplies.

The mountains hold a large share of the nation's hydropower potential. The Da River alone has a potential capacity of 50 billion kw/h, which is 19 per cent of the total national hydropower potential.[25] The Hoa Binh dam provides much of the electrical power used in the north and also helps to protect Hanoi and the Red River Delta from flooding. Most of the undoubted benefits of this project have flowed to the lowlands, however, while the social, economic, and environmental costs have mostly been borne locally. A large number of Muong households, who formerly lived in the valley flooded by the reservoir, lost their wet-rice fields and had to relocate onto steep slopes in the watershed surrounding the dam where they make a precarious living from shifting cultivation. The proposed Ta Bu dam, in Son La Province, will flood an even larger area and force relocation of many tens of thousands of minority people, mainly Thai. The social and environmental impacts of this project are so adverse that none of the international development assistance agencies is willing to support it, but the Vietnamese government is determined to build it using domestic funds.

Perhaps the greatest shortcoming of efforts to exploit the natural resources of the uplands is the absence of mechanisms to ensure that a fair share of the benefits stay in the affected localities. Thus it was almost a decade after the completion of the Hoa Binh dam before electrical power lines were constructed serving the minority villages in the Da River watershed. Revenues from the dam belong to the state and do not flow directly into the provincial budget. Most mines are operated by state enterprises under ministerial control and again contribute little or nothing to local budgets. Most of their workers are brought in from the lowlands.

Commercial logging, land clearance for production of cash crops such as coffee, and shifting cultivation by ethnic minorities have severely damaged once abundant forest resources in the uplands. Forest cover declined from 43 per cent in 1943 to about 28 per cent in 1996, and the quality of the surviving forests was also severely degraded. Although logging and land clearance for planting of coffee and other industrial crops are responsible for much greater loss of forest area than shifting cultivation, the state continues to place most of the blame for deforestation on minority shifting cultivators.

Traditionally, many upland minority groups depended on shifting cultivation (also called slash-and-burn farming or swidden agriculture) to meet their subsistence needs. Under favourable conditions of low population density and abundant areas of forest such as traditionally existed in the Central Highlands, shifting cultivation produced relatively abundant crops with minimal labour requirements, but this system of agriculture is anathema to communist development planners who view it as a primitive means of production. Since the early 1960s, the state has attempted to eliminate shifting cultivation and resettle minority populations in fixed communities. In the late 1950s, H'Mong and Dao from the high mountains were moved to valley land where they were assigned wet-rice fields in fixed settlements. According to official statistics, 167,000 households from 630 villages in the northern mountains have been more or less successfully settled and now practise fixed cultivation.[26] In reality, however, many communities that have been officially classified as practising fixed cultivation in fact continue to engage in swiddening. In Tay communities I studied in Hoa Binh Province, for example, the people, realizing that shifting cultivation was illegal, began referring to their swiddens as 'mixed gardens' (*vuon tap*) when reporting to district officials. The latter duly reported that shifting cultivation had almost totally been eliminated in their district, although one could look out of the window at the district People's Committee offices and see swiddens on the surrounding hills.

The persistence of shifting cultivation is often explained by officials in terms of the supposed 'backwardness' and lack of knowledge of minority farmers. In my experience, however, upland farmers generally recognize that swiddening is no longer a sustainable productive system and would like to find alternatives. The main constraint on change is not the attitudes of the farmers but the lack of viable alternative agricultural systems for sloping lands. The area suitable for wet-rice cultivation is limited and most of it has already been developed. Tree-based cropping systems can be productive and sustainable, but expansion of areas under perennials is constrained by lack of capital, the long delay between the time the trees are planted and the time when farmers earn any income from them, and restricted and unstable markets. Many mountain areas are suitable for rearing livestock and sale of livestock has become a major source of cash income for many upland households. Restriction of shifting cultivation and re-forestation of fallowed swiddens is reducing the area of pasture, however. Unless and until better alternatives can be developed, shifting cultivation will continue to be practised in the mountains.

In response to widespread deforestation, the state has banned all logging of natural forests and initiated major reforestation programmes. The results of these efforts have been mixed; illegal logging continues in remaining areas of natural forest, even inside national parks and nature reserves, and the area of mature natural forest continues to decline. But reforestation efforts have enjoyed considerable success in parts of the midlands and many formerly barren hills are now covered with trees. Nationally, according to a 2001 estimate by the Forest Inventory and Planning Institute, forests covered 33 per cent of Vietnam's land area compared to 28 per cent just five years earlier.[27]

Problems of national integration

Because minorities inhabit approximately three-quarters of its national territory, including strategically sensitive border areas with China, Laos and Cambodia, retention of their loyalty is of critical importance to the state's survival, explaining the tremendous emphasis official rhetoric places on maintenance of national unity. Ho Chi Minh's call for 'unity, unity, great unity' (*doan ket, doan ket, dai doan ket*) is constantly invoked in government propaganda campaigns.

Official literature either wholly ignores or denies the existence of separatist movements. It has even been claimed that contrary to tendencies towards greater ethnic differentiation in prehistoric times in other parts of the world, Vietnam is unique in that for many thousands of years all the ethnic groups residing in the territory now encompassed by the national borders have aspired to the creation of a unified state![28] But there is considerable evidence that integration of some tribal groups into the nation-state has not been as rapid or successful as official claims of total national unity would have one believe. During the Resistance War, French commandos organized anti-communist guerrilla units among the H'Mong in the northern mountains and, as recently as 1958, a short-lived H'Mong rebellion, allegedly instigated by the Saigon regime with covert encouragement from Taiwan, gained control over several districts in Ha Giang Province near the northern border with China.

In 1946, using divide-and-rule tactics to stimulate ethnic fragmentation of the independence movement, the French promised the Montagnards that the Central Highlands would be governed separately from the rest of Vietnam and in 1950 they declared that the Central Highlands were an autonomously-governed Crown Domain called the Pays Montagnards du Sud (PMS). A special Montagnard division was recruited to defend this territory and Montagnard officers trained to lead it. Although autonomous more in name than practice, the PMS contributed to the generation of a sense of common identity among the previously fragmented tribal groups. After the French defeat in 1954, the newly established Republic of Vietnam abolished the PMS and incorporated the Central Highlands directly into the state.

During the liberation war in the south (1958–75), the Montagnards exhibited divided loyalties. Many supported the National Liberation Front (NLF) while others, especially E-De and Gia-Rai tribesmen, enlisted in paramilitary units the US organized to fight against the Kinh-led NLF. A separatist movement referred to as FULRO (United Front for the Liberation of the Oppressed Races) fought against both the NLF and the Saigon regime.[29] Some members of FULRO continued armed resistance into the late 1980s. Integration of tribal groups into the nation-state remains problematic as evidenced by the spreading of a millenarian movement with separatist overtones among H'Mong in the northern mountains[30] and recent protest demonstrations involving minorities in the Central Highlands. It is the latter movement that the authorities perceive as the most serious threat to national unity.

In early 2001, protest demonstrations involving some thousands of minority villagers suddenly erupted in many districts and provincial capitals in the Central Highlands. The authorities responded by saturating the area with police and military forces, quickly bringing overt protests to a halt. Many alleged ringleaders were arrested and soon publicly recanted their actions. Subsequently, some hundreds of ethnic minority Vietnamese fled across the border seeking refuge in Cambodia where they have become the focus of a continuing acrimonious debate between the Vietnamese and Khmer governments and the United Nations High Commissioner for Refugees. According to official Vietnamese statements, the demonstrations and refugee movement were entirely attributable to the activities of outside agitators who tricked and deceived innocent people into believing that their way of life was being threatened by the policies of the Vietnamese state. It is clear to outside observers, however, that a number of inter-related factors have contributed to the spread of discontent among the minorities. These include the massive influx of Kinh migrants into the Central Highlands since 1975, the loss of minority control over their traditional land, state policies towards religion and the emergence of ethnonationalism among the minorities.[31]

Kinh in-migration into the Central Highlands

As recently as 1943, ethnic minorities accounted for 95 per cent of the population of the Central Highlands provinces whereas their current share of the population has fallen to barely 33 per cent as the result of massive in-migration of Kinh settlers after 1975. Thus, in little more than half a century, the tribal peoples of the Central Highlands have been transformed into a minority within their own territory.

Alienation of minority lands

The massive resettlement of Kinh in the Highlands was accompanied by the extensive alienation of lands the minorities formerly occupied. Vast tracts of the best quality forestland were incorporated into the state farms and state forest enterprises on which the newly arrived Kinh were settled. More recently, waves of spontaneous migrants, often themselves ethnic minorities (Tay, Nung), from land-scarce provinces in the northern mountains, have displaced local minorities from better lands located near roads, with the former owners forced to move ever deeper into the forests. As a consequence of growing land scarcity, traditional shifting cultivation, which once provided a relatively stable livelihood to the minorities, is no longer either a productive or sustainable way of farming.[32]

State policies towards religion

Although the Vietnamese Constitution guarantees freedom to practise or not practise religion, exercise of this right is tightly circumscribed, with only officially recognized religious groups permitted to operate openly. Many minorities are adherents of unrecognized, and hence illegal, evangelical Protestant sects that have been growing rapidly in membership since 1975. Official efforts to suppress this movement have been vigorous and heavy-handed, with members suffering various types of harassment and many pastors being jailed.

Ethnonationalism

Beginning in the latter days of French colonial rule, the diverse and previously autonomous Montagnard tribal groups of the Central Highlands began to de-velop a sense that they shared a common culture that set them apart from the Kinh. This spirit of ethnonationalism was particularly strong among graduates of schools run by Christian missions that brought together students from diverse tribes. It was further solidified by involvement of young men from different ethnic groups in the American Special Forces-led paramilitary forces and, subsequently, the FULRO movement. Although any public expression of ethnonationalist sympathies was totally prohibited after reunification, the movement has recently re-emerged in a rather dramatic fashion.

And although the Vietnamese state has blamed all signs of unrest among the minorities on a handful of outside agitators, it is deeply concerned about the situation in the Central Highlands and has launched a massive propaganda effort designed to counter the emergence of ethnonationalism. Kinh cadres are now receiving training in minority languages and the use of minority languages on radio and television has suddenly dramatically increased. Cadres from provincial and district governments have been sent to the villages to live together with the minority people and the army has assigned 'civic action' teams to many Montagnard settlements.

Some foreign policy ramifications of the minorities

Ethnic issues have considerable impact on Vietnam's foreign relations. Key issues relate to minorities that have territories straddling Vietnam's borders with China, Laos and Cambodia, the situation of the Hoa (Sino-Vietnamese) community in Vietnamese society, and the human rights and religious freedom of the minorities.

Minorities that overlap Vietnam's borders with China, Laos and Cambodia

A number of minorities live in border zones and maintain contact with their relatives living on the other side of the border. The Tay, Nung and H'Mong, for example, are found on both sides of the border with China. The H'Mong, Kho-mu and Thai maintain connections with kin in Laos, and the Gia-Rai and Khmer have connections to relatives in Cambodia. Such ethnic relations facilitate informal trade as well as the smuggling of drugs and other contraband goods and people. They are also the cause of concern to security officials who fear that such transboundary minorities may be potential fifth columnists in the event of war. During the 1979 border war with China, several well-known Tay senior officers in the Vietnamese People's Army came under suspicion because of their close ties with China, and a number were forced into retirement. Since Vietnam now enjoys friendly relations with all neighbouring states, concerns about the loyalty of border zone minorities have largely abated but border security is still a major preoccupation of the central authorities.

The situation of the Hoa (Sino-Vietnamese) in Vietnamese society

Officially sanctioned discrimination against the Hoa in the latter part of the 1970s, including seizure of property and covert official pressures on them as boat people to leave Vietnam, was a factor in China's decision to launch its armed incursion into Vietnam's northern border provinces in 1979. Since the launching of the reform effort in the late 1980s, official treatment of the remaining Hoa has greatly improved and their situation in Vietnamese society no longer appears to be a significant source of tension in Sino-Vietnamese relations.

Human rights and religious freedom of the minorities

Criticisms by the US Congress and the State Department of Vietnam's human rights record, especially its repression of unauthorized religious movements among the minorities, has become a growing source of friction in relations with the United States. This criticism is fed by active lobbying of Congress by communities of Montagnard and H'Mong refugees resident in the United States, some of whom are allied with fundamentalist Christian sects, and left-over Cold Warriors seeking new justifications for anti-communism. Quite incredible stories about diabolical plots by the Vietnamese state against the minorities are picked up and circulated on the Internet. Vietnam has added fuel to the fire by denying foreign observers access to large parts of the highlands and by its repeated claims that no real problems in ethnic relations exist and that any signs of unrest among the minorities are actually the work of dangerous outside agitators. No quick resolution of this issue can be anticipated and it is likely to remain an irritant in Vietnam–American relations for some time to come.

Conclusion

By global standards, the Vietnam state's handling of relations with its minorities has been relatively enlightened. Although there continue to be many serious problems, there has been no genocide and no ethnic cleansing. Members of minorities have full citizenship accompanied by constitutional guarantees of the rights to use their languages and preserve their cultures. Misguided campaigns to suppress religious practices considered to be 'superstitions' have occurred, but the majority Kinh have also suffered from such efforts. Social prejudice based on the belief that many minorities are 'backward' is prevalent among the Kinh but in recent years it appears to have lessened. The Party and the state have frequently expressed their strong commitment to maintaining Vietnam as a multi-ethnic nation in which all citizens, regardless of ethnic identity, have the same rights and duties. The national ideal is to fully integrate minorities into the national life while permitting, even encouraging, a carefully circumscribed degree of multiculturalism.

There are, however, many obstacles to achieving this ideal. The minorities are, to a large extent, economically and socially marginal. The greatest problems facing the minorities relate to education, poverty and access to resources. The poor education minorities receive compared to the Kinh, prevents them from moving into positions offering higher pay and status, and locks most into a lifetime of subsistence farming. Despite great government efforts in recent years, the poverty rate (especially among the Khmer and the mountain groups) is much higher than among lowland Kinh. Worse, the gap between incomes in the lowlands and the mountains is rapidly widening. We can largely explain the prevalence of poverty by the very limited natural resource base from which the minorities must extract their livelihoods and the continued rapid environmental degradation in the mountains. Good agricultural land is scarce, the ratio of population to land high and rapidly increasing, the quality of soil declining and crop yields falling. At the same time, demand for cash is growing, causing people to overexploit natural resources, resulting in even more rapid environmental degradation. One can argue that the mountain minorities are caught in a vicious downward spiral that will make them ever more marginal players in the national economy and society.[33]

Increasing economic and social marginalization may fuel separatist sentiments among some minorities, which will remain a potential source of unrest, especially in the Central Highlands. But their numbers are small compared to the national population, they lack any real military force, and have no foreign powers actively supporting them. Thus, ethnic separatism poses no real threat to the security of the state although it is likely to remain the cause of acute anxiety for the authorities.

Notes

All photographs of Vietnam by A. Terry Rambo.

1 Most of the field research on which this chapter is based was carried out while I was the East-West Center Representative in Vietnam (1996–2000), my work being funded by the Ford Foundation, the Swedish International Development Cooperation Agency, the John D. and Catherine T. MacArthur Foundation, the Rockefeller Brothers Fund and the Keidanren Nature Conservation Fund. I am grateful to colleagues at the Center for Natural Resources and Environmental Studies (CRES) of the Vietnam National University, Hanoi and at the Center for Agricultural Research and Environmental Studies (CARES) of Hanoi Agricultural University for all of their help, both intellectual and personal, over the years. I would especially like to acknowledge the help of Le Trong Cuc, Coordinator of the CRES Upland Working Group, who was my counterpart in Vietnam.
2 General Statistical Office, *Population and Housing Census Vietnam 1999: Completed Census Results*, Hanoi: Statistical Publishing House, 2001, p. 21, Table 1.6.
3 Official spellings are employed for the names of minority groups throughout this chapter. The first time the group is mentioned, alternative names/spellings are listed in parentheses, e.g. Tay (Tho).
4 Dang Nghiem Van, Chu Thai Son and Luu Hung, *Ethnic Minorities in Vietnam*, Hanoi: The Gioi Publishers, 2000, p. 2.
5 John T. McAlister Jr, 'Mountain minorities and the Viet Minh: A key to the Indochina War', in Peter Kunstadter (ed.), *Southeast Asian Tribes, Minorities, and Nations*, Princeton, NJ: Princeton University Press, 1967, pp. 771–844.
6 John S. Ambler and Oscar Salemink, 'Media and minorities: The communication of upland development in Vietnam', Paper presented at EUROVIET III Conference, Amsterdam, July 1997.
7 Le Trong Cuc and A. Terry Rambo (eds), *Bright Peaks, Dark Valleys: A Comparative Analysis of Environmental and Social Conditions and Development Trends in Five Communities in Vietnam's Northern Mountain Region*, Hanoi: National Political Publishing House, 2001, p. 205, Table 6–25.

8 Dang Nghiem Van, *Ethnological and Religious Problems in Vietnam*, Hanoi: Social Sciences Publishing House, 1998, pp. 10–11.

9 Dang Nghiem Van, *Ethnological and Religious Problems*, p. 25.

10 Dang Nghiem Van, 'Nhung van de xa hoi hien nay o Tay Nguyen' ('Contemporary social problems in Tay Nguyen'), in Vietnam Committee for the Social Sciences, *Tay Nguyen tren duong phat trien* (*Tay Nguyen on the Road to Development*), Hanoi: Nha xuat ban khoa hoc xa hoi, 1989, pp. 67–151.

11 Tran Huu Son, *Van hoa HMong* (*H'Mong Culture*), Hanoi: Nha xuat ban van hoa dan toc, 1996.

12 'Marriage directive', *The Nation* (Bangkok), 31 March 2002, p. 6.

13 Deanna Donovan (ed.), *Policy Issues of Transboundary Trade in Forest Products in Northern Vietnam, Lao PDR and Yunnan PRC*, Washington, DC: World Resources Institute, Washington, 1998.

14 Khong Dien (ed.), *Nhung dac diem kinh te-xa hoi cac dan toc Mien nui Phia bac* (*Socio-economic Characteristics of Northern Mountain Minorities*), Hanoi: Nha xuat ban khoa hoc xa hoi, 1996, p. 243.

15 National Center for Social Sciences and Humanities, *National Human Development Report 2001*, Hanoi: The Political Publishing House, 2001, p. 39, Table 2.6.

16 Tran Tri Doi, *Ngon ngu va phat trien Van hoa Xa hoi* (*Language and the Development of Culture and Society*), Hanoi: Nha xuat ban van hoa thong tin, 2001.

17 Joint Report of the Government–Donor NGO Working Group, *Attacking Poverty: Vietnam Development Report 2000*, Hanoi: The World Bank in Vietnam, 1999, p. 15, Figure 1.4.

18 Le Trong Cuc and Rambo, *Bright Peaks*, pp. 237–8.

19 Le Trong Cuc and Rambo, *Bright Peaks*, p. 241.

20 Joint Report, *Attacking Poverty*, p. 15, Figure 1.4.

21 Nguyen Thi Hang, 'Van de xoa doi giam ngheo va thuc hien chinh sach nguoi co cong voi cach mang o vung dan toc thieu so' ('Problems of hunger eradication and reduction of poverty and realization of policies for revolutionary workers in the ethnic minority regions'), in *Cac dan toc thieu so Viet nam the ky XX* (*Vietnam's Ethnic Minorities in the Twentieth Century*), Hanoi: Nha xuat ban chinh tri quoc gi, 2001, pp. 195–205.

22 'Northern provinces get more aid, urged to build up strengths', *Viet Nam News* (23 July 2001), p. 1.

23 Hoang Xuan Ty, 'Cach phan loai dat va su dung dat vung nui cua nguoi Thai Den Moc Chau, Mai Son, Son La' ('Classification and use of mountain land by Black Thai in Moc Chau, Mai Son, Son La Province'), in Hoang Xuan Ty and Le Trong Cuc (eds), *Kien thuc ban dia cua dong bao vung cao trong nong nghiep va quan ly tai nguyen thien nhien* (*Local Knowledge of Highland Peoples in Agriculture and Management of Natural Resources*), Hanoi: Nha xuat ban nong nghiep, 1998, pp. 97–8.

24 Khong Dien, *Nhung dac diem kinh te-xa hoi*, p. 35.

25 Khong Dien, *Nhung dac diem kinh te-xa hoi*, p. 19.

26 Phan Huu Dat, 'Su phat trien cua cac dan toc thieu so Viet Nam trong the ky XX' ('Development of ethnic minorities in Vietnam in the twentieth century'), in *Cac dan toc thieu so Viet nam the ky XX* (*Vietnam's Ethnic Minorities in the Twentieth Century*), Hanoi: Nha xuat ban chinh tri quoc gia, 2001, p. 74.

27 AP news service, 8 January 2001.

28 Dang Phong, *Kinh te thoi nguyen thuy o Viet-nam* (*Primeval Economy of Vietnam*), Hanoi: Nha xuat ban khoa hoc xa hoi, 1970, p. 26.

29 Oscar Salemink, '*Mois and maquis*: The invention and appropriation of Vietnam's Montagnards from Sabatier to the CIA', in George W. Stocking (ed.), *Colonial Situations: Essays on the Contextualization of Ethnographic Knowledge*, History of Anthropology Vol. 7, Madison: University of Wisconsin Press, 1991, pp. 243–84.

30 Tran Huu Son, *Van hoa HMong*.

31 'An independent WriteNet researcher', *Vietnam: Indigenous Minority Groups in the Central Highlands*, UNHCR Centre for Documentation and Research, WriteNet Paper No. 05/2001.

32 Bui Minh Dao, *Trong trot truyen thong cua cac dan toc tai cho o Tay Nguyen* (*Traditional Agriculture of Indigenous Ethnic Groups in the Central Highlands of Vietnam*), Hanoi: Nha xuat ban khoa hoc xa hoi, 2000.
33 Neil L. Jamieson, Le Trong Cuc and A. Terry Rambo, *The Development Crisis in Vietnam's Mountains*, Honolulu: East-West Center Special Report No. 6, 1998.

Further reading

Although a vast literature exists on Vietnam's ethnic minorities, most publications are in French or Vietnamese. The literature in English is relatively few in quantity and uneven in quality. Dang Nghiem Van, Chu Thai Son and Luu Hung's *Ethnic Minorities in Vietnam* (Hanoi: The Gioi Publishers, 2000), provides brief descriptions of each of the fifty-four minority groups. The two volumes of the US Army's Ethnographic Study Series, *Minority Groups in the Republic of Vietnam* (Washington, DC: Department of the Army Pamphlet No. 550–105, 1966), and *Minority Groups in North Vietnam* (Washington, DC: Department of the Army, 1972), summarize the available literature on all northern and southern minority groups.

General works on Vietnam's ethnic minorities

Dang Nghiem Van, *Ethnological and Religious Problems in Vietnam*, Hanoi: Social Sciences Publishing House, 1998.
Rambo, A. Terry, Robert R. Reed, Le Trong Cuc and Michael R. DiGregorio (eds), *The Challenges of Highland Development in Vietnam*, Honolulu: East-West Center, 1995.
Van de Walle, Dominique and Dileni Gunewardena, 'Sources of ethnic inequality in Viet Nam', *Journal of Development Economics*, 2001, vol. 65, pp. 177–207.

The minorities of the Central Highlands

Condominas, Georges, *We Have Eaten the Forest: The Story of a Montagnard Village in the Central Highlands of Vietnam*, New York: Hill and Wang, 1977.
Evans, Grant, 'Central Highlanders of Vietnam', in R.H. Barnes, Andrew Gray and Benedict Kingsbury (eds), *Indigenous Peoples of Asia*, Ann Arbor, MI: Association for Asian Studies, 1995, pp. 247–71.
Hickey, Gerald Cannon, *Free in the Forest: Ethnohistory of the Vietnamese Central Highlands, 1954–1976*, New Haven, CT: Yale University Press, 1982.
Hickey, Gerald Cannon, *Sons of the Mountains: Ethnohistory of the Vietnamese Central Highlands to 1954*, New Haven, CT: Yale University Press, 1982.
Hickey, Gerald Cannon, *Shattered World: Adaptation and Survival among Vietnam's Highland People during the Vietnam War*, Philadelphia: University of Pennsylvania Press, 1993.
Salemink, Oscar, '*Mois and maquis:* The invention and appropriation of Vietnam's Montagnards from Sabatier to the CIA', in George W. Stocking (ed.), *Colonial Situations: Essays on the Contextualization of Ethnographic Knowledge*, History of Anthropology Vol. 7, Madison: University of Wisconsin Press, 1991, pp. 243–84.

The mountain minorities of northern Vietnam

Donovan, Deanna, A. Terry Rambo, Jefferson Fox, Le Trong Cuc and Tran Duc Vien (eds), *Development Trends in Vietnam's Northern Mountain Region*, Hanoi: National Political Publishing House, 1997.

Le Trong Cuc and A. Terry Rambo (eds), *Bright Peaks, Dark Valleys: A Comparative Analysis of Environmental and Social Conditions and Development Trends in Five Communities in Vietnam's Northern Mountain Region*, Hanoi: National Political Publishing House, 2001.

McAlister, John T. Jr, 'Mountain minorities and the Viet Minh: A key to the Indochina War', in Peter Kunstadter (ed.), *Southeast Asian Tribes, Minorities, and Nations*, Princeton, NJ: Princeton University Press, 1967, pp. 771–844.

Michaud, Jean, 'The Montagnards in northern Vietnam from 1802 to 1975: A historical overview from exogenous sources', in J. Michaud and J. Ovesen (eds), *Turbulent Times and Enduring Peoples: The Montagnards of Mainland South-East Asia*, London: Curzon Press, 1999.

Novellino, Dario, 'The limits and implications of food production among the H'mong people of the Northern Highlands (Vietnam)', *Soma*, 1998, no. 2, pp. 55–76.

Sikor, Thomas, 'Agrarian differentiation in post-socialist societies: Vietnamese transformations', *Development and Change*, 2001, vol. 32, no. 5, pp. 923–49.

8 Ethnicity in the Philippines

R.J. May[1]

The Philippines is a nation of some 7,000 islands, 83 million people (in mid-2001) and 168 'living languages'.[2] The principal lines of ethnic cleavage were created more by colonial policies, particularly those of the Spanish administration, than by primordial ethnic attachments.

The Spanish colonial regime lasted from 1565 until the Philippines' cession to the Americans in 1898. To a substantial extent, it defined the identity of Filipinos in terms of the indigenous population's religious relationship to the Spaniards. The status of Chinese immigrants was more ambivalent, but intermittent pressures on the Chinese (alternating with attacks on Chinese communities and the deportation of migrants) to blend into Filipino rural society laid the basis for a relatively high degree of integration compared with most of the Philippines' Southeast Asian neighbours. In essence the half century of American colonialism maintained the ethnic construct of the Spanish regime.

The legacy of these policies is a nation comprising three major ethnic blocs: an economically and politically dominant majority population of 'mainstream' Filipinos, mostly Christian and substantially Westernized; a minority group of indigenous cultural communities or 'tribal' Filipinos concentrated in relatively remote and mountainous areas; and a smaller population of Muslim Filipinos (or, as many of them prefer to be called, Philippine Muslims) concentrated in the south. There is also a relatively small, but influential, ethnic Chinese population. All three major groups are predominantly of Malay, Austronesian-speaking stock. There has long been intermarriage among them, as well as with foreign migrants and settlers such as the Chinese, Spaniards and Americans. In terms of material culture and ethnic relations, however, the two most significant cleavages are those between mainstream and Muslim Filipinos, and between mainstream Filipinos and indigenous cultural communities.

The following presents a brief description of the four main ethnic groups, attempting to place them within their historical context, but with most stress on the last third of the twentieth century and beyond. It then goes on to examine the main areas of ethnic cleavage and contention in the Philippines.

The major ethnic groups

Mainstream Filipinos

Using language as a marker of ethnicity, there are, depending on definition, between approximately 80 and 170 language groups in the Philippines. The authoritative *Ethnologue* lists 168 living and 3 extinct languages, but these figures include foreign languages spoken in the Philippines and language dialects.[3] A more modest figure might be around ninety languages. Of these, however, eight language groups account for about 86 per cent of the Philippine population. Ranked in descending order, they are: Cebuano (Sugbuanon), Tagalog, Ilocano, Hiligaynon (Ilonggo), Bicolano, Waray, Pampangan (Kapampangan) and Pangasinan. Five are lowlands languages of Luzon; the other three (Cebuano, Hiligaynon and Waray) are languages of the Visayan Islands. All are languages of the mainstream Filipino population. Even though there are actually more first speakers of Cebuano than of Tagalog, the latter language (that of the ancestral people around the capital Manila) became the official national language in 1937 and the basis for Filipino/Pilipino, the language recognized in the 1987 Constitution, along with English, as the official language. An estimated 55 per cent of the population speak Filipino.

Reflecting their long interaction first with Spanish colonialism and then with US colonialism, mainstream Filipinos are predominantly Christian (about 83 per cent of the total Philippine population is Roman Catholic and about 9 per cent Protestant), and more Westernized than most of their Asian neighbours. This is sometimes expressed in the old cliché, 'three hundred years in the convent and fifty years in Hollywood'.[4] Filipinos have high rates of outmigration, both as permanent emigrants, particularly to the United States and more recently Australia, and as overseas contract workers mainly in Singapore, Hong Kong, Japan, the Middle East and Europe.

Plate 8.2 Tingguian woman, San Andres, Abra 1905 (Worcester Photographic Collection, University of Michigan, reprinted with permission.)

Plate 8.3 Bontoc Igorots in automobile, Manila, 1905 (Worcester Photographic Collection, University of Michigan, reprinted with permission.)

Among mainstream Filipino groups, language, local cuisine, and cultural forms such as music and dance remain significant ethnic markers, and ethnicity defined in terms of language and locality has been identified as a factor explaining voting patterns in Philippine presidential and senatorial elections, and as a factor influencing senior appointments to the armed forces during the Marcos years.[5] But ethnic differences within mainstream Filipino society are not pronounced and have seldom been a subject of significant political debate.[6]

Indigenous cultural communities

Tribal Filipinos or indigenous cultural communities are essentially those groups that resisted or avoided substantive contact with Spanish colonialism. They are concentrated in the mountainous interior of Luzon (the Cordilleras) and the hinterland of Mindanao, with smaller groups in the Visayan islands and Palawan. In 1969 the Commission on National Integration identified thirty-six non-Muslim cultural communities, nineteen on Luzon and seventeen in the Visayas and Mindanao.[7] In 1985 the Roman Catholic Church's Episcopal Commission on Tribal Filipinos listed forty-six groups,[8] representing in total about 10 per cent of the national population.

Because of their historic resistance to outside forces, the indigenous cultural communities have generally retained more of their traditional culture and social organization, including the institution of *datu* or head of the community. During the unrest in the Cordilleras in the 1970s and 1980s (see pp. 150–1), for example, the traditional peace pact (*bodong*) was employed in peace negotiations. In recent times some groups have pursued cultural tourism and the production of traditional crafts as a source of cash income. For a while in the 1980s and 1990s, the T'boli people of South Cotabato maintained a craft shop in Metro Manila, selling traditional fabrics, jewellery and cast metal figurines. But indigenous cultural communities' isolation has also had costs. Education and incomes in most cultural communities are relatively low, and as loggers, miners, agribusinesses, lowland settlers and even the state have pushed forward the frontiers of settlement and large-scale commercial activity, tribal peoples have been susceptible to land-grabbing and other forms of exploitation, and have often been forced to engage in unskilled wage labour to survive. The spread of missions and conversion to Christianity, while conferring some undoubted benefits, have also frequently undermined traditional social structures and social practices. Meanwhile, young people from cultural communities migrate out to towns to join the mainstream.

From the 1970s, however, first in the Cordilleras and then in Mindanao and more widely, indigenous cultural communities have become politically mobilized to assert their rights, especially land rights.

The Moros

Philippine Muslims account for about 5 per cent of the population, but, despite their small number, have been clearly the main issue in ethnic group/state relations, which is why they are considered first in the next section. Since the early Spanish conquest of Muslim settlements in Luzon and the Visayas, the Muslim Filipino population has been concentrated in western and central Mindanao, the Sulu Archipelago, and southern Palawan, with a significant population also around the Quiapo district in metro Manila. It comprises thirteen language groups. Historically, these Muslim groups, as with other Philippine ethnic groups, were frequently in conflict, but Islam provided something of a unifying force, especially during the escalating conflict between Christian and Muslim Filipinos in Mindanao in the 1970s (see p. 143). The term 'Moro', which earlier had a pejorative connotation, was widely adopted by Philippine Muslims as a badge of ethnic identity.

Like mainstream Filipinos, Philippine Muslims are of Malay stock, are primarily lowlands rice farmers (though the Tausug, Samal and the partly-Islamized Badjao 'sea gypsies' are mostly maritime peoples), and share many cultural traits with other Filipinos. But, as a result of their long engagement with the Islamic world, social structures tend to be more hierarchical, with an established aristocracy of sultans and *datus*, and the early education of Philippine Muslims is primarily through Islamic schools (*madaris*). Many continue their studies in the Middle East or Malaysia. There is also a long-standing literary tradition, and Philippine Muslims engage in metal crafts as well as the weaving of textiles and mats, and woodcarving. The brass ceremonial urns (*gador*) and silver-inlaid betel boxes (*loto-an*) of the Maranao are well represented in museums and private collections around the world, and the *Sarimanok*, a bird with a long tail, generally represented in wood and brass with a fish in its beak, has become a national as well as a Maranao icon. Music and dance of the Philippine Muslims relate more closely to those of Indonesia and Malaysia than to those of mainstream Filipinos.[9] As with the non-Muslim cultural communities, the areas in which the Philippine Muslim population is concentrated are among the poorest in the Philippines, and education levels are relatively low.

The Moros strongly resisted the intrusions of the Spanish colonial regime and, for a while, those of the United States. Outbreaks of armed resistance continued throughout the US colonial period and in the years after independence. From around the 1960s there was something of a resurgence of Islamic consciousness among Philippine Muslims, with the building of mosques and *madaris* and an increase in the number of people performing the *haj*.[10] There were also increasing demands for the restitution of Muslim ancestral lands and for a separate Islamic state (see pp. 143–4).

The Chinese

Chinese Filipinos (Filipinos of ethnic Chinese ancestry) and Philippine Chinese (citizens and non-citizens of the Philippines who identify with China) constitute perhaps around 0.5 per cent of the Philippines population.[11]

A rapid increase in the number of Chinese in the Philippines in the second half of the nineteenth century, and the visible economic success many of them

Plate 8.4 Traditional Maranao house, Lanao del Sur, Philippines (Photograph by R.J. May.)

enjoyed sparked anti-Chinese sentiment in the last decades of Spanish rule, which in turn, encouraged the growth of Chinese ethnic community organizations. Anti-Chinese riots occurred in 1919 and 1924, and demands for the nationalization (that is, Filipinization) of certain economic activities were incorporated in the Commonwealth Constitution of 1935. But notwithstanding this, the Chinese community generally prospered during the US colonial period and the descendants of Chinese immigrants were assimilated into Filipino society.

Following independence from US colonialism in July 1946, economic nationalist policies were implemented in several areas, including the retail and import trades, and the rice and corn industries, to the detriment of non-citizen Philippine Chinese.[12] Non-citizens were also excluded from some professions, and a 'Filipino First' policy was applied to certain government contracts. Under Ferdinand Marcos, the 1973 (martial law) Constitution prohibited the establishment of schools 'exclusively for aliens' and the government sought to Filipinize curricula, teaching staff and management in Chinese schools. At the same time, Marcos lifted the immigration quota to allow so-called 'overstaying Chinese' to remain in the country, facilitated the acquisition of citizenship by Chinese residents, used his executive authority to encourage Chinese participation in a range of economic activities, and supported the integration of ethnic Chinese generally. In a speech to the Federation of Filipino-Chinese Chambers of Commerce and Industry in 1966 President Marcos said: 'I have Chinese blood in me . . . perhaps the great leaders of our country all have Chinese blood.'[13] By 1990 Chinese ownership accounted for about one-third of the top 1,000 manufacturing corporations in the Philippines, and Chinese Filipinos were prominent in a range of businesses and professions and in politics.

During the presidency of Corazon Aquino (1986–92), who had come to office through a People Power Revolution, the question of 'overstaying Chinese' was raised again, with Immigration and Deportation Commissioner Miriam Defensor-Santiago estimating the number of illegal aliens at over 100,000. An executive order gave them twelve months to register and apply for naturalization, but following a legal challenge this programme was suspended. A decade later, in 1999, the chair of the Senate National Defense Committee expressed concern that up to 120,000 Chinese nationals may have entered the country illegally since 1996, posing a potential security and economic risk.[14] Yet, despite such concerns, the long history of integration has probably made the ethnic Chinese in the Philippines more thoroughly integrated than in any other country in Southeast Asia, with the possible exception of Thailand.

Ethnic groups and the state in the Philippines

The Moros and Muslim separatism

Although Spain never achieved lasting sovereignty over the Moros, Mindanao and Sulu were included in the territory ceded to the United States in 1898. By 1913 Moro resistance to US rule in Mindanao and Sulu had been effectively subdued and administration of the predominantly Muslim areas was transferred from the US army to civilian authorities.

Although US officials made some attempt to accommodate Philippine Muslim customs and Islamic law, US policy was nevertheless aimed essentially at assimilating the Moros into mainstream Christian Filipino society. From 1914 integration was pursued through a 'policy of attraction'. In Muslim areas, the government allocated substantial spending to roads, schools, hospitals and other services; education was made compulsory, and scholarships were provided for Muslims to study in Manila and in the United States. Muslims began to participate in the emerging political system. The United States administration also encouraged migration to Mindanao from the populous northern islands of Luzon and the Visayas through the provision of timber and mining concessions and land for plantations and cattle ranches. Between 1903 and 1939 the population of Mindanao, estimated at around 500,000 at the end of the Spanish period, had grown by 1.4 million. Increasingly, the new settlers encroached on ancestral Muslim and tribal lands.

In 1920 control of Mindanao and Sulu was passed from the United States administration to the Philippine legislature, and in 1935 to the newly established

Commonwealth. In the latter year a group of 120 Moro *datus* from Lanao petitioned the US president, repeating earlier requests either to give the Moros political independence or to let them remain under US rule. Christian Filipinos, they claimed, discriminated against Muslims and treated them abusively.[15] Under an administration dominated by Christian Filipinos, the 'policy of attraction' did indeed lapse, and there was an increasing incidence of clashes between Muslims and Christian settlers.

Following independence in 1946, there was a further heavy influx of settlers into Mindanao, doubling the population in several provinces between 1948 and 1960. By the end of the 1960s disputes over land between the Muslim population, tribal peoples and Christian settlers were becoming more frequent and more violent, and the growing number of settlers was threatening the electoral bases of several Muslim politicians.

In 1954 a special committee of the Philippine Congress was set up to report on 'the Moro problem', especially with regard to peace and order in Mindanao and Sulu. Partly as a result of its report a Commission on National Integration (CNI) was established in 1957. The CNI, however, was regarded with suspicion by most Philippine Muslims, who resented being referred to as a 'national minority' and saw the real objective of the commission to be the destruction of Philippine Muslim identity under the guise of 'national integration'. Apart from providing scholarships to Muslim students, the CNI achieved little before its abolition in 1975.[16] Two further reports were produced in 1963 and 1971 by a Senate Committee on National Minorities, which identified in-migration and land-grabbing as the major sources of conflict in Mindanao, but the Senate committee maintained the view that the solution to the Moro problem should be sought through social and political integration and economic development.

In 1968 tensions between Muslims and Christians were heightened by an incident in which a number of Muslim recruits to the armed forces, reportedly being trained for an invasion of the Malaysian state of Sabah, were shot during an alleged mutiny. That year a Muslim (later Mindanao) Independence Movement was created to push for a separate Bangsa Moro (Moro nation). From this point, armed clashes between Muslim and Christian groups escalated, and by 1971 Muslim Mindanao and Sulu were in a state of rebellion. A government task force was sent to Mindanao to mediate between the rival groups, but had little success. Official sources acknowledged that by the end of the year clashes between Muslim and Christian groups and the military had killed over 1,500 people.

In the early 1970s the Moro National Liberation Front (MNLF) emerged at the forefront of the Moro movement, demanding a separate homeland, the return of ancestral land to Muslims and reform within Muslim traditional society. The leader of the MNLF, and its military arm, the Bangsa Moro Army (BMA), was Nur Misuari, one of several young Philippine Muslims who had received guerrilla warfare training in West Malaysia in the late 1960s. The international Islamic community also became involved in the conflict, supplying arms and finance to the MNLF, sending two fact-finding missions to Mindanao, accusing the Marcos government of genocide and threatening to cut off oil supplies.

The Marcos government's response to the MNLF was multi-faceted. Its primary response was a military one. The decision to impose martial law in the Philippines in 1972 was partly rationalized in terms of the conflict in Minadano, and the Armed Forces of the Philippines (AFP) launched a major offensive against the MNLF/BMA, which resulted in heavy casualties on both sides and a massive displacement of people. The AFP was assisted in this by local Civil Home Defense Force (CHDF) units, which acquired a formidable record for human rights abuses and general indiscipline, and extremist Christian right-wing vigilante groups. Marcos also announced a package of social and economic measures intended to placate separatist demands, including a commitment to the codification of Shari'a law and the creation of a Southern Philippines Development Authority to promote and coordinate economic development in the region. A third strategy, encouraged by reports of surrenders of BMA soldiers in the mid-1970s, was the commencement of a series of peace negotiations with the MNLF, through the mediation of the Organization of Islamic Conference (OIC), the Islamic Council of Foreign Ministers (ICFM), and Libyan President Muammar Qaddafi. These initiatives culminated in the signing of an agreement in Tripoli in December 1976, which provided for a ceasefire and set out tentative provisions for a broader political settlement. The latter included Muslim-dominated political autonomy in thirteen provinces of Mindanao, Sulu and Palawan, which the MNLF considered to be the minimum claim for a Moro homeland. Further talks were scheduled for early 1977 to discuss the details of implementation, but negotiations collapsed and the ceasefire was abandoned.

The main sticking point in negotiations in 1976–7 concerned the geographical boundaries of Moro autonomy. By 1980, as a result of heavy in-migration, the proportion of Muslims in Mindanao's population (which had been estimated at 76 per cent in 1903) had fallen to 23 per cent. Of the (then) twenty-three provinces in Mindanao and Sulu, only five (and in Mindanao only two) still had a Muslim majority. The MNLF, which had already compromised on its original claim to the whole of Mindanao, Sulu and Palawan, nevertheless insisted that the area of Muslim autonomy should include the thirteen provinces of historical Muslim dominance. In 1977 Marcos proposed to put the issue to a plebiscite in these provinces. Realizing that this would produce a negative vote, Misuari accused the government of violating the Tripoli Agreement. Marcos nevertheless proceeded to appoint a provisional government and to organize a referendum on the form of the autonomy. The MNLF rejected an invitation to participate in the provisional government and boycotted the referendum, which predictably rejected the MNLF's claim and endorsed a more limited proposal put forward by President Marcos. Marcos's proposal involved the creation of two small autonomous regions in the Muslim-dominated areas of Western Mindanao and Sulu, and Central Mindanao. Elections for the two regional assemblies in 1979 were boycotted by most Muslim groups, and, with limited powers, inadequate funding and low levels of perceived legitimacy, the two regional autonomous governments were largely ineffective and did nothing to overcome the grievances of Philippine Muslims.

At about the same time, the Moro movement began to lose momentum. A number of Moro fighters surrendered to the Philippine government under amnesty arrangements, while others, as part of 'lost commands', turned to brigandage. More significantly, the MNLF split into three factions, along personal, ethnic and ideological faultlines. The main MNLF group, under the leadership of Misuari (a Tausug) and with the support of the OIC, was geographically centred in Sulu and ideologically the most progressive of the three. A more religiously oriented Moro Islamic Liberation Front (MILF), led by Hashim Salamat, an Iranun from Maguindanao, drew its support mainly from western Mindanao. A third faction, the MNLF-Reformist Group (MNLF-RG), led by Dimas Pundato, had its support base among the Maranao people of Lanao. Another group, the Bangsa Moro Liberation Organization (BMLO), a socially conservative, mostly Maranao group headed by Macapantan Abbas, also emerged in this period, but both it and the MNLF-RG appear to have largely faded away by the late 1980s. Fighting continued sporadically during the late 1970s and early 1980s, and Misuari and Salamat maintained the international campaign for a separate Bangsa Moro, but the Marcos regime was facing challenges on other fronts, and many Philippine Muslims had become weary of the fighting and the social dislocation it imposed. In 1981 the national government created a Ministry of Muslim Affairs; its activities appear to have been mainly concerned with organizing the annual *haj* and Qur'an-reading competitions, accrediting *madaris*, and supporting the implementation of Shari'a.

The Moro movement received a boost, however, following the overthrow of President Marcos in 1986. Marcos's opponents had earlier held talks with Misuari, promising to address Muslim demands if elected. In September 1986 Misuari returned to the Philippines and met with new President Aquino in Sulu. Subsequently, talks were held in Jeddah under the auspices of the OIC, at which Misuari and the Philippine government agreed to continue negotiations on autonomy through a joint commission. The MILF and MNLF-RG were invited to join the talks but the MILF rejected the invitation and launched an attack on government installations in western Mindanao.

Negotiations between the MNLF and the Aquino government broke down in mid-1987. By this time, however, a new Constitution had been enacted, which made specific provision for the creation of an Autonomous Region of Muslim Mindanao (ARMM), and a Cordillara Autonomous Region in the north – see p. 151.

The process by which the ARMM was established was deeply flawed and reflected the insensitivity to Philippine Muslim demands that had long been a source of Moro grievance. For example, the regional consultative commission charged with drafting the organic act for the Autonomous Region of *Muslim* Mindanao actually had Muslims in a minority on the commission; it was served by a secretariat drawn from the (Christian) Ateneo de Manila University in Manila, and one of its first and most intensive debates was over whether the region was to be called ARMM, as the Constitution mandated, or simply Mindanao Autonomous Region.[17] Nevertheless, by 1989 an organic act had been drafted and was put to a plebiscite in the thirteen provinces and nine cities covered by the Tripoli Agreement, but only four provinces, and no cities, voted to be part of the ARMM. The various Moro factions again boycotted the elections for the regional assembly, and the ARMM, like its predecessors, was generally seen as lacking credibility. Despite President Aquino's good intentions, the new autonomy arrangements thus did little to satisfy the demands of Philippine Muslims.

In 1992 Aquino was succeeded as Philippines' president by General Fidel Ramos, who had been closely involved with the Mindanao conflict as head of the Philippine Constabulary under Marcos. In his first year of office he visited Libya and, with backing from Qaddafi and others, revived negotiations with the MNLF. In 1996 these efforts were rewarded with the signing of a Peace Agreement between the Philippine Government and the MNLF.[18] The Agreement, subtitled 'The Final Agreement on the Implementation of the Tripoli Agreement', provided for a Special Zone of Peace and Development (SZOPAD) in the area covered by the Tripoli Agreement, and the creation of a Southern Philippines Council for Peace and Development (SPCPD) to 'control and/or supervise . . . appropriate agencies of the government that are engaged in peace and development activities in the area [of the SZOPAD]'. The powers of the SPCPD were described as an extension of the powers of the president and funds for the SPCPD and its associated institutions were to come initially from the president. Provision was also made for a Consultative Assembly headed by the chair of the SPCPD and dominated by members of the MNLF, a *Darul Iftah* (religious advisory council) appointed by the SPCPD chairman, and for the integration of 7,500 former BMA fighters into the AFP and the Philippines National Police.

Potential jurisdictional problems between the existing ARMM and the newly created SPCPD were bypassed when Misuari, having returned to the Philippines and been appointed chair of the SPCPD, was elected governor of the ARMM in September 1996. The more difficult issue of the boundaries of Muslim autonomy was deferred, but the Agreement provided for the inevitable referendum on the expansion of the ARMM to cover the area of the SZOPAD, to be held within two years of the establishment of the SPCPD. In fact, the referendum was not held until August 2001.

In some quarters the 1996 Peace Agreement was hailed as an historic breakthrough, ending decades – if not centuries – of Muslim–Christian conflict. Among Christian communities within the SZOPAD, however, the agreement aroused deeply entrenched fears and distrust. Some Christian leaders denounced the agreement and opposed it in Congress. The legality of President Ramos's action in securing the agreement was even challenged in the Supreme Court. As a result of this opposition, the executive order intended to give effect to the Peace Agreement was a significantly watered down version of the document signed with Misuari. Furthermore, although Misuari was able to secure a limited amount of external funding, the SPCPD/ARMM leadership continually complained that it was not receiving adequate funding. Early in 1999, Misuari warned that, unless conditions improved, former MNLF/BMA fighters would return to the hills (indeed as early as 1997 there were reports of former MNLF guerrillas joining the MILF). To add to his problems, the administration of the SPCPD/ARMM was accused of inefficiency, mismanagement and nepotism, and Misuari's leadership was challenged within the MNLF.[19]

Another limitation of the 1996 Peace Agreement was that it was specifically an agreement with the MNLF. The MILF, which during the early 1990s appears to have grown significantly in strength and militancy and which was said to be undergoing a transition from a guerrilla force to a 'semi-conventional army', was not party to the negotiations leading to the 1996 agreement and continued the armed struggle for a separate Bangsa Moro. Intermittent attempts were made during the Ramos presidency to establish a dialogue with the MILF, and formal peace talks were resumed under Ramos's successor, Joseph Estrada. Following MILF attacks on non-Muslim communities in early 2000, however, Estrada abandoned the talks and declared 'all-out war' against the MILF.

In August 2001, despite objections from Misuari and the MNLF, the long-awaited referendum on the proposed expansion of the ARMM was held. Not surprisingly, of the (now) fifteen provinces and nine cities covered by the SZOPAD, only five provinces and one city voted in favour. Shortly after this, elections for the ARMM took place and in the election for governor, Misuari was displaced by a rival candidate supported by the newly incumbent president, Gloria Macapagal-Arroyo. Misuari subsequently made good his threat to return to the hills, launching an armed attack on government troops before fleeing to Malaysia, where he was arrested and repatriated.[20]

Meanwhile, in the early 1990s another renegade Muslim group emerged in the western Mindanao-Sulu area. The Abu Sayyaf was founded by a former MNLF supporter, Abdurajak Janjalani, who had received religious training in Libya before returning to the Philippines where he became a charismatic preacher and advocate of a separate Islamic state in the south. He recruited a small but committed following, some of whom had fought with the *mujahideen* in Afghanistan and appear to have had links with radical Muslim groups overseas, including al-Qaida. A confrontation with police in 1998 killed Janjalani but his group survived, primarily carrying on kidnapping and extortion.[21] In 2000 Abu Sayyaf attracted international publicity with a series of kidnappings, which included several Europeans and Americans. Its ransom demands included recognition of an independent Islamic state, the release of international terrorists held overseas, the banning of foreign fishing vessels from the Sulu Sea and protection for Filipinos in Sabah, as well as payments of up to $US1 million per hostage. Some hostages were executed. Others were released following intervention by President Qaddafi.

Initially other Muslim groups, including the MNLF and the MILF, condemned Abu Sayyaf and dissociated themselves from it. Following the destruction of the World Trade Center on 11 September 2001, however, the situation became more complex. The United States was already providing specialist military advisers to assist with training in counter-terrorism after Abu Sayyaf groups had taken American hostages. As US air strikes against the Taliban in Afghanistan began,

Plate 8.5 Mosque on the shores of Lake Lanao, Marawi City, Philippines (Photograph by R.J. May.)

Plate 8.6 Market in Marawi City, Philippines (Photograph by R.J. May.)

there was a protest rally in the Islamic City of Marawi, during which crowds burned an American flag and shouted support for Osama bin Laden; hundreds of Philippine Muslims reportedly volunteered to go to Afghanistan to fight with the Taliban.[22] Increasingly, Philippine Muslims have accused the Macapagal-Arroyo government of joining the United States in a war against Islam.

These developments, along with the arrest of Misuari and the continuing slow progress in talks with the MILF, are a reminder that many Philippine Muslims have little identification with the government in Manila, and retain a strong sense of being part of the international community of Islam.

Cultural communities and indigenous peoples' rights

When the American administration took over from Spain it accepted the categorization of the indigenous population into Christian, Muslim and (other) non-Christian peoples. A Bureau of Non-Christian Tribes (BNCT) was created in 1901, with the task of investigating the boundaries, social organizations, beliefs, manners and customs of the 'pagan and Mohammedan tribes', with a view 'to determining the most practicable means for bringing about their advancement and material prosperity'.[23] The BNCT was disbanded shortly thereafter and, after some vicissitudes, a new 1914 policy sought to foster 'a more rapid spread of civilization' by 'cultivating confidence and goodwill between the non-Christians and their Christian neighbors'.[24] Overall responsibility for the non-Christians was delegated to an officer under the Secretary of the Interior, but was exercised increasingly by provincial and municipal authorities. Within three years, dissatisfaction with the new system had resulted in the reconstitution of the BNCT, with a new mandate to work for the moral, material, economic, social and political development of the non-Christian regions and the 'fusion' of the Christian and non-Christian populations.[25]

Several later policy initiatives endorsed this emphasis on assimilation of the non-Christian peoples, including the Muslims, into the larger Christian Filipino society, Christian missions supporting the state's objectives. This tendency was strengthened as political authority was passed on to the Philippine legislature; indeed, one of the first actions of the National Assembly, following the declaration of the Commonwealth in 1935, was to abolish the BNCT. The administration of non-Christian peoples was left to the Department of the Interior, though in recognition of its specific circumstances in the south, a Commission for Mindanao and Sulu was appointed.

Meanwhile, though some communities in remote areas remained virtually untouched, the spread of Christian missions resulted in the Christianization of many 'non-Christian tribes', and in-migration from the populous lowlands of Luzon and the Visayas into relatively underdeveloped frontier areas – in some cases sponsored by the national government – encroached on tribal lands, sometimes resulting in violent confrontations. Under royal doctrine, the Spanish crown had acquired ancestral lands in the Philippines, and in 1898 these lands had passed to the US government. Although in 1909 a United States Supreme Court decision upheld the constitutional right of Filipinos to their ancestral lands, land rights were frequently violated, and many Muslim and tribal Filipinos lost their traditional lands to outsiders. In the early decades of independence, conflicts over encroachment on tribal lands increased, especially in Mindanao where government-sponsored resettlement and spontaneous migration led to a very rapid rise in population.

In 1957 the Commission on National Integration (CNI) was established to advance the non-Christian Filipinos or cultural minorities and integrate them into the rest of society. But, although it was given extensive responsibilities in relation to business and agriculture, education and training, credit and other matters, the CNI was poorly funded and had achieved little when it was abolished in 1975. The philosophy of integration continued to dominate approaches to tribal Filipinos throughout the 1960s and 1970s. However, little was achieved in the way of tangible policy benefits for cultural minorities, and often the rhetoric of integration provided a cover for loggers, miners, agribusiness and migrant settlers to exploit tribal lands.

Under the Marcos regime, the situation of tribal Filipinos deteriorated significantly. In 1968 the Presidential Assistant on Tribal Minorities (usually abbreviated as PANAMIN) was created by a wealthy Marcos crony, Manuel Elizalde. The previous year Elizalde had been appointed Presidential Adviser on National Minorities with cabinet status. Following the abolition of the CNI in 1975, PANAMIN was given formal responsibility for non-Muslim minorities. The activities of PANAMIN became one of the scandals of the Marcos regime. Among other things, Elizalde was accused of using his power to grant access to tribal lands to loggers, miners and agribusinesses. PANAMIN also became involved in the forced relocation of people from areas of Muslim and Communist insurgency and in the employment of tribal Filipinos in counter-insurgency operations.[26] In 1983 Elizalde left the Philippines and the following year, amid rumours of financial irregularities, PANAMIN was dissolved. Its functions, including the counter-insurgency programme, were transferred to the Ministry of Muslim Affairs, which was consequentially renamed Office of Muslim Affairs and Cultural Communities (OMACC). Like its predecessors, OMACC was given a range of economic, social and cultural responsibilities but little financial or administrative capacity.

In the same period, increased migration into Mindanao and the spread of lowland settlers into the interior of Luzon, Mindoro and Palawan, combined with acquisition of ancestral lands by government-supported corporations and proposed land alienation for national development projects, provoked increasingly militant responses from some tribal groups. From around 1976 the Communist New People's Army (NPA) became active in the Cordillera region. PANAMIN officials were called in, and a Kalinga Special Development Region was declared, but the government also deployed the military, including CHDF units, in counter-insurgency operations. In central Cordillera a major hydro-electric project of the National Power Corporation threatened the ancestral lands of the Kalinga and other cultural communities inhabiting the Chico River basin, while the logging activities of the Cellophil Resources Corporation in the western Cordillera impacted severely on the ancestral domain of the Tingguians.

In the late 1970s the leftist National Democratic Front (NDF) was proposing the formation of a Cordillera People's Democratic Front to assert demands for regional self-determination. In 1984 a Cordillera Peoples Alliance (CPA) was established, claiming the support of some 120 groups representing 25,000 members. Although it denied links to the NDF, the CPA employed similar leftist rhetoric. The same year legislation for Cordillera regional autonomy was introduced into the national Parliament.

Beyond the Cordilleras – in Zambales and Bataan, in Mindoro and across Mindanao – other cultural communities became politically mobilized in opposition to land-grabbing by cattle ranchers, agribusinesses and in-migrant settlers, who were frequently backed by government security forces, including CHDF units and vigilante groups. In 1977 church-backed community groups on Mindanao organized the first convention of tribal communities on Mindanao, leading to other groups demanding indigenous rights over the next decade.

When the People Power Revolution toppled Marcos in 1986, the demands of cultural communities were thus firmly on the agenda. This was reflected in the 1987 Constitution, which declares that 'the state recognizes and promotes the rights of indigenous cultural communities within the framework of national unity and development . . . [and] shall protect the rights of indigenous cultural communities to their ancestral lands' (Art.XII s.5). Community rights to ancestral domain were excluded from the government's agrarian reform programme. The constitution also guarantees 'the rights of indigenous cultural communities to preserve and develop their cultures, traditions, and institutions' (Art.XIV s.17). Although both these statements of principle were qualified by overriding concern for national unity and development, the People Power Constitution, in rhetoric at least, thus marked a significant shift from earlier policies of effective assimilation.

As noted above in relation to the ARMM, the 1987 Constitution also provided for the creation of autonomous regions in Muslim Mindanao and the Cordilleras, under the 'general supervision' of the president. By 1986, however, the complexities of Cordillera politics threatened the viability of a Cordillera autonomous region. Following the fall of Marcos, renegade priest Conrado Balweg, who had left his parish to join the NPA in the early 1980s, abandoned it and formed a Cordillera Peoples Liberation Army (CPLA). Subsequently, he negotiated a traditional peace pact with the Aquino government, which foresaw the creation of an autonomous Cordillera state based on indigenous institutions. An Interim Cordillera Regional Administration was established, and a regional consultative commission was created to draft the necessary organic law for the proposed Cordillera Autonomous Region. As in Muslim Mindanao, however, the process soon ran into problems. The CPA and the CPLA adopted opposing positions, while other political leaders from the region attempted to occupy the middle ground. When the organic act was submitted to plebiscite in the six provinces and one city in the region in 1990, only one province voted for it. The proposed autonomy arrangements were subsequently expanded and a further plebiscite was held in 1998, but with much the same result. A Cordillera Administrative Region remains, with a regional assembly and executive, but it has few powers and limited credibility.[27]

Apart from the constitutional provisions relating to cultural communities, the Aquino government took several initiatives in its early years. The OMACC was divided into three separate offices: of Muslim Affairs, Southern Cultural Communities and Northern Cultural Communities. The latter two were charged with coordinating the activities of government agencies dealing with cultural communities, and assisting development by providing livelihood programmes, loans, training programmes, cultural projects, and assistance in formulating land use plans for ancestral landholders. In a major reorganization of the Department of Environment and Natural Resources (DENR) – whose new head was a prominent human rights activist – an Indigenous Communities Affairs Division was created. Under Marcos, the Bureau of Forestry Development had been generally seen as acting against the interests of cultural communities, especially in granting timber licence agreements to outside loggers and prohibiting the traditional practice of *kaingin* (swidden) agriculture. Under the new DENR the number of timber licence agreements was substantially reduced and cultural communities were offered certificate-of-stewardship contracts that gave security of tenure to forest land, and were provided with agro-forestry technology conditional upon their undertaking reforestation and soil conservation work. In 1989, an Ancestral Domain Bill was drafted within the DENR and, as an interim measure, certificates of ancestral domain claims were issued to indigenous cultural communities through a Special Task Force on Ancestral Lands. By June 1998 certificates had been issued to over 50,000 beneficiaries, covering an area of about 2.5 million hectares.

The initiatives introduced during the Aquino administration were pursued by Aquino's successor, President Ramos. In addition, under Ramos the DENR initiated consultations with mining companies, partly to safeguard the rights of cultural communities in relation to ancestral lands, and award them royalties from minerals revenue. Cases involving ancestral land rights were brought before the Philippines Human Rights Commission. Cultural communities were specifically targeted under the Ramos government's Social Reform Agenda to alleviate poverty.

The most significant policy development, however, was the 1997 passage of the Indigenous People's Rights Act (IPRA), which grew out of the earlier Ancestral Domain Bill. Bills introduced into the Senate and the House in 1996 had encountered strong opposition, particularly over the definition of 'ancestral domain' and the granting to indigenous peoples of a right of veto over development projects. Notwithstanding this, the legislation was passed, and came into effect in October 1997. Following discussions with interested groups through a consultative assembly, Implementing Rules and Regulations were promulgated in mid-1998. The IPRA is intended broadly 'to recognize, protect and promote the rights of Indigenous Cultural Communities/Indigenous Peoples [ICCs/IPs]'. Apart from provisions guaranteeing social justice and human rights, recognizing and protecting cultural integrity, and recognizing 'the inherent right of ICCs/IPs to self-governance and self-determination', the IPRA contains potentially far-reaching provisions concerning ancestral domain and ancestral lands.

Ancestral domain, briefly, is defined as 'all areas generally belonging to ICCs/IPs . . . occupied or possessed by ICCs/IPs . . . communally or individually since time immemorial . . . and which are necessary to ensure their economic, social and cultural welfare'; it includes 'lands which may no longer be exclusively occupied by ICCs/IPs but which they traditionally had access to [sic] for their subsistence and traditional activities, particularly the home ranges of ICCs/IPs who are still nomadic and/or shifting cultivators', and it specifically includes 'minerals and other natural resources' within ancestral domains. Ancestral lands are defined more narrowly as 'land occupied, possessed and utilized by individuals, families and clans' of ICCs/IPs since time immemorial.

Not surprisingly, in a country prone to litigation, the IPRA quickly came under challenge, particularly from the mining industry. After only a few mining agreements had been approved, however, an environmental disaster at a copper mine in Marinduque, and growing protests from indigenous cultural communities over prospective mining operations in areas of ancestral domain, led to the suspension of further approvals. In April 1998 a former Supreme Court associate judge petitioned the Court to declare the IPRA unconstitutional, on the grounds that it conflicted with principles enshrined in the 1987 Constitution. Over 100 cultural communities opposed the petition and the Philippines Commission on Human Rights sought to be represented at hearings. Eventually the validity of the IPRA was upheld. Meanwhile indigenous cultural communities, and the NPA, threatened militant action against mining companies in several parts of the country, invoking memories of the turbulent 1970s. In 2002 major issues of concern to indigenous cultural communities included a proposed dam on the Agno River in northern Luzon, a prospective mining development on B'laan ancestral land in South Cotabato, and moves to deny ancestral land claims in special economic zones.

Conclusion

The Philippines is a country of many linguistic and cultural groups, but the major ethnic divides – between mainstream predominantly-Christian lowlands Filipinos, indigenous cultural communities and Philippine Muslims – are essentially a product of colonial history. After years of attempted assimilation, under the Spanish and US colonial regimes and successive Philippine governments, and, more recently, attempts to accommodate the demands of the minority peoples, these cleavages remain a source of conflict and a challenge to future governments.

Notes

1 This chapter draws on an earlier paper by the author, published in Michael E. Brown and Sumit Ganguly, *Government Policies and Ethnic Relations in Asia and the Pacific*,

Cambridge, MA: MIT Press, 1997. I am indebted to Alan Robson for his comments on a draft of this paper.

2 This figure is from Barbara F. Grimes, *Ethnologue: Languages of the World*. 13th edn. Dallas, Txs: Summer Institute of Linguistics, 1996, p. 747. The subject of language is discussed below.

3 Grimes, *Ethnologue*, pp. 747–64.

4 For a non-academic overview of (mainstream) Filipino culture and customs, see Alfredo and Grace Roces, *Culture Shock! Philippines*, Singapore: Times Books International, 1985.

5 See Hirofumi Ando, 'A study of voting patterns in the Philippine presidential and senatorial elections, 1945–1969', *Midwest Journal of Political Science*, 1969, vol. 13, no. 4, pp. 567–86; Cynthia Enloe, *Ethnic Soldiers: State and Security in a Divided Society*, Harmondsworth: Penguin Books, 1980, pp. 176–9.

6 A similar conclusion was reached by Benedict Anderson, 'Introduction', in *Southeast Asian Tribal Groups and Ethnic Minorities: Prospects for the Eighties and Beyond*, Cultural Survival Report No. 22, Cambridge, MA: Cultural Survival, Inc., 1987. David Brown, in his study of ethnicity and the state in Southeast Asia (*The State and Ethnic Politics in Southeast Asia*, London: Routledge, 1994), significantly does not mention the Philippines.

7 Loethiny S. Clavel, *They Are Also Filipinos*, Manila: Bureau of Printing, 1969.

8 *Tribal Forum*, 1985, vol. 6, no. 5.

9 For an excellent overview of Philippine Muslim culture, see Peter G. Gowing, *Muslim Filipinos: Heritage and Horizon*, Quezon City: New Day Publishers, 1979. Also see Nagasura T. Madale, *The Muslim Filipinos: A Book of Readings*. Quezon City: Alemar-Phoenix Publishing House, 1981.

10 Gowing, *Muslim Filipinos*, pp. 186–7, and R.J. May, 'The Philippines', in Mohammed Ayoob (ed.), *The Politics of Islamic Reassertion*, London: Croom Helm, 1981, p. 218.

11 This estimate is projected from a 1975 estimate by C.J. McCarthy of the number of people 'either entirely or partly speaking Chinese dialect at home or among themselves, and observing Chinese cultural manners and social patterns'. Charles J. McCarthy, 'The Chinese in the Philippines today and tomorrow', *Fookien Times Philippines Yearbook 1975*, Manila: The Fookien Times Yearbook Pub, p. 348.

12 As a result of the influx of Chinese immigrants in the late nineteenth and early twentieth centuries, in 1954 'the majority of the Chinese in the Philippines did not have Filipino citizenship' (Theresa Chong Cariño, *Chinese Big Business in the Philippines: Political Leadership and Change*, Singapore: Times Academic Press, 1998, p. 29).

13 Quoted in Arturo G. Pacho, 'Policy agenda of the ethnic Chinese in the Philippines', PhD dissertation, Kent State University, Ann Arbor: University Microfilms International, 1984, p. 103.

14 *Manila Times*, 11 May 1999.

15 Gowing, *Muslim Filipinos*, pp. 169–70.

16 For a critical assessment of the work of the CNI, specifically in relation to Philippine Muslims, see Filipinas Foundation, *An Anatomy of Philippine Muslim Affairs*, Makati: Filipinas Foundation, 1971.

17 For an insider critique of the process, see M.S. Lalanto and Nagasura Madale, *Autonomy for Mindanao: The RCC Untold Story*, n.p.: B-lal Publishers, 1989.

18 Ramos's own account of negotiations, together with most of the key documents, is contained in Fidel V. Ramos, *Break Not the Peace: The Story of the GRP-MNLF Peace Negotiations, 1992–1996*, Quezon City: Friends of Steady Eddie, 1996. Also see Eliseo R. Mercado, *Southern Philippines Question: The Challenge for Peace and Development*, Cotabato City: Notre Dame Press, 1999.

19 See Eric Gutierrez and Marites Danguilan-Vitug, *ARMM After the Peace Agreement*, Occasional Paper No. 3, Quezon City: Institute for Popular Democracy, 1997; Eric Gutierrez, *The Problems of Peace*, Occasional Paper No. 5, Quezon City: Institute for Popular Democracy, 1997; Emil P. Bolongaita and Beethoven Morales, *A Perilous Peace: The Challenges to Democratic Governance in the Autonomous Region in Muslim Mindanao*,

Policy Forum Papers No. 4, Makati: Washington SyCip Policy Forum, Asian Institute of Management, 1997; Marites Danguilan Vitug and Glenda M. Gloria, *Under the Crescent Moon: Rebellion in Mindanao*, Quezon City: Ateneo Center for Social Policy and Public Affairs, Institute for Popular Democracy, 2000; R.J. May, 'Muslim Mindanao, four years after the Peace Agreement', in *Southeast Asian Affairs 2001*, Singapore: Institute of Southeast Asian Studies, 2001, pp. 263–75.

20 R.J. May, 'Beyond ethnic separatism: Recent developments in the southern Philippines', in *Strategic Update 2001*, Canberra: Australian Defence Studies Centre, 2001, pp. 17–20.
21 Mark M. Turner, 'Terrorism and secession in the southern Philippines', *Contemporary Southeast Asia*, 1995, vol. 17, no. 1, pp. 1–19; Nathan G. Quimpo, 'Dealing with the MILF and Abu Sayyaf: Who's afraid of an Islamic state?', *Public Policy*, 1999, vol. 3, no. 4, pp. 38–62.
22 *Philippine Daily Inquirer*, 10 October 2001.
23 Cited in Gowing, *Mandate in Moroland: The American Government of Muslim Filipinos 1899–1920*, Quezon City: New Day Publishers, 1977, p. 67.
24 *Report of the Philippine Commission to the Secretary of War*, 1915, cited in Violeta B. Lopez, *The Mangyans of Mindoro: An Ethnology*, Quezon City: University of the Philippines Press, 1976, p. 114.
25 The work of the BNCT is examined critically in Gowing, *Mandate in Moroland*, pp. 305–9; and in Lopez, *The Mangyans of Mindoro*, pp. 106–10.
26 See Joel Rocamora, 'The political uses of PANAMIN', *Southeast Asian Chronicle*, 1979, vol. 67, pp. 11–21; Chip Fay, 'Counter-insurgency and tribal peoples in the Philippines: A report by Survival International USA', Washington, DC: Survival International USA, 1987. A particular point of controversy was the alleged 'discovery' of the Tasaday, see Thomas N. Headland (ed.), *The Tasaday Controversy: Assessing the Evidence*, AAA Scholarly Series Special Publication No. 28, Washington, DC: American Anthropological Association, 1992.
27 The Cordillera autonomy issue is examined in detail in Rollie Buendia, 'The case of the Cordillera: An unresolved national question', *Philippine Journal of Public Policy*, 1987, vol. 31, no. 2, pp. 157–87; Maximo B. Garming, *Towards Understanding the Cordillera Autonomous Region*, Manila: Friedrich Ebert Stiftung, 1989; Steven Rood, *Issues in Creating an Autonomous Region for the Cordillera, Northern Philippines*, CSC Working Paper No. 11, Baguio: University of the Philippines College Baguio, Cordillera Studies Center, 1989; and Cordillera Studies Center, *Issues on Cordillera Autonomy: General Summary*, CSC Working Paper No. 18, Baguio: University of the Philippines College Baguio, Cordillera Studies Center, 1991.

Further reading

There have been numerous local histories and anthropological accounts of different groups, among the more interesting of which are E. Arsenio Manuel, *Manuvu Social Organization* (Quezon City: Community Development Research Council, University of the Philippines, 1973); Violeta B. Lopez, *The Mangyans of Mindoro: An Ethnology* (Quezon City: University of the Philippines Press, 1976) and Stuart Schlegel, *Tiruray Subsistence* (Quezon City: Ateneo de Manila Press, 1979). B.R. Rodil, *The Minoritization of the Indigenous Communities of Mindanao and the Sulu Archipelago* (Davao City: Alternate Forum for Research in Mindanao, 1994), provides a complete listing of cultural communities in the Philippines.

Accounts of government policies and actions towards cultural communities may be found in Peter G. Gowing, *Mandate in Moroland: The American Government of Muslim Filipinos 1899–1920* (Quezon City: New Day Publishers, 1977); Frank L. Jenista, *The White Apos: American Governors on the Cordillera Central* (Quezon City: New Day Publishers, 1987); papers by P. Bion Griffin, and Jonathan Y. Okamura, in *Southeast Asian Journal of Social Science*,

1988, vol. 16, no. 2, Special Issue on 'National Policy and Minority Cultures in Asia', edited by David Y.H. Wu; and R.J. May, 'Ethnicity and public policy in the Philippines', in M.E. Brown and S. Ganguly (eds), *Government Policies and Ethnic Relations in Asia and the Pacific*, Cambridge, MA: MIT Press, 1997, pp. 321–50.

The ethnic situation and government policies in the Cordilleras of northern Luzon – which is home to a number of cultural communities and which became an area of contestation during the Marcos regime – are described in William Henry Scott, *The Discovery of the Igorots: Spanish Contacts and the Pagans of Northern Luzon* (Quezon City: New Day Publishers, 1974); and Howard T. Fry, *A History of the Mountain Province* (Quezon City: New Day Publishers, 1983).

There is an extensive literature on the Philippine Muslims. The best overviews are Peter G. Gowing, *Muslim Filipinos: Heritage and Horizon* (Quezon City: New Day Publishers, 1979) and Cesar A. Majul, *Muslims in the Philippines*, 2nd edn (Quezon City: University of the Philippines Press, 1973).

Studies which focus on the Moro separatist movement, the Mindanao conflict and the peace process include Gowing, *Muslim Filipinos*; Wan Kadir bin Che Man, *Muslim Separatism: The Moros of Southern Philippines and the Malays of Southern Thailand* (Singapore: Oxford University Press, 1987); International Studies Institute of the Philippines (ISIP), *Papers on the Tripoli Agreement* (Quezon City: ISIP, UP Law Complex, University of the Philippines, 1986); R.J. May, 'The Philippines', in Mohammed Ayoob (ed.), *The Politics of Islamic Reassertion* (London: Croom Helm, 1981), pp. 211–32, 'The Moro movement in southern Philippines', in R. Stewart and C. Jennett (eds), *Politics of the Future: The Role of Social Movements* (Melbourne: Macmillan Australia, 1989), pp. 321–39, and 'Muslim Mindanao, four years after the Peace Agreement', in *Southeast Asian Affairs 2001* (Singapore: Institute of Southeast Asian Studies, 2001), pp. 263–75; Fidel V. Ramos, *Break Not the Peace: The Story of the GRP–MNLF Peace Negotiations, 1992–1996* (Quezon City: Friends of Steady Eddie, 1996); Thomas M. McKenna, *Muslim Rulers and Rebels: Everyday Politics and Armed Separatism in the Southern Philippines* (Berkeley: University of California Press, 1998); Eliseo R. Mercado, *Southern Philippines Question: The Challenge for Peace and Development* (Cotabato City: Notre Dame Press, 1999); Mara Stankovitch (issue ed.), *Compromising on Autonomy: Mindanao in Transition, Accord 6/1999* (London: Conciliation Resources); and Marites Danguilan Vitug and Glenda M. Gloria, *Under the Crescent Moon: Rebellion in Mindanao* (Quezon City: Ateneo Center for Social Policy and Public Affairs and Institute for Popular Democracy, 2000).

On the Chinese in the Philippines, see Eufronio M. Alip, *Ten Centuries of Philippine–Chinese Relations (Historical, Political, Social, Economic)* (Manila: Alip Sons, 1959); Edgar Wickberg, *The Chinese in Philippine Life, 1850–1898* (New Haven, CT: Yale University Press, 1965); Antonio S. Tan, 'The emergence of Philippine Chinese national and political consciousness', PhD dissertation, University of California, Berkeley (Ann Arbor: University Microfilms, 1970), chapters 2–7; and Theresa C. Cariño, *Chinese Big Business in the Philippines: Political Leadership and Change* (Singapore: Times Academic Press, 1998).

9 Ethnicity and the politics of ethnic classification in Thailand

Pinkaew Laungaramsri

Thailand as a modern nation is often characterized as unique in its ethnic and cultural homogeneity, and through the supposed ability of Tai culture to assimilate distinctive characteristics. 'Tai-ness' as a collective identity is constituted by shared commonality of language, religion and monarchy. To be Thai is to be loyal to three principles/pillars: *chat* or nation (speaking Thai as a manifestation of membership in the Thai nation), *satsana* or religion (being Thai as being Buddhist), and *phra mahakrasat* or the King (devotion to the monarchy).

Ethnic studies and studies of nationalism and the formation of the Thai nation-state in the past decade have posed significant challenges to this view of cultural unity/uniformity. 'Tai-ness', some argue, is in fact a key element of Tai political expansion onto non-Tai populations, a process Condominas calls irreversible Tai-ization.[1] The construction of 'Tai-ness' as a collective identity of the Thai population therefore reflects the politics of ethnic relations in which ethnic homogenization is fundamental to the process of nation-building.

Contemporary ethnicity theory draws attention to ethnicity in relation to nationalism and modernization. Central to this relationship are the processes in which nation-state and its nationalistic and modernizing projects shape ethnic identifications, as well as the ways in which people see themselves in relation to the nation. Ethnic categories in the modern Thai nation are, therefore, not simply constituted by shared/common identity but represent a powerful instrument of confinement and control by the modern state. At the same time, ethnicity is by no means an immediate given but is constantly achieved/created through a process of negotiation. Ethnic identification thus contains the possibility of counter-discourse in which ethnic minorities are also actors active in their responses to national intervention.

This chapter examines ethnicity in Thailand in the context of state-formation and modernization. It traces the history of ethnic heterogeneity in Thailand and examines the ways in which ethnic differences have been downplayed within the process of nation-building. Central to this process is national integration, which involves the naturalizing mechanism of inclusion and exclusion. While ethnic categorization represents the Thai state's attempts at normative stabilization, ethnic identification involves complex processes of negotiation and articulation between active self-formation of ethnic minorities on the one hand, and powerful dominant norms on the other. Dialectical interaction and slippage between imposed identities and lived identities/realities are thus key elements that characterize contemporary ethnicity in modern Thai society.

Ethnic heterogeneity in Thailand

Official narratives about the peoples of Thailand maintain that the vast majority of the population are ethnic Thai who speak Thai as their common language. The 1990 Population and Housing Census showed that 95 per cent of the populace were Thai who were Buddhists, while about 4 per cent were Muslims.[2] The Census also maintains that Central Thai is the official language that is understood everywhere, while cultural differences are discussed in terms of regional distinctiveness. Such depictions, while creating a false cultural homogeneity of Tai-speaking peoples, also conflate the heterogeneous, domestic Tai languages with Thai or 'standard Thai', the national language taught in schools and based on the Siamese or Central Tai dialect.

Although a large majority of the peoples of Thailand speak languages related to the Tai language family, these languages are distinctive. While people who speak Central Tai as their first language at home constitute approximately 30 per cent of all Tai-speakers in Thailand, the majority of the population speak related Tai dialects and live in the north, the northeast, and the south of Thailand.[3] These peoples are known as Khon Muang (literally people of the principalities), Khon Isan (literally people of the northeastern region who speak Lao) and Khon Pak Tai (literally people of the southern region). Tai as a language family is also spoken by a large number of people living across the Thai borders such as the Shan or Tai Yai of Shan State in Burma, the Black and White Tai in northern Vietnam, the Yunnanese Tai in southern China, and the Laotians in Laos.

Tai-ness is also a social identification. Jit Phumisak argued that self-identification with 'Tai-ness' connotes a specific sense of 'social(ized)' person/people (*khon thang sangkhom*) as opposed to the merely human or 'natural' person/people (*khon thang thammachat*).[4] Tai identity therefore is closely associated with '*muang*' (principality, society). Thus 'Tai' refers to 'society' people or people of the *muang*, as distinct from the non-Tai who live in the hills.

Ethnic relations and social differentiation between the Tai and non-Tai in pre-modern times is therefore characterized by the hill and valley distinction. The most distinctive cultural characteristics of the valley people, apart from the practice of wet-rice farming, are their adherence to Theravada Buddhism, and Sanskrit language, both symbols of civilization. The hill people, on the contrary, practice swidden agriculture and adhere to animism.

The apparently radical opposition between the valley and the hill peoples is, however, belied by their symbiotic relationship. Original hill inhabitants such as the Karen, the Lawa, the Thin and the Khamu in the northern and western parts of Thailand see themselves as closely related to the local Tai peoples. This is true particularly for the Karen, who have been settled in the north and west of

Plate 9.1 Akha people joining the Thai Loy Krathong Festival in Chiang Mai city (November 2002) (Photograph by Panadda Boonyasaranay.)

Siam since the thirteenth century. Their place within the pre-modern Tai society was that of an 'in between' and they were considered 'the holder of the wild for the sown'.[5] Other hill peoples, on the other hand, are relatively recent immigrants to Thailand and are, to a certain extent, culturally distinctive. These ethnic groups are the Hmong and the Mien, who migrated into northern Thailand from southern China by way of Laos, and the Akha, Lahu, and Lisu who migrated to northern Thailand from Burma between the mid-nineteenth and early twentieth century.[6] In the jungles of Phrae and Nan provinces reside the Mlabri, a small group of hunting and gathering people who originated from Laos. It is estimated that ethnic hill peoples in northern Thailand constitute 1.3 per cent of the total population.[7]

In the northeastern part of Thailand, also known as Isan, the population predominantly comprises ethnic Laos or Tai-Lao-speaking peoples who have migrated into the region since the fourteenth century. These peoples are by no means homogeneous. Various subgroups of Lao Phuan, Phu Tai, Yo and Tai Korat are also inhabitants of the northeast.[8] Non-Lao speaking groups have settled in the southern part of Isan, including the Khmer and original dwellers such as the Kuai, the So and the Nyakur.

In southern or peninsular Thailand, ethnic identity reflects the political–religious history of the region and the distinctive ecological system, the population combining inland agriculture with coastal fishing for their livelihood. The predominant group is that of the Malay-speaking Muslims living in the four provinces of Pattani, Yala, Narathiwat and Satun, an influential minority in terms of population and separatist political movements in the 1960s and 1970s. On the border between Thailand and Malaysia, the Sam Sam – Thai-speaking Muslims – are another ethnic group. These people speak the old southern Thai dialect blended with Malay words and are often officially regarded as good subjects, as opposed to the rebellious Malay-speaking Muslims.[9]

The urban sector of Thai society comprises various non-Tai peoples as well. The largest immigrant group is the Chinese, who migrated into Thailand during the nineteenth century. The Chinese form significant urban communities throughout the country, particularly in major cities. The early Chinese immigrants were important as labourers as well as middlemen in the export sector of the economy. However, many Chinese descendents or *luk chin* (literally 'children of Chinese') have become highly influential figures, particularly in the political and economic spheres. To a certain extent, these Thai-born Chinese have assimilated into Thai society and have acquired Thai citizenship. Many of them have also intermarried with the Thai people.

Indians form a small group of immigrants or descendants of immigrants living in Bangkok and other major urban areas. Indian people in Thailand are divided into Hindus, Sikhs and Muslims and are closely linked with the textile trade. Another small group of immigrants or descendants of immigrants is the Vietnamese, who came into Thailand in the middle of the nineteenth century and after the end of the French-Indochina War in 1954. Most of the Vietnamese settled in the northeast of Thailand.

Within Thai official discourse, the heterogeneity of ethnic peoples in Thailand has often been regarded as problematic in the process of nation-building. Since the mid-twentieth century, assimilation has been the major mechanism of incorporation of the diverse ethnic groups living within the bounded nation-state. Central to the assimilation process is the state's attempt to create an identity of Thai-ness, and to differentiate 'distinctive characteristics' separating Thai from the non-Thai. This process has been carried out through the institutionalization of Thai nationalism.

Nation-state, nationalism, and state–ethnic relations

Ethnic identity is often seen as being created through self-identification based on a sense of shared interests emerging out of social processes and interactions, both within and between similar as well as distinctive groups. However, ethnic identification can also be an imposition, a product of policies designed by the nation-state for the classification of its citizenry. Central to the process is ethnic categorization, a powerful instrument of both identification and control of ethnicity by the administrative state. In order to understand the relationship between state and ethnic identity in Thailand, it is thus essential to pay attention to the politics of cultural difference within the nation-state, particularly in the context of nationalism.

The creation of the bounded 'geo-body' of Siam, renamed Thailand in 1939, was a response to the threat of colonial expansion by European powers in the late nineteenth century.[10] *Chat*, a Sanskrit derived term was initially used to mean people who share a common language and culture, and subsequently came to mean a national, political community or the nation. In the early twentieth century, after the threats of European colonial power had receded, the promulgation of Thai nationalism was primarily a response to 'internal threats'. King Vajiravudh (1910–24), in his campaign against the Chinese, put forward an idea of Thai-ness based upon the shared national heritage of the Thai language, Buddhist religion and loyalty to the ruling Chakkri monarchy.[11] The Chinese, who did not share in this common heritage, were perceived as a threat to the Thai nation and were, in fact, labelled 'the Jews of the Orient' by the king. The expansion of the Chinese population, their increasing domination of the economic sector and their control over commerce were seen by the Thai elite as major threats to the sovereignty of the Thai nation.

Thai nationalism, therefore, is not only a process of creating a unified national identity, but is also importantly a production of internal threats and enemies. In the eyes of the state, cultural differences and the diversity of the people living within the Thai nation were seen as a threat to national stability. King Vajiravudh, through the implementation of the first Nationality Law of 1912, both initiated and set a precedent for later state attempts to homogenize and unify the Thai nation's ethnic diversity. The king believed that granting Thai citizenship to the Chinese children who were born in Thailand would reduce these children's attachment to China and Chinese nationalism.[12] After the Second World War, the homogenization process was carried out and made possible through various means, including the standardization of the Thai language as the national language and its enforcement through state compulsory education. The prohibition of using languages other than Thai as the primary language of instruction in schools came into effect in the 1930s, as part of the military government's project of national assimilation. As a consequence, non-Thai languages have been made subordinate to Thai and do not have official recognition.

Significantly, the construction of 'Thai-ness' went hand in hand with the identification of what is non-Thai as that which is 'problematic' and a 'threat'. Ethnic categorization was a fundamental mechanism for the identification of cultural and ethnic differences and the 'problems' they posed, and therefore crucial to the processes of assimilating ethnic minorities into the nation. It is noteworthy that while state attempts at systematic classification of ethnic peoples began as early as the late nineteenth century, ethnic categorization as a 'rhetoric of control'[13] in fact emerged in the mid-twentieth century, a product of Cold War ideologies of national security (*khwam mankhong haeng chat*) and territorial integrity. While 'Thai-ness' was characterized by a seemingly bounded, essential and natural culture, ethnic classifications also created fixed and essentialized non-Thai identities. The demarcation of the geographical and cultural boundaries of the modern Thai nation-state led not only to the territorial incorporation within the boundary of the nation of peoples with diverse cultural practices, but also to the cultural exclusion of people who do not partake of the bounded Thai identity.

Ethnic categorization and the discourse about ethnic minorities

In official discourses, all the non-dominant groups of people are defined as *chon klum noi* or ethnic minorities, regardless of their distinctive histories, cultures and languages. The notions of indigenous and native peoples (*khon dung doem*) are absent from the state's perception of the non-Thai minorities, despite the fact that many of them are original inhabitants of what is today Thailand. The term *chon klum noi* was used by the Thai government during the Cold War period of the mid-twentieth century to refer to ethnic groups of races (*chua chat*), languages, religions, customs, traditions and beliefs that are distinctive from those of 'the majority' of the country.[14] The term also has a political implication, identifying 'minority' status with a potential 'problem' for the nation and thus linking it to the notion and concerns of 'national security'. As Suwit Suthanukul, the then-secretariat of the National Security Council, clearly states '[Ethnic minorities] are not a problem by themselves as long as they are still loyal to the nation in general and [as long as] their distinctive practices do not pose a threat to national security.'[15]

Ethnic minorities within official classification are divided into five groups comprised of the Chinese (*chao chin*), the hill tribe peoples (*chao khao*), the Vietnamese immigrants (*chao yuan opphayop*), the Thai Muslims (*chao Thai Muslim*) and others. Under the category of others are refugee groups such as the '*chin haw*' (Chinese), refugees from Burma (*phu phlad thin sanchat phama*) and those from Indochina (*phu opphayop liphai chak indochin*). During the Cold War period, the Thai state identified the Chinese, the hill tribe peoples, the Vietnamese immigrants and the Thai Muslims as the most 'contentious' groups, in fact, as 'problems' that needed to be solved.[16] At the turn of the twenty-first century, however, the concerns of the Thai state regarding *chon klum noi* (ethnic minorities) were focused on the hill tribe peoples (*chao khao*), the Thai Muslims and refugees from Burma.

Within the discourse of *chon klum noi*, several ethnic groups are absent, particularly the 'Lao' of the northeast and the Yuan or Khon Muang of the north. Keyes notes that the promotion of inclusive nationalism by the Thai state has turned the 'Lao' and the 'Khon Muang' into ethno-regional groups rather than ethnic minorities, where cultural differences are seen as regional distinctions rather than as ethnic differences.[17] In explaining why ethnic groups in the northeast are not perceived as *chon klum noi* (ethnic minorities) by the state, Khachadpai Burutpat, the then-deputy-secretariat of the National Security Council, argues that (these people) are actually Thai because they have never caused any problems to the government administration.[18] The regional distinctiveness of the 'Lao' is not regarded as a problem by the state, because 'the more development expands [in the northeast region], the greater the chance that these people will become real Thais'.[19] The silencing of ethnic differences in the northeast has not only downplayed the Lao identity but has also rendered invisible the non-Laos who live at the margin of the northeast region, particularly the Kui. This marginalization process, however, has constantly been contested in various forms of ethnoregionalism, by the very people classified ethnic-neutrally as *khon isan* or people of the northeast.

In the north, diverse ethnic lowlanders have been subsumed under yet another regional category of 'Thai-ness' and come to be known simply as 'Khon Nua' (people of the north), which replaces their self-identification as 'Khon Muang' (people of the polity). Historically, ethno-regionalism as a response to national integration and centralization, though not as strong as in the northeast, was evident in several millenarian movements. Nevertheless, the cultural distinctiveness of the Khon Muang has become commercially valuable with the rise of tourism in the northern region, particularly in the city of Chiang Mai since the 1990s. Various cultural artifacts have been selected as representative of an exclusively northern culture, for example hand-made cotton (while silk is rejected as distinctive of the northeast). But while the Khon Muang are regarded as akin to the dominant Thai, the non-Thai category is often identified with the *chao khao* (hill tribe peoples). Of all the ethnic minorities in Thailand, *chao khao* (hill tribe peoples) has been the category that has attracted the most attention of the Thai state.

Chao khao *(hill tribe peoples)*

The term *chao khao* (hill tribe peoples) refers to the minorities residing in the highlands of northern Thailand. This term was introduced during the early twentieth century and became a dominant referent in the discourse about people on the border. The term 'hill tribes' was made official in 1959 with the formation of the Central Hill Tribe Committee (CITTC).

One literal translation of *chao khao* is 'people of the hills'. However, the term *khao*, apart from meaning hills or mountains, is also a third-person pronoun, connoting the 'other'. When contrasted with *chao rao*, literally 'those of us' or 'we people', the expression falls into opposition to 'us'. Likhit Theerawhekhin, drawing on a senior Border Patrol Police official's notion, gave the following definition of *chao khao*:

> [They are] minorities who settle in the hill areas under 10,000 feet above sea level; partaking of similar traditional customs, spoken languages, beliefs, occupations and habits among each other; sharing common administrative systems [with the Thai], but obviously distinct in terms of customs and spoken languages. And [they] believe in animism.[20]

The official discourse of 'hill tribes' above clearly lumps together every group of highlanders under the same category, despite their distinctive cultural identities and histories. Thus the Karen, who perceive their own place as more among the lowlanders than with the highlanders, and who feel no affinity with hill peoples of the higher slopes, are put into the same gross ethnic identification with other highland tribes.[21]

Thus, the definition of 'hill tribes' did not come from the hill peoples' self-identification, but emerged from state (re)conceptualization and categorization of the people living in the border areas in relation to the dominant lowlanders, reflecting the Cold War mentality of the time. 'Hill tribes' do not necessarily live in the mountains. The concept is assigned to nine ethnic minority groups, the Karen, the Hmong, the Lisu, the Aka, the Lahu, the Yao, the Khamu, the Htin and the Lua, even though some of the people so classified are no longer mountain dwellers.[22] On the other hand, the category excludes other ethnic groups who also live in the mountainous areas, such as Khon Muang, the Haw Chinese and the Shan. In some official accounts such as those of the National Security Council, *chao khao* are reduced to only six tribes by leaving out the Khamu, the Hitn and the Lua.[23]

Although some hill peoples practise a type of agriculture little different from that in other upland regions, *chao khao* do not count as upland farmers (*chao rai*). This is because the term 'hill tribes' does not refer simply to groups of ethnic highland minorities possessing distinctive cultures, but also refers to certain stereo-typical practices, including particular types of cultivation. The expression also has a specific geo-political implication. As the Border Patrol Police's definition of *chao khao* quite clearly implies, *chao khao* people as a category is situated outside the realm of belonging and therefore denied 'ownership of the country'. Instead, they are constantly subjected to state control.

So hill people find themselves with little space in the nation's life. During the 1960s, '*panha chao khao*' or 'the hill tribe problem' emerged as government rhetoric. The 'problem' was in fact a product of the changing relations between the modern state and the peripheral peoples due to changing ideas about the frontier. The impact of the alterations on the lives of hill peoples is twofold. First, the notion of the 'border' has come to represent demarcated and fixed territories of the modern nation-state. However, the traditional agricultural and social practices of the hill peoples, which continue today, involve moving back and forth within what have come to be several national territories, and are thus perceived as practices that undermine the sacredness of the border, and hence the sovereignty of the state. Second, since citizenship as a marker of fixed national/social identity is generally circumscribed by the idea of permanent settlement, hill peoples' mobility within and across territories is often made to connote ethnic minorities' disloyalty to the nation. So it appears that the basic reason why hill tribe peoples are not seen as full Thai citizens is because their mobility has come to signify the absence of ties with the nation-state. Within the discourse of 'the hill tribe problem', these people pose three dangerous threats needing urgent control in the interests of Thai national security: migratory behaviour, opium growing and shifting cultivation.

Plate 9.2 A Hmong woman from Ban Huay Hoy, Chiang Mai (Photograph by Panadda Boon-yasaranay.)

The three labels: migratory insurgent, opium producer and forest destroyer

The first label for 'hill tribes' – as borderless migrants and communist insurgents – began to be used in the mid-twentieth century. State policies towards hill peoples, however, did not target every group of ethnic hill tribe, omitting, for example, the Karens. On the other hand, attention was strongly focused on the Hmong people, who were considered potentially the most 'dangerous' group.[24] During the 1960s and 1970s, the mobility of the Hmong came to signify the ethnic group's political independence. Government officials created and constantly utilized the expression 'Red Meo' in their rhetoric to paint an insurgent picture of the Hmong as well as other of highland groups. The mis-use of the 'communist label' by government officials was in fact a major factor in initially forcing a number of Hmong people to join the communist insurrection. The movement itself, however, as Cooper argues, was 'an ethnic rebellion rather than a chapter in communist revolution'.[25]

In the early 1960s, the Thai king undertook to become a bridge to ethnic minorities in northern Thailand, to bring them into the consolidated modern state.[26] As Tapp argues, the most prominent endeavour of the Royal Highland Development Project was to win the hearts and minds of the Hmong, the ethnic minority who had previously suffered tremendously from their subordinate relationship with the rulers of lowland Tai states.[27]

The promotion of the Royal Project went ahead alongside state attempts to control the movement of hill peoples through resettlement programmes. In the 1960s, resettlement was based on the idea of 'relocation' into 'settlement areas'. By stabilizing the residence and livelihood of these hill peoples in the more accessible low-lying areas, under the eyes of the authorities, border problems would perhaps be controlled. However, the idea of '*nikhom*' or 'settlements' as a means to secure the border areas eventually failed, as many hill peoples escaped from the prison-like camps. Yet authorities still promote *nikhom* for the hill peoples as an effective means to accelerate assimilation.

The second label for hill peoples – as opium producers – also feeds the security paranoia of the modern state. While opium production had been a significant source of national income for the Thai state for more than a century, international pressure forced the Thai government to ban the sale and consumption of opium in 1958. Before then, the Thai government derived considerable profit from trade in this commodity and encouraged its cultivation so strongly that it became an integral part of the economies of some highland ethnic minorities, particularly that of the Hmong.

After the opium ban, the United States and international agencies such as the United Nations introduced massive amounts of cash and development projects to replace opium in the highlands. However, as world market demand for opium continued to expand, its high value encouraged illegal trade and official government corruption. Opium eradication projects consequently became another avenue of benefit for local officials. It was the hill peoples engaged in the production of opium who suffered most from new penalties. Their harvests were confiscated, poppy fields burnt or bombed, and cultivators arrested. During the communist suppression of the 1960s and 1970s, the conflation of opium production with national security problems provided even more power for local Thai bureaucrats to extort levies and taxes from those continuing to produce opium. Since the 1980s, the politics of opium have played a significant role in shaping the status of ethnic minorities. However, by the turn of the century, the state's concern about opium had faded as crop substitution programmes expanded significantly. Nonetheless, massive expansion of narcotic production and consumption in the form of amphetamines have become a serious concern for the state in the twenty-first century, particularly in northern Thailand and along the Thai-Burmese borders. As some hill people have been involved in this trade, the connection between 'hill tribes' and 'narcotics trader' has deepened the negative label of hill peoples as 'destroyers of the nation'.

The third label for the hill peoples – as shifting cultivators and thus forest destroyers – represents the most prominent and long-standing characteristic associated with the 'hill tribes' in official as well as public discourses. This stereotype continues to shape social and political attitudes toward hill people. With its long tradition in this region, shifting cultivation has been practised by both lowland Thais and the upland hill peoples. Over the past several decades, however, shifting cultivation has been increasingly viewed by the Thai state as a problematic and dangerous pattern of agriculture.

The rationale underlying the state's prejudice against shifting cultivation lies in the political economy of this mode of production, within the politics of territorial control of the forests. Historically, the colonial administration in this region, and its imposed commercial forestry, was an initial enforcement of 'protection against hill cultivation'.[28] The main aim of this regulation was to protect the value of teak forests. In Thailand, however, the position of the swiddeners only became vulnerable when international prejudice against shifting cultivation became felt in the mid-twentieth century. In the early colonial period of forest commercialization, hill peoples were seen as a more or less essential seasonal labour force for timber companies. In particular, the labour power of the Karen and local northern Thais with their elephants was in great demand. After the Second World War, international influence on forestry and nature conservation, especially by the Food and Agriculture Organization (FAO) led to a systematic control of shifting cultivation by the Thai government. Since the mid-twentieth century, the Royal Forestry Department, following the FAO's guidelines, has been the chief institution combating this form of agriculture. Shifting cultivation has come to be regarded as a major indicator of forest destruction. At the same time, as the value of timber, particularly teak, increased in the world market, many came to see shifting cultivation as the major impediment to economic exploitation of the forests. With the rise of nature conservation ideology in the 1960s, many have also viewed shifting cultivation as the cause of the 'destruction of pristine nature'.

Hill peoples have thus come to be seen as destroyers of the national economy through 'irrational' and 'destructive' agricultural practices. Official resettlement as a strategy employed by forestry authorities represented a significant attempt by the government to end 'the shifting cultivation problem'. In giving reasons for the relocation of hill peoples in April 1986, a forestry official stated, 'the Hmong entered Thailand deliberately to destroy the forest. Ethnic Thais practice slash-and-burn agriculture only because of the example set by the hill tribes.'[29]

The Thai state's policy of ending shifting cultivation continues to characterize contemporary state–ethnic relations in the periphery of northern Thailand. Among the three labels – insurgents, opium producers and forest destroyers – the last represents the most contentious image, pushing hill peoples into a most vulnerable position within Thai society. However, within the changing political and economic climate of the late twentieth century, in which tourism came to reshape the northern landscape, the rise of ethno-tourism has provided hill peoples with some negotiating and economic power. Tribal handicrafts have generated significant sources of income for some hill peoples, and are sold in regional, national and international markets. The emergence of jungle tours and adventure businesses, some operated by hill people themselves, have provided some rationale for the 'hill tribes' to remain in their 'place' in the forests, despite the fact that what is preserved and accentuated in the modern discourse of tourism is but another variant construction of the 'hill tribe' as object/other.

The 'Thai Muslims' and the politicization of religion

Unlike other categories of ethnic minorities (*chon klum noi*), the Thai state has granted the 'Thai Muslims' in southern Thailand recognition as the original inhabitants of the region.[30] However, their minority status is understood by the Thais as having significant political implications, derived from their practise of a distinctive religion, Islam.

While, generally, Thais call the Muslim people in the southern border provinces *khaek* (guests, visitors), the Muslims refer to themselves as Melayu people.[31] Religious difference has long been a source of political dissidence. In the area designated as 'the four southern border provinces' (*si changwat chaidaen phak tai*), which include Pattani, Yala, Satun and Narathiwat, central governments enforced coercive assimilationist strategies during the mid-twentieth century. They strictly forbade the use of the Malay language and certain practices of Islam. Compulsory education used the Thai language, and emphasized central Thai perspectives. At the same time, government officials were mainly from central Thailand, knew no Malay language and often disliked Islamic culture. The state's downplaying of ethnic differences between Thais and Malays signified an attempt to force an assimilation of Malay identity, so that the Malay Muslims became increasingly caught in the political infringements of the dominant Thai nation-state.

During the Cold War, the Communist Party of Malaysia movement along the Thai-Malaysia border[32] and the rise of separatist movements within the south of Thailand itself accelerated the state's wish to assimilate 'the Thai Muslim minority'. Particularly important was the Patani United Liberation Organization (PULO), which was successful in gaining support among the people of the southern border. Thus the government came to regard the four southern provinces as the biggest political threat to national security, requiring immediate suppression, and labelled the separatists as 'terrorist bandit movements' (*khabuankan chon ko kan rai*). In the 1970s, with the military government in power, ethnic insurgency expanded, and clashes between the separatist movements and the government increased in the four Muslim border provinces.

The changes in the political climate in Thailand since the 1980s, however, have resulted in a relaxation of some of the coercive policies towards the Malay Muslims. Although the government still enforces Thai as the language of communication, it has dealt with religious differences more flexibly. More Thai Malay officials have been appointed to local posts. Many Thai Malay people join political parties, particularly the Democratic Party, the major constituencies of which are in the south. Several Muslim politicians have become prominent in Parliament and government. The king fosters public recognition of Islam and provides patronage to the Office of Islamic Affairs (*samnak chula ratchamontri*).

The increasingly democratic environment in contemporary Thailand, particularly with the new Constitution of 1997, which recognizes cultural and religious diversity and the right to cultural and religious differences, has provided some room for the southern Malay Muslims within the Thai nation. The decline of the separatist movements has been partly a result of the government's policy towards the Muslim minorities over the past decade. Nevertheless, the state's questions and concerns regarding national security are still apparent in its perceptions of the southern border and practices of Islam. Concurrently, the attempt to assert religious and ethnic distinctiveness by Islamic fundamentalists through violent actions is still present in the southern provinces of Thailand.

The immigrant and border politics

Immigrants represent one of the most ambiguous ethnic categories of the non-Thai minorities. Thailand is not a signatory to the United Nations Refugee Convention and the Thai state's policies towards people who cross into its territory as a result of war are ambivalent and contradictory. The government's designation of this group of people varies, ranging from *phu opphayop* (immigrant), *phu phad thin* (displaced people), *phu khao muang phit kod mai* (illegal immigrant) to *phu li phai* (refugee). While the Indochinese refugees who entered Thailand during the mid-twentieth century were allowed to receive aid from the United Nations High Commission for Refugees (UNHCR), the ethnic peoples from Burma who sought asylum in Thailand during the late twentieth century were not granted the status of refugees. After many years of negotiations, in 1998 Thailand finally agreed to allow the UNHCR a role in aiding people from Burma living at the border, but continued to regard them not as refugees but as illegal immigrants.

Since the mid-1990s, relations between the governments of Thailand and Burma have been improving, leading to a tightening of policies against ethnic people entering Thailand from Burma. While allowing the entry of those fleeing armed fighting, people abused by the Burmese military in other ways, such as through forced relocations, forced labour or even forced impregnation are not permitted to seek asylum in Thailand. Some of the ethnic minorities from Burma, such as the Karen and Karenni, who left the country to flee armed conflict, are allowed to reside in the refugee camps. Other asylum seekers, such as the Shan people, are denied the same protection and thus become illegal immigrants.

Towards the end of 1999 and during early 2000, tough policies towards Burmese refugees were enforced as a result of several movements of Burmese dissidents attacking targets in Thailand. Restrictions on the refugees' mobility and the closing down of the Maneeloy Center, the major camp for Burmese students and dissidents, were among the measures taken to ensure Thailand's national security.

Official records of the US Committee for Refugees estimate that at the end of 2000, there were approximately 217,000 refugees living in Thailand. These comprised 115,000 ethnic Karens and Karennis living in camps, 100,000 ethnic Shans living among the local population, 1,700 former Burmese students and urban refugees living at a special camp or in Bangkok, and a small number of Indochinese refugees.[33] However, the total number could be twice as high, since official statistics do not include undocumented migrant workers living in hiding in many major cities.

The border as a cultural and political space represents an arena in which identities are both imposed and rejected. Control over border areas and movements of people entering this space are therefore tantamount to control of ethnic identity. The shifting policies and practices of the Thai state toward immigrants over the past several decades reflect the changing political economy of the border and border identities. Government policies restricting immigration were created and implemented in the period after the Second World War, even though initially immigrants were often regarded as a significant source of the labour force necessary to Thailand's economic development. Many of these earlier immigrants, such as the Chinese and Vietnamese who came into Thailand in the late nineteenth century, were allowed to settle in the country, and some were also granted Thai citizenship. Despite the fact that migrant workers continue to be a significant part of the labour force and of the Thai economy, particularly in agro-industry, changing state policy and the refusal to grant legal status to these immigrants have made these people very vulnerable.

Border crossing by immigrants and refugees from neighbouring countries after the Second World War was of political concern to the Thai state because of communist expansion in the region. In the 1960s, many Vietnamese sought asylum in Thailand, followed by Lao and Cambodian refugees in the 1970s. While the border became the strategic space of national security, the control of refugees along the border was part of the policy to counter communist operations across the border. By the end of the twentieth century, border security issues in the northeast had subsided as Thailand improved its relations with Laos, Vietnam and Cambodia, and the refugees had been repatriated and resettled. The issue of border security, however, resurfaced in the northern and western parts of Thailand, where ethnic insurgents fought the military in Burma, while the Burmese military continues to attack insurgents along the Thai-Burmese borders.

Conclusion

The modern Thai nation-state was built on a policy of ethnic, religious and cultural homogenization, which was begun early in the twentieth century. Ethnicity in Thailand not only involves changing alignments of social groups within flexible boundaries, but also shifting constructions of, as well as disjunction between, the Thai and non-Thai identities. Ethnic categorization as designed by the state represents a significant mechanism of political and cultural incorporation and the transformation of ethnic diversity, or non-Thai identification, into the modern Thai nation. This process, however, involves the fixing of ethnic identification, as is manifest in the exercising and deployment of the discourse on *chon klum noi* (ethnic minorities). Within the dominant narrative of ethnic minorities, the distinctive identifications of Thais and non-Thai Others have become politicized and rendered counter-productive to national integrity.

The birth of the modern Thai state and its nationalist ideology have also created an ambivalence within state–ethnic relations. The history of national assimilation of the subordinated ethnic groups is also the history of suppression of ethnic heterogeneity, and produced uneven opportunities for different ethnic groups in terms of integration into national cultures, economies and political systems. Ethnic tension and conflict between the Thai state and the Lao, the Yuan, the Malay Muslims and the Chinese between the beginning and the middle of the twentieth century were integral in the creation of nationalism and the making of Thai homogeneity. In contemporary Thailand, however, state policies toward ethnic diversity have become more tolerant, while the processes of national assimilation involve both incorporation and ideological manipulation of subordinate minorities for the benefit of the dominant group. The state has promoted cultural diversity and distinctiveness and encouraged pride in distinctive cultural values, and these notions have become part of the discourse about Thai-ness (*khwam pen thai*) in which the recognition of diverse ethnic and cultural components of peoples is seen as essential to the Thai nation and even to Thai-ness itself. This policy, however, rests upon a process of selection whereby certain aspects of traditional cultures, particularly elements of material culture, win the status of the 'authentic'. This cultural essentialism has its commercial purposes, particularly in the tourist industry where diverse cultural features and artifacts have been turned into commodities.

Yet, within the increasingly de-consolidated Thai national ideology, which allows more space for ethnic heterogeneity, tensions regarding diversity within the nation remain. In the north of Thailand, the contentious relation between the state and hill peoples is still circumscribed by the politics of ethnicity through the three official identifications of the hill peoples as insurgents, opium producers and forest destroyers. Complex identification processes in which both inclusion and exclusion have been simultaneously used as strategy for national integration remain fundamental and dominant in policies towards ethnic minorities. Such identification, however, is dialectical and responsive. The articulation of identification from the margin and the constant negotiation over ethnic differences continue to shape the relationship between ethnicity and nation-state in modern Thailand.

Notes

1 G. Condominas, 'Essay on the evolution of Thai political systems', in G. Condominas, *From Lawa to Mon, from Saa' to Thai: Historical and Anthropological Aspects of Southeast Asian Social Space*, Canberra: Research School of Pacific Studies (Occasional Paper of the Department of Anthropology), 1990, pp. 28–91.
2 R. Gray, 'The role of population census for providing statistics on disadvantaged groups in Thailand', available online at http://216.../gray_final_paper.doc.+thailand, _statistic,+population,+ethnic+minorities$hl=t (25 May 2002).
3 C. Keyes, *Thailand: Buddhist Kingdom as Modern Nation-State*, Boulder, CO and London: Westview Press, 1987, p. 15.
4 J. Phumisak, *Khwampenma khong Kham Sayam Thai Lao lae laksana thangkansangkhom khong chuchat (Etymology of the Terms Siam, Thai, Lao and Khom, and the Social Characteristics of Ethnonyms)*, Bangkok: Social Sciences Association of Thailand, 1976, cited in A. Turton (ed.), *Civility and Savagery: Social Identity in Tai States*, Richmond, Surrey: Curzon Press, 2000, p. 11.
5 D. Marlowe, 'In the mosaic: The cognitive and structural aspects of Karen–other relationships', in C. Keyes (ed.), *Ethnic Adaptation and Identity: The Karen on the Thai Frontier with Burma*, Philadelphia: Institute for the Study of Human Issues, 1979, pp. 165–214.
6 Keyes, *Thailand*, p. 21.
7 According to the Department of Public Welfare (1997), the total numbers of the major hill tribes are 704,057 (Karen: 353,574, Hmong: 126,300, Lahu: 85,845, Akha:

56,616, Mein: 48,357, and Lisu: 33,365), cited in M. Ritchie and B.Yang, 'Demographic and social survey of tribal people', Chiang Mai, CONTO and World Concern, September, 1999. Smaller groups of hill peoples total 58,792 (H'tin: 32,755, Lua: 15,711, Khamu: 10,153, and Mlabri: 173), Prachuab *et al.* 1996, cited in D. McCaskill and K. Kampe (eds), *Development or Domestication? Indigenous Peoples of Southeast Asia*, Chiang Mai: Silkworm, 1997, p. 23.

 8 V. Grabowsky (ed.), *Regions and National Integration in Thailand 1892–1992*, Wiesbaden: Harrassowitz, 1995, p. 108.

 9 R. Nishii, 'Emergence and transformation of peripheral ethnicity: Sam Sam on the Thai-Malaysian border', in Turton (ed.), *Civility and Savagery*, pp. 180–200.

10 See Thongchai Winichakul, *Siam Mapped: A History of the Geo-body of a Nation*, Honolulu: University of Hawaii Press, 1994.

11 See W. Vella, *Siam under Rama III, 1824–1851*, Locust Valley, NY: J.J. Augustin, Association for Asian Studies Monographs IV, 1957.

12 Khachadphai Burutpatra, *Chon klum noi nai Thai lae khwam man khong khong chad* (*Ethnic Minorities in Thailand and National Security*), Bangkok: Phrae Phittaya Press, 1983, p. 16.

13 R. Rosaldo, 'The rhetoric of control: Ilongots viewed as natural bandits and wild Indians', in B. Babcock (ed.), *The Reversible World: Symbolic Version in Art and Society*, Ithaca, NY: Cornell University Press, 1978, pp. 240–57.

14 Khachadphai, *Chon klum noi nai Thai*, 1983, p. 2.

15 Suwit Suthanukul, 'Chon klum noi khong chat: prasobkan khon prathed Thai' ('Ethnic minorities of the nation: Experience from Thailand'), in Kusuma Sanitwongsa Na Ayuthaya (ed.), *Roi rao nai sangkhom Thai: buranakan kab panha khwam mankhong khong chad* (*Fractures in Thai Society: National Integration and the Problem of National Security*), Bangkok: Faculty of Social Science, Chulalongkorn University, 1988, p. 4.

16 Khachadphai, *Chon klum noi nai Thai*, 1983, pp. 1–5.

17 C. Keyes, 'Cultural diversity and national identity in Thailand', in M. Brown and S. Ganguly (eds), *Government Policies and Ethnic Relations in Asia and the Pacific*, Cambridge, MA: MIT Press, 1997.

18 Khachadpai, *Chon klum noi nai Thai*, 1983, p. 1.

19 Khachadpai, *Chon klum noi nai Thai*, 1983, p. 1.

20 Likhit Theerawekhinm (ed.), *Chon klum noi nai phrathed Thai* (*Ethnic Minorities in Thailand*), Bangkok: Phrae Phittaya Press, 1978, p. 68.

21 C. Kammerer, 'Territorial imperatives: Akha ethnic identity and Thailand's national integration', in J. McKinnon and B. Vienne (eds), *Hill Tribes Today: Problems in Change*, Bangkok: White Lotus-Ostrom, 1989, p. 262.

22 B. Vienne, 'Facing development in highlands: A challenge for Thai society', in McKinnon and Vienne (eds), *Hill Tribes Today*, p. 36.

23 Khachadpai, *Chon klum noi nai Thai*, 1983, p. 66.

24 Kammerer, 'Territorial imperatives', pp. 282–3; N. Tapp, *Sovereignty and Rebellion: The White Hmong of Northern Thailand*, Oxford, New York: Oxford University Press, 1989, p. 32.

25 R.G. Cooper, *The Tribal Minorities of Northern Thailand: Problems and Prospects*, Southeast Asian Affairs, Singapore: Heinemann Educational (Asia), 1979, pp. 323–32.

26 Keyes, *Thailand*; Tapp, *Sovereignty and Rebellion*.

27 N. Tapp, 'Squatters or refugees: Development and the Hmong', in G. Wijeyewardene (ed.), *Ethnic Groups across National Boundaries in Mainland Southeast Asia*, Singapore: Institute of Southeast Asian Studies, 1990, p. 154.

28 A. Jorgensen, 'Forest people in a world of expansion,' *Transactions of the Finnish Anthropological Society*, 1979, no. 2, pp. 82–3.

29 A. Eudey, '14 April 1986: Eviction orders to the Hmong of Huai Yew Yee village, Huai Kha Khaeng Wildlife Sanctuary, Thailand', in McKinnon and Vienne (eds), *Hill Tribes Today*, p. 256.

30 Suwit, 'Chon klum noi khong chat', p. 11.

31 A. Idris, 'Tradition and cultural background of the Patani region', in Grabowsky (ed.), *Regions and National Integration in Thailand 1892–1992*, p. 206.
32 Khachadphai, *Chon klum noi nai Thai*, 1983, p. 175.
33 http://www.refugees.org/world/countryrpt/easia_pacific/thailand.htm (5 October 2002).

Further reading

For a comprehensive analysis of various state strategies of ethnic classification and national integration including ethno-regionalism see Charles F. Keyes, *Isan: Regionalism in Northeastern Thailand* (Ithaca, NY: Cornell University, Southeast Asian Program, Data Paper 65, 1967) and 'Hegemony and resistance in northeastern Thailand,' in V. Grabowsky (ed.), *Regions and National Integration in Thailand 1892–1992* (Wiesbaden: Harrassowitz, 1995), pp. 154–82, Thongchai Winichakul, 'The others within: Travel and ethno-spatial differentiation of Siamese subjects 1885–1910', in A. Turton (ed.), *Civility and Savagery: Social Identity and Tai Space* (Richmond, Surrey: Curzon Press, 2000), pp. 38–62, R. Renard, 'The differentiatial integration of hill people into the Thai state', in A. Turton (ed.), *Civility and Savagery*, pp. 63–83, and Hjorleifur Jonsson, 'Rhetorics and relations: Tai states, forests, and upland groups', in E. Paul Durrenberger (ed.), *State, Power and Culture in Thailand* (Monograph 44/Yale: Southeast Asia Studies, 1996).

On national integration, marginalization and ethnic responses see Ratana Boonmathya, 'Contested Concepts of Development in Rural Northeastern Thailand', unpublished dissertation (department of Anthropology, University of Washington, 1997), Komartra Chuengsatiansup, 'Living on the Edge: Marginality and Contestation in the Kui Communities of Northeast Thailand', unpublished dissertation (Department of Anthropology, Harvard University, 1998), Peter Cuasay, 'Time Borders and Elephant Margins: Among the Kuay of South Isan, Thailand', unpublished dissertation (Department of Anthropology, University of Washington, 2002), Leo Alting von Geusau, 'Akha internal history: Marginalization and the ethnic alliance system,' in A. Turton (ed.), *Civility and Savagery*, pp. 122–58, and Kwancheewan Buadaeng, 'Negotiating Religious Practices in Changing Sgaw Karen Community in North Thailand', unpublished dissertation (Department of Anthropology, University of Sydney, 2000).

10 Myanmar/Burma

Bertil Lintner

In 1989, Burma's military government changed the name of the country to Myanmar. The reason, it said, was that the British colonial power had named it 'Burma' after the main ethnic group in the country, the Burmese, who inhabit the central plains. 'Myanmar', it was argued, included the Burmese and all other 'ethnic races', including the Shan, the Karen, the Mon, the Kachin and more than 100 other nationalities. This is, however, historically and linguistically highly dubious. The once-British colony has always been called Burma in English and *bama* or *myanma* in Burmese.

The best explanation of the difference between *bama* and *myanma* is to be found in the old *Hobson-Jobson Dictionary*, which remains a very useful source of information: 'The name [Burma] is taken from Mran-ma, the national name of the Burmese people, which they themselves generally pronounce Bam-ma, unless speaking formally and empathically.'[1]

Both names have been used interchangeably throughout history, with Burma being more colloquial and Myanmar more formal. Burma and Myanmar (and Burmese and Myanmar) mean exactly the same thing, and it is hard to argue that the term 'Myanmar' would include any more people within the present union than the name 'Burma'.

There is no term in any language that covers both the Burmans and the minority peoples, since no country with the borders of present-day Burma existed before the arrival of the British in the nineteenth century. Burma, with its present boundaries, is a colonial creation rife with internal contradictions and divisions.

There is another dimension to the recent name changes in Burma. It was not only the names of the country and the capital (from Rangoon to Yangon) that were 'changed'; in the minority areas names also changed, and here it was a real change. A few examples from Shan State: Hsipaw became Thibaw, Hsenwi became Theinli or Thinli, Kengtung became Kyaingtong, Mong Hsu became Maing Shu, Lai-Hka became Laycha, Pangtara became Pindaya and so on. The problem here is that the original names all have a meaning in the Shan language; the 'new' names are Burmanized versions of the same names, with no meaning in any language. Since the new names are no more 'indigenous' than the old, the ethnic minorities did not appreciate the change, which deprived the

Plate 10.1 Shan woman husking rice

Shan of their historic names in favour of a Burman-sounding name. In this chapter, I have decided to use the 'old' names of the country as well as localities, because to do otherwise would only add to the confusion caused by the unpopular 'name-changes' of 1989.

Until Burma's ethnic problem is addressed in a sensible manner, the country's ethnic strife is likely to continue. Burma will remain a source of political, social and economic despair in a region that, over the past few decades, has developed more rapidly than any other part of the world, while Burma itself has stagnated.

Background

According to the 1931 census – the last proper census ever taken in the country – the Burmans made up 60 per cent of the total population.[2] They are believed to have come down from the Tibetan plateau in the north and settled in the Irrawaddy plain between the ninth and the eleventh centuries. They were an agrarian people who established small, relatively self-sufficient villages.

Their first ethnic clash occurred with the Mon, or Talaing, a people related to the Khmer of present-day Cambodia. The Mon had been living in the coastal areas of southern Burma long before the arrival of the Burmans, and they were the first to come into direct contact with Indian civilization, adopt Theravada Buddhism, develop a written script, and adapt Indian law to their local needs.[3]

The Karen are another people who also lived in southern Burma when the Burmans arrived about a millennium ago.[4] They suffered more at the hands of the Burman invaders than any other people in the region. They were treated as inferiors and, unlike the Mon, were discouraged from intermingling with the Burmans. Those Karen who lived under direct Burman rule were forced to provide *corvée* labour for their new masters, heavy taxes being imposed on them.[5] There were frequent raids into unadministered Karen territory by the politically more advanced lowland Burmans. Many references in Karen folklore attest to hardship and suffering.

The Karen were resentful enough that they willingly fought alongside the British against the Burmans when the latter conquered the country in stages in 1824–6, 1852 and 1885, and eventually made it a province of British India. Subsequently, many Karen were recruited into the army and the colonial police. For the first time in history, many of them also went to school. The arrival of the missionaries among the Karen and other tribal minorities of Burma resulted in social, cultural, economic and educational transformation. In the 1920s and early 1930s, Christian Karen constituted 22 per cent of the student body at the University of Rangoon, while they were only about 2 per cent of the total population of Burma.[6]

According to the 1931 census, there were 1.37 million Karen in Burma, or nearly 8 per cent of the population at that time – a significant increase on earlier estimates. But the name Karen actually includes a number of different tribes, of which the Sgaw had become the largest and most widely dispersed by the end of colonial rule. They were found all over the Irrawaddy delta, from the area around Prome down to the Arakan coast in the west and the hills along the Thai border in the east. The other main tribe, the Pwo, lived almost exclusively along the sea coast from Arakan down to Mergui in Tenasserim Division, where they intermingled with the Mon. A third subgroup, the Bwe, were found in the vicinity of Toungoo and in the territory extending from the foothills east of that city into the Karenni states bordering Thailand.

Besides the Karen, the Shan were the most numerous of Burma's many ethnic groups, forming 7 per cent of the population in the 1930s. They are not related to any other ethnic group in Burma. The Shan established an abundance of principalities, varying in size and importance, known as the Shan States. These were 'pacified' by the British over the years 1885–90. The thirty or so Shan States on the northeastern Shan plateau achieved a status different from that of Burma proper, which was a directly administered British colony. They became protectorates and the British recognized the authority of the Shan princes, or *saohpas*, who enjoyed a status somewhat similar to that of the rulers of the Indian princely states.[7] The Shan people, and the numerous hill tribes who inhabit the mountains surrounding their valleys, are today found on all sides of the borders in this region – in Burma, Thailand, Laos, China and even in northwestern Vietnam. There are also Shans in Kachin and Karenni states.

Partly because of their separate administrative status, the pre-war nationalist movement that swept central Burma never affected the Shan states. The colonial machinery was very light there. By the same token, very little was done to exploit the rich natural resources of the area and improve it economically. The colonial epoch meant peace and stability for the Shan states – but also an economic and political standstill.[8]

There was even less development in the hills surrounding the Shan valleys. These highlands were inhabited by a variety of hill peoples, mostly Tibeto-Burman in origin – Kachin, Lahu, Lisu and Akha – who were comparatively recent arrivals in the area. The movement of Kachin from the mountains of southern China and eastern Tibet was still going on when the British entered the area in the early twentieth century. But there were also tribes which had been there at least as long as the Shan, if not before them, such as the Mon-Khmer-speaking Palaung and Wa. The Palaung, who lived mainly in Tawngpeng state in the north, have developed into relatively prosperous tea-growers, while the Wa were headhunters well into modern times: the British never fully conquered their wild hills east of the Salween River, adjacent to the Chinese frontier. Nor has any government of independent Burma ever administered the Wa Hills.

The southern Shan states were inhabited by a Karen subgroup, the Thaungthu or Pa-O. Although related to the Karen, they had adopted Buddhism from the Shan and developed their own literature. To the south of the Shan states was another Karen subgroup that had come under Shan influence, but in a different way: the Karenni (literally 'Red Karen'), who had remained animist or been converted by Christian missionaries – but who had adopted Shan political culture and established their own principalities ruled by local *saohpas*.

In the northeastern-most corner of the Shan states is another colonial anomaly: a district called Kokang inhabited by ethnic Chinese of Yunnanese stock. The area became British under the Anglo-Chinese Burma Treaty of 4 February 1897, mainly because the colonial power wanted to control part of the cross-border trade with China. Kokang was placed under indirect British rule through the Shan *saohpa* of Hsenwi, west of the Salween River.

The Kokang Chinese live at an altitude where not even dry paddy farming is practicable and they have traditionally had to depend on various cash crops – tea, corn or opium – to buy rice from the more developed valleys. The people controlling the local opium trade were other Chinese groups, mostly immigrants from Yunnan. Many of them came from the Muslim, so-called Panthay, minority of southern China, descendants of Kublai Khan's Arab and Tartar soldiers who settled in the Dali area of western Yunnan and married local women.

Another minority also lived under the *saohpa* of Hsenwi. The warlike Kachin had managed to migrate that far south before the British were able to control such movements of peoples within their Burmese territories. The first Kachin are believed to have arrived in northern Burma from Tibet more than a millennium ago. A mountain people, over the centuries they drove the Chin (see p. 178), Palaung and Shan out of most of the north.

Although the Kachin, like the Karen, encompassed numerous tribes, the distinctions between them have had little divisive effect. There were the Jinghpaw, the Maru, the Lashi, the Atzi, the Lisu and the Rawang – but these represented

Plate 10.2 Nagas in the hills near the Indian border (in loincloths)

Plate 10.3 Naga children

Plate 10.4 Naga women

Plate 10.5 Kachin girls in church

linguistic groups rather than actual tribes. Far more important bonds were formed by an intricate system of clans cutting across tribal barriers and binding together a remarkably tight-knit society.[9]

Just before the turn of the century, a Swedish-American Baptist missionary, Ola Hanson, arrived in the Kachin hills. He was not the first Western missionary to come to the north, but he was by far the most energetic. The Kachin, until then animists, converted to Christianity faster than any other ethnic group in Burma, leaving but few pockets of animism. After Hanson had put their language into the Roman alphabet, the Bible was translated into Kachin and they achieved a relatively high literacy rate.[10]

Akin to the Kachin were two other Tibeto-Burman tribes in the northwest: the Naga and the Chin. The latter are also closely related to the Mizo of northeastern India. Like the Kachin, the Chin were animists until the arrival of Christian missionaries. Politically, hereditary chiefs and an aristocracy ruled the northern Chin tribes, while many of the southern Chin had a democratic type of organization, with each village governed by an elected council.

Unlike the Kachin, who were never conquered by any Burman state, the Chin were forced to pay tribute to the court in Mandalay. But they were sturdy fighters and, along with the Kachin and Karen, came to make up the backbone of the colonial army in pre-Second World War days.

The Naga, another hill people in the northwest, inhabited the remote mountain regions immediately to the north of the Chin area. Like the Chin, they spoke an abundance of local dialects, and were grouped into clans and virtually independent village clusters. Stevenson states that there were approximately 75,000 Naga in Burma in 1941, and that the greater portion of this number came under 'a gentle form of regular administration' only in 1940.[11]

While the Naga tribes on the Indian side of the border converted to Christianity at about the same time as the Kachin of Burma, and obtained their own Roman script as well, the Burmese Naga lived in isolation. There were no roads, no towns, only villages on hilltops surrounded by stockades. The Naga were headhunters and feared by the plainspeople, few of whom ventured into their wild mountains.[12]

To the south of the Chin and Naga Hills was a territory contrasting sharply with this primitive wilderness, the Arakan region, which a densely forested mountain range separated from Burma, making it possible for the Arakanese to maintain their independence from various Burmese empires. Moorish, Arab and Persian traders introduced Islam to the Arakan coast very early on. Some stayed and married local women. Their offspring became the forefathers of yet another group, which much later was to become known as the Rohingya. They speak a Bengali dialect.[13]

Against this backdrop of complex ethnic mosaic and centuries of mistrust, modern Burma emerged: a Burman-dominated, central heartland on both sides of the Irrawaddy River, surrounded by a horse-shoe shaped ring of mountain ranges inhabited by altogether more than a hundred different Tibeto-Burman, Mon-Khmer and Tai nationalities. But even inside this 'horse-shoe', there were some important minorities: the Indians and the Chinese, who dominated trade and commerce in virtually every urban centre across the country.

During the British era, thousands of Indians were brought in to work on the railways, in the postal services and the civil administration. Many Indians went into business and, being more familiar with modern finance and commerce than the Burmans, they soon came to control a disproportionately large share of the country's economy. Before the Second World War, 45 per cent of Rangoon's population was of South Asian origin – Hindu, Muslim or Sikh.

Generally speaking, the Burmese looked down on any person of South Asian origin referring to them as *kala*, a pejorative term meaning 'foreigner' or 'Indian'.[14] The Burmese have traditionally felt much closer to the Chinese than to the Indians. Although the Chinese have been entering Burma for centuries, they have generally intermarried quite freely. The relatively small size of the Chinese community in Burma – estimated at somewhat over 300,000 immediately before the outbreak of the Second World War – also accounts for the low level of hostility against the Sino-Burmese compared to the situation in other Southeast Asian countries. The urban Chinese – mostly Cantonese and Fujianese – formed part of the mainstream economy of Burma and had little contact with other, upcountry Chinese minorities such as the Panthay Muslims and the Kokang Chinese in the Shan states.

Pax Britannica provided the stability that was needed to keep this intricate jigsaw puzzle of nationalities, tribes, immigrant communities, linguistic and religious groups functioning as one administrative entity. But the Second World War pitted many of the nationalities against one another, and old animosities flared anew. The Burman nationalist movement sided with the Japanese, while many hill peoples – notably the Karen and the Kachin – formed guerrilla units, which fought alongside the British and the Americans against the Japanese.

When the war was over Burma's political process gained momentum once again. On 12 February 1947, Aung San and twenty-three representatives of the Shan, the Kachin and the Chin signed the historic Panglong Agreement. This was a key document in post-war relations between the frontier peoples and the central authorities in Rangoon. The day on which the agreement was signed is still celebrated officially every year in Burma as Union Day, a national holiday.[15]

The minorities were promised autonomy, and the Shan princes were even granted the right to secede from the Union of Burma after a ten-year period – that is, in 1958 – should they be dissatisfied with the new federation. This right was also granted to the Karenni states and ensured under the first Burmese Constitution.[16] The Panglong Agreement, as well as the new Constitution, further stipulated that a Kachin State be formed, but without the right to secede.

Policy post-independence

Everything was ready for the declaration of independence of the new Union of Burma – at an auspicious hour on the night of 4 January 1948 – when tragedy struck. On 19 July 1947, the leader of Burma's independence struggle Aung San was assassinated, along with six other state leaders. The new leader and independent Burma's first Prime Minister, U Nu, was a talented, intellectual politician but hardly the strong statesman the country needed during its first difficult years of independence.

Army units rose in mutiny, the powerful Communist Party of Burma (CPB) went underground to organize guerrilla forces, and the Karen, Karenni and Mon minorities took up arms, demanding separate states or secession from the Union. When the ten-year 'trial period' as part of the Union was up in 1958, many young Shan took to the hills to demand independence. In 1961, the Kachin minority in the far north formed the Kachin Independence Army (KIA), which quickly gained control over most of Kachin State as well as the Kachin-inhabited areas of northeastern Shan State.

Burma's governments tried to resolve the ethnic insurgencies with a mixture of military campaigns and politics. The minorities were represented in the Upper House, or the Chamber of Nationalities, in the bicameral Parliament, and a Shan, Sao Shwe Thaike, was given the ceremonial post of the first president of the Union. The first Constitution guaranteed freedom of speech, religion and assembly, and the country had the liveliest press in the region, with over thirty newspapers in the 1950s. Apart from the leading ones in Burmese and English, there were also five in Chinese, two in Hindi and one each in Urdu, Tamil, Telugu and Gujarati. The minorities published journals and periodicals in their own languages.

But the military campaigns against the ethnic and communist insurgents also led to an unprecedented expansion of the country's armed forces. In 1949 the chief of the army, General Ne Win, probably had no more than 2,000 men under his command. By 1955, the strength of the armed forces had increased to 40,000 men, and in 1962 the three services – the army, the navy and the air force – totalled 104,200 men.[17] The army had its own trading houses, shipping line, newspapers, schools and hospitals.

The army eventually took over the state – on 2 March 1962. The month before, U Nu had convened the Nationalities' Seminar in Rangoon in order to discuss the future of the frontier areas and to find a political solution to the long-running ethnic crisis. But before any decision could be made, Ne Win's army seized power and detained all the meeting's participants. Burma's federal Constitution was abolished and replaced by centralized rule under a military-controlled Revolutionary Council. This was followed by the introduction of a new 'state ideology', the Burmese Way to Socialism, which led to the nationalization of all private enterprises – and the exodus of their mostly Indian and Chinese owners. The newspapers were also nationalized, and a new press law ordained that all media publish in Burmese or English.

Burma's new, centralized state structure was enshrined in a new Constitution, adopted in 1974. The country remained a Union, but in name only. There were seven divisions for the areas dominated by the Burmans – Rangoon, Tenasserim, Irrawaddy, Magwe, Mandalay, Pegu and Sagaing – and seven states for the minorities: Mon State, Karen State, Karenni (Kayah) State, Shan State, Kachin

Plate 10.6 Kachin rebel soldiers with anti-aircraft gun

Plate 10.7 Kachin rebel soldiers standing to attention

State, Chin State and Arakan (Rakhine) State. But in reality, there was no difference between the states and the divisions, and the military held a firm grip on power.

In the border areas, the ethnic insurgencies flared anew, and the country went into a state of self-imposed isolation. By the mid-1980s, there were around 20,000–25,000 ethnic insurgents in the country, apart from 15,000 communist rebels, of whom the vast majority also came from ethnic minorities. The Rangoon government controlled the central heartland, but the outlying areas were guerrilla zones or revolutionary base areas. Apart from a failed attempt in 1963 to negotiate with the rebels, the new military-dominated government launched several offensives in the border areas, and by 1988 the armed forces had increased to 185,000 men. There seemed to be no solution in sight to Burma's ethnic problems, and minority culture and literature survived only in rebel-held areas, and in exile in Thailand, where many of the ethnic rebels had offices and safe-houses.

The next watershed in modern Burma's history came in 1988, when the entire country rose up against the military-dominated government. Millions of people marched in every major town and village across the country to demand democracy and an end to the disastrous Burmese Way to Socialism. The minorities also took part in these demonstrations, often dressed in their traditional costumes. Aung San's charismatic daughter, Aung San Suu Kyi, emerged as the leader of the movement for democracy, which effectively undermined the army's claim to be the successor to the independence forces of the 1940s.

The protests shook Burma's military establishment, which responded fiercely. Thousands of people were gunned down as the army moved in to shore up a regime overwhelmed by popular protest. The crushing of the 1988 uprising was more dramatic and much bloodier than the better publicized events in Beijing's Tiananmen Square a year later.[18]

Following the massacres in Rangoon and elsewhere, more than 8,000 pro-democracy activists fled the urban centres for the border areas near Thailand, where a multitude of ethnic insurgencies, not involved in the drug trade, were active. The Burmese military now feared a renewed, potentially dangerous insurgency along its frontiers: a possible alliance between the ethnic rebels and the Rangoon and other urban pro-democracy activists. But these Thai-border-based groups – Karen, Mon, Karenni, and Pa-O – were unable to provide the urban dissidents with more than a handful of weapons. None of the ethnic armies could match the strength of the CPB, whose 15,000 troops then controlled territory along the Sino-Burmese border in the northeast. Unlike the ethnic insurgents, the CPB had vast quantities of arms and ammunition, which were supplied by China from 1968 to 1978 when it was Beijing's policy to support communist insurrections in Southeast Asia. Although the aid had almost ceased by 1980, the CPB still had a large stockpile of munitions.[19]

Despite government claims of a 'communist conspiracy' behind the 1988 uprising, there was at that time no linkage between the anti-dictatorship, pro-democracy movement in central Burma, and the orthodox, Marxist-Leninist leadership of the CPB. However, given the strong desire for revenge for the bloody events of 1988, it is plausible to assume that the urban dissidents would have accepted arms from any source. Thus, it became imperative for the new junta that had seized power on 18 September 1988 – the State Law and Order Restoration Council (SLORC) – to neutralize as many of the border insurgencies as possible, especially the CPB.

A situation that was potentially even more dangerous for the SLORC arose in March and April 1989 when the hill-tribe rank-and-file of the CPB, led by the military commanders who also came from the various minorities in its northeastern base area, mutinied against the party's ageing, mostly Burman political leadership. On 17 April 1989, ethnic Wa mutineers from the CPB's army stormed party headquarters at Panghsang on the Yunnan frontier. The old leaders and their families – about 300 people – escaped to China while the former CPB army split along ethnic lines and formed four different, regional resistance armies. The main one, the United Wa State Army (UWSA) led by Chao Ngi Lai, comprised the bulk of the old CPB's fighting force, or approximately 10,000 men, at the time of the mutiny. The figure was soon to increase as the UWSA began procuring more weapons from China and Thailand to strengthen its forces. The Wa Hills form the centre of the CPB's old 'liberated zone' – and are a major opium-growing area. The old CPB's units in Kokang, Kachin State and eastern Shan State also formed new, regional armies.

Suddenly, there was no longer any communist insurgency in Burma, only ethnic rebels, and the SLORC worried about potential collaboration between these four new, well-armed forces in the northeast and the ethnic minority groups along the Thai border, as well as the urban dissidents who had taken refuge there. The ethnic rebels sent a delegation from the Thai border to Panghsang to negotiate with the CPB mutineers soon after the break-up of the old party – but the authorities in Rangoon reacted faster, with more determination, and with much more to offer than the ethnic rebels. Within weeks of the CPB mutiny, the chief of Burma's military intelligence, Khin Nyunt, helicoptered up to the border areas to meet personally with leaders of the mutiny.

Step by step, alliances of convenience were forged between Burma's military authorities and various groups of mutineers. In exchange for promises not to attack government forces and to sever ties with other rebel groups, the CPB mutineers were granted unofficial permission to engage in any kind of business to sustain themselves – which, in Burma's remote and underdeveloped hill areas inevitably meant opium production. Rangoon also promised to launch a 'border-development programme' in the former CPB areas, and the United Nations and its various agencies were invited to help fund those projects.

Ironically, at a time when almost the entire population of Burma had turned against the regime, scores of former insurgents rallied behind the ruling military, lured by lucrative business opportunities and unofficial permission to run drugs with impunity. With the collapse of the communist insurgency in 1989, several smaller ethnic armies also gave in. The 2,000-strong Shan State Army (SSA), which for decades had waged a war for autonomy for Shan State, made peace with Rangoon on 24 September 1989, and was granted timber concessions in the Hsipaw area in northern Shan State. They were followed by smaller groups of Pa-O and Palaung rebels who also operated in Shan State.

The Kachin Independence Army (KIA), which with 8,000 men in arms was Burma's most powerful ethnic rebel army and controlled most of Kachin State in the far north of the country, entered into an agreement with the SLORC in October 1993, and signed a formal ceasefire deal with Rangoon in February 1994. As a result, several pro-democracy activists, who had fled to the KIA-controlled area, surrendered in July of the same year. By 1997, more than a dozen ethnic rebel armies had made peace with Rangoon. As the twenty-first century dawned, only a handful of groups along the Thai border remained in armed opposition to Rangoon.

In the beginning, at least, the Wa actually had fairly well-articulated political demands. On 3 November 1994, their leader, Chao Ngi Lai, summoned a meeting of the UWSA and seven other groups that had also made peace with Rangoon, and an umbrella organization called the Peace and Democratic Front (PDF) was formed. It consisted of the four former CPB groups as well as a number of ethnic rebel armies that had made peace with Rangoon after the lucrative deal the ex-communists had struck with the state. At its first meeting in the Wa Hills, the PDF urged Rangoon to release all political prisoners, including Aung San Suu Kyi who had been detained in 1989. The Front also demanded that the SLORC should recognize the victory of her party, National League for Democracy (NLD) in a general election, which the new military regime had agreed to hold in May 1990.

But these policies were abandoned when Chao Ngi Lai suffered a stroke the following year. His successor as Wa leader, Pao Yuchang, was not interested in the welfare of the Wa people – and much more inclined to take over the already booming trade in opium and heroin. His brother-in-law Su Ching-pao took charge of most of the drug business. Around 1996 or 1997, methamphetamines were added to the list of drugs produced in the Wa area, and the UWSA also became involved in a range of other business activities such as gun-running, assisting illegal immigrants from China to escape down to Thailand, and even the production of counterfeit VCDs, DVDs and CDs with American and Chinese movies. According to estimates by Western anti-narcotics officials, the combined wealth of the Pao family is now in the order of two billion Chinese yuan, or US$243 million, much of it invested in Rangoon, Mandalay and Yunnan.

The threat from the border areas had been thwarted, but the consequences for the country and the rest of the world, which was hit by a flood of narcotics, were disastrous. Following the massacres of 1988, continuous human rights abuses, lack of rights for the ethnic minorities – and the fact that the government decided to ignore the outcome of an election organized by itself – Burma became an international pariah, and the subject of yearly condemnations in statements and resolutions issued by the United Nations.

The Myanmafication of Burma

Though the 1988 pro-democracy uprising failed to end military rule in Burma, it did force the authorities to give up the Burmese Way to Socialism. Later that year, Burma introduced a new foreign investment law, and private enterprise was once again allowed. This was done partly to appease the international community, which had in no uncertain terms condemned the carnage of 1988, but also because the Burmese economy had hit rock bottom after twenty-six years of misrule and mismanagement. While it is true that other countries, such as China and Vietnam, were also heading towards a market economy, the Burmese military has never thought it appropriate to pay attention to foreign models.

The consequences of these reforms for the army were significant. The Burmese Way to Socialism had provided the army with ideological underpinnings, which had prevented splits and factionalism before 1988. A new 'state ideology' was needed, and it emerged as an extreme form of nationalism based on Buddhism. The state-controlled media suddenly became filled with reports of generals presenting gifts to senior Buddhist monks, and glorified tales of Burma's history and past kings. The original idea of a Union of Burma, which the democratic forces equated with a federal system, and the diversity that had been recognized at the Panglong conferences in 1946 and 1947 was replaced by a new concept of nationhood: Myanmar. The authorities claimed there were 135 'national races', all united under the common name 'Myanmar'. National reconsolidation, not national reconciliation, became the new slogan.

On 31 May 1989, the SLORC formed the Committee for the Compilation of Authentic Data on Myanmar History to rewrite Burmese history to suit the new policies. The most extreme example of the ultra-nationalist approach to Burmese history was to claim not only that the Burmese had always been in Burma, but that the entire human race actually originated there. In 1997, intelligence chief Khin Nyunt learnt of the existence of some very rare fossils from Pondaung in the central plains, and, under military auspices, the (Myanmar) Fossil Exploration Team was put together. At a seminar in Rangoon a year later, Khin Nyunt proclaimed: 'The Myanmar people are not visitors from a faraway land who settled here. Life began in this Myanmar environment of land, air and water. Their roots are here.'[20]

Few scholars took these findings and statements seriously, and it is also doubtful whether the country's ethnic minorities were impressed. The outcome of the May 1990 general election clearly indicates otherwise. While the NLD swept the Burmese heartland, the military-sponsored National Unity Party won only ten seats, and local pro-democracy parties, based on ethnicity, captured most of the remaining seats.[21] The outcome of the election shows that although the ethnic minorities supported the pro-democracy movement in principle, they also wanted to safeguard their own interests. In the minority areas, people very clearly identified themselves with parties representing their respective ethnic groups. The ceasefire agreements with the armed rebel groups operating in the minority areas have not changed this perception. Even if they have rallied behind the regime – which since November 1997 calls itself the State Peace and Development Council (SPDC) – they have maintained their ethnic identity and, very often in vain, tried to promote ethnic issues.

The NLD's response to this has been entirely different from the SLORC/SPDC's. The ethnic conflict was addressed in the NLD's official programme, adopted in 1989:

> The forty-year history of [ethnic] relations has been a chapter of misfortune verging on the tragic. Along Burma's extended borders from the extreme north to the far south there are no less than thirteen groups of insurgents – a situation which is sapping the strength and resources of the nation. The development of the country has suffered greatly since approximately 40 per cent of the national budget has to be devoted to defence requirements. For these reasons we must seek a lasting solution to the problems of the ethnic minorities . . . it is the aim of the League to secure the highest degree of autonomy consonant with the inherent rights of the minorities and the well-being of the Union as a whole.[22]

In an interview with the Thailand-based *Irrawaddy* magazine, Aung San Suu Kyi stated in April 2002: 'We think that to be a true and lasting union it would have to be of a federalist nature.' But she remained strongly opposed to the idea that the ethnic states should have the right to secede, adding, 'but as you probably know, the ethnic nationalities are not asking for secession. They are just asking for their rights within a true federal union.'[23]

In brief, there are two entirely opposite views of what Burma is, or should be: the military's centralized and ethnically monolithic 'Myanmar', and a democratic, federal union that recognizes diversity envisaged by the NLD and the regional parties. The incompatibility of the two concepts may be the main reason why there seems to be no solution in sight to the country's long ethnic conflict. And then there is the view of the minorities, who are demanding more autonomy than even the NLD would be prepared to accept.

Conclusion

Before the 'Myanmar' concept was invented, Burma's official statistics showed that 68 per cent were Burman, 8.9 per cent Shan, 6.6 per cent Karen, 4.4 per cent Arakanese, and 12.1 per cent 'Others', that is, smaller ethnic groups as well as Chinese and Indians.[24] The figure for the Burmans is probably too high, as it seems to include most of the Mon population as well as Tavoyans and other groups in Mon State and Tenasserim Division, which do not necessarily think of themselves as Burmans. This makes Burma's ethnic balance extremely delicate, and any future government, democratic or non-democratic, would find it hard to keep the country together.

Part of the problem is that the SLORC/SPDC has clearly not thought of the consequences of its policy of 'Myanmafication'. All education in Burma is in 'the Myanmar language', that is, Burmese. If there is a Myanmar language, how can the term 'Myanmar' include all the ethnic groups in the country? The use of minority languages is very clearly discouraged, though people speak their own language at home and among members of their own group, and their literature is kept alive mainly through religious institutions. Shan and Mon are taught in local Buddhist monasteries, and the Kachin, Chin and Karen churches publish Bibles and hymn books in their own languages. Newspapers are still only printed in Burmese and English, with the sole exception of a Chinese-language weekly paper, *Miandian Huabao*, which has been published in Rangoon since November 1998. The changes of local place names to make them sound more 'Myanmar' (i.e. Burmese) is another extremely unpopular move by the present regime.

But the problem is not as simple as a clear-cut conflict between Burma's ethnic minorities and the country's Burman majority. Differences in religion, languages, and social and economic development also exist between the various minorities. The Shan, valley-dwelling cultivators of wet paddy, have often clashed with poorer, slash-and-burn hill tribes such as the Kachin and the Pa-O. While most Kachin tribes rallied behind the KIA in the 1970s and 1980s, the Rawang in the far north remained staunchly loyal to the central government. In 1988, the Mon and the Karen rebel armies clashed at the Three Pagodas Pass near the Thai border in a conflict over control over territory. The emergence of a new drug empire in the Kokang district and the Wa Hills has created a new 'upper class' of gangster-entrepreneurs, who, thanks to the ceasefire agreement with the government, act with impunity even in the towns. There have been several shoot-outs in Rangoon night clubs, and traffic accidents in Rangoon and Mandalay, where Kokang Chinese or Wa have been guilty, but never arrested or prosecuted.

Nor has Burma's ethnic problem been an entirely domestic affair. The foreign policy ramifications of Burma's ethnic insurgency have often been overlooked, and it is important to remember that, until the late 1980s, it was Thailand's policy to maintain buffers along its Burmese frontier, and the Shan, Mon and Karen rebel armies were able to obtain supplies from the Thai side in exchange for acting as an unofficial 'border police'. The Thais wanted to prevent a link-up between the CPB and its own communist insurgents – apart from cashing in on the lucrative trade in consumer goods across the border. Under the previous socialist system, more than 80 per cent of all consumer goods in Burma were smuggled in through rebel-held border areas.

The Shan have enjoyed a close relationship with their Thai cousins, also including close cultural contacts. Shan monks usually go to Thailand for higher education. There are also several Mon monasteries in Thailand, which attract Mon from across the border. Karen and Kachin churches in Thailand maintain links with congregations on the Burmese side.

Plate 10.8 Young recruits for the Karen rebel army (in an open field)

Plate 10.9 Karen children dancing in rebel camp near the Thai border

For many years, China supported the CPB insurgency, and the Chinese have maintained close contacts with its successor armies, the UWSA as well as the other three components of the former communist army. Despite their involvement in the drug trade, the UWSA and its allies have been able to buy construction materials, machinery, petrol, food and even weapons from China. Burma's government has not protested against this, because since 1988 China has been the SLORC/SPDC's foremost foreign ally – and supplier of military hardware. In order to counter China's influence, India gave some support to the KIA in the early 1990s, but that ceased when the Kachins made peace with Rangoon in 1993–4.

With the end of the Cold War and the communist threat in the region, it should not be too difficult to undertake a thorough, objective study of the Burmese civil war, free of Cold War considerations, with the aim of finding a lasting solution, though such a study would still have to be undertaken outside Burma itself. The shaky business deals the ruling military has reached with some rebel groups hardly serve as models for such a solution: these agreements have merely frozen the ethnic problems without addressing the underlying issues that caused the minorities to take up arms in the first place.

Further, in Burma, the ethnic conflict is closely linked to the war on drugs. No anti-drug policy in Burma has any chance of success unless it is linked to a real political solution to the conflict and a meaningful democratic process in Rangoon. The alternative is continuing ethnic strife, which will keep the drugs flowing – and the country will remain a social, economic and political basket case.

Notes

All Myanmar/Burma pictures copyright Hseng Noung Lintner.

1 Col. Henry Yule and A.C. Burnell, *Hobson-Jobson: A Glossary of Anglo-Indian Words and Phrases, and of Kindred Terms, Etymological, Historical, Geographical and Discursive*, New Delhi: Munishiram Manoharlal Publishers, 1979 (new edition edited by William Crooke), p. 131.

2 Josef Silverstein, *Burmese Politics: The Dilemma of National Unity*, New Brunswick, NJ: Rutgers University Press, 1980, p. 9.

3 Silverstein, *Burmese Politics*, p. 14.

4 Harry Marshall, *The Karens of Burma*, New York: AMS Press, reprint, 1980 (original published by the University of Columbus, OH, 1922), pp. 5–6.

5 Silverstein, *Burmese Politics*, p. 16.

6 J. Russel Andrus, *Burmese Economic Life*, Stanford, CA: Stanford University Press, 1948, p. 27.

7 For a succinct history of Shan–Burman relations during the British era, see Chao Tzang Yawnghwe, *The Shan of Burma: Memoirs of a Shan Exile*. Singapore: Institute of Southeast Asian Studies, 1987, pp. 45–82.

8 Chao Tzang Yawnghwe, *The Shan of Burma*. See also Bertil Lintner, 'The Shans and the Shan State of Burma', *Contemporary Southeast Asia*, March 1984, vol. 5, no. 4.

9 For a comprehensive study of the Kachins, see Edward R. Leach, *Political Systems of Highland Burma: A Study of Kachin Social Structure*, London: G. Bell, 1954.

10 For a detailed history of the Kachin Baptist church, see Herman G. Tegenfeldt, *A Century of Growth: The Kachin Baptist Church of Burma*, South Pasadena, CA: William Carey Library, 1974.

11 H.N.C. Stevenson, *The Hill Peoples of Burma*, Calcutta: Longmans & Green, 1945, p. 15.

12 For a description of the Burmese Nagas, see Bertil Lintner, *Land of Jade: A Journey through Insurgent Burma*, Edinburgh and Bangkok: Kiscadale and White Lotus, 1991, pp. 87–8.

13 For a comprehensive account of the Rohingyas and other Muslim communities in Burma, see Moshe Yegar, *The Muslims of Burma: A Study of a Minority Group*, Wiesbaden: Otto Harrassowitz, 1972.

14 For a comprehensive history of the Indian community in Burma, see Nalini Ranjan Charkravarti, *The Indian Minority in Burma: The Rise and Decline of an Immigrant Community*, London: Oxford University Press, 1971.

15 For the full text of the Panglong Agreement, see Silverstein, *Burmese Politics*, pp. 107–8.

16 *The Constitution of the Union of Burma*, Rangoon: Supdt., Govt. Printing and Stationery, 1947, pp. 56–7 (Chapter X: Right of Secession).

17 Information supplied by Col. Michael Bremridge, British Defence Attaché in Rangoon, February 1989.

18 For an account of the 1988–9 pro-democracy uprising, see Bertil Lintner, *Outrage: Burma's Struggle for Democracy*, London and Bangkok: White Lotus, 1990.

19 For an account of the 1989 CPB mutiny, see Bertil Lintner, *The Rise and Fall of the Communist Party of Burma*, Ithaca, NY: Cornell Southeast Asia Program, 1990.

20 Gustaaf Houtman, *Mental Culture in Burmese Crisis Politics*, Tokyo: Institute for the Study of Languages and Cultures of Asia and Africa, Tokyo University of Foreign Studies, 1999, pp. 143–5.

21 *To Stand and be Counted: The Suppression of Burma's Members of Parliament*, a report compiled by the All-Burma Students Democratic Front, Bangkok 1998.

22 Programme of the National League for Democracy, mimeo, 1989, pp. 2–3.

23 *Irrawaddy*, April 2002, vol. 10, no. 3, p. 9.

24 *Population Census*, Rangoon: Ministry of Home and Religious Affairs, 1983.

Further reading

Boucaud, André and Louis Boucaud, *Burma's Golden Triangle: On the Trail of the Opium Warlords* (Hong Kong: Asia 2000, 1988). A personal account of several treks together with Karenni, Karen, Pa-O and Shan rebels.

Elliott, Patricia, *The White Umbrella* (Bangkok: Post Books, 1999). A biography of Sao Nang Hearn Kham, the widow of Burma's first president, Shan leader Sao Shwe Thaike.

Falla, Jonathan, *True Love and Bartholomew: Rebels on the Burmese Border* (Cambridge: Cambridge University Press, 1991). A detailed study of the culture, history and rebel movement of the Karen of Burma.

Houtman, Gustaaf, *Metal Culture in Burmese Crisis Politics* (Tokyo: Institute for the Study of Languages and Cultures of Asia and Africa, Tokyo University of Foreign Studies, 1999). A thesis discussing Burma's ethnic problems and the meaning of the name change of the country in 1989.

Leach, Edward R., *Political Systems of Highland Burma* (London: The London School of Economics and Political Science, 1954; revised edn 1964). A study of Kachin social structure.

Lintner, Bertil, *Land of Jade: A Journey through Insurgent Burma* (Edinburgh: Kiscadale Publications; Bangkok: White Lotus, 1990). An account of an eighteen-month trek, from October 1985 to April 1987, through rebel-held areas in Sagaing Division, Kachin State and Shan State. Second edn: *Land of Jade: A Journey from India through Northern Burma to China* (Bangkok: White Orchid Press, 1996).

Lintner, Bertil, *The Kachin: Lords of Burma's Northern Frontier* (Chiang Mai: Teak House Publications, 1997). A portrait of the Kachin (Jinghpaw, Jingpo or Singpo) of northern Burma, western Yunnan and northeastern India.

Lintner, Bertil, *Burma in Revolt: Opium and Insurgency Since 1948* (Chiang Mai: Silkworm Books, 1999). A history of Burma's ethnic strife and the intertwined opium problem.

Marshall, Andrew, *The Trouser People* (London and New York: Viking, 2002). A personal account of travels in today's Burma, including visits to the Wa Hills and the Sino-Burmese border.

Milne, Leslie, *The Shans at Home* (New York: Paragon Book Reprint Corp., 1970; first published in 1910). Anthropological notes on Shan customs and traditions.

Mirante, Edith T., *Burmese Looking Glass: A Human Rights Adventure and a Jungle Revolution* (New York: Grove Press, 1993). A lively and very personal account of several trips to rebel bases along the Thai-Burma border.

Saimong Mangrai, Sao, *The Shan States and the British Annexation* (Ithaca, NY: Cornell University Southeast Asia Programme, Data Paper no. 57, 1965). A history of the Shan States written from a Shan viewpoint.

Sargent, Inge, *Twilight over Burma: My Life as a Shan Princess* (Honolulu and Chiang Mai: University of Hawaii Press and Silkworm Books, 1994). A moving book about an Austrian lady who married Sao Kya Hseng, a Shan prince who disappeared after the military takeover in 1962.

Silverstein, Josef, *Burmese Politics: The Dilemma of National Unity* (New Brunswick, NJ: Rutgers University Press, 1980). An analysis of Burma's struggle for political unity up to the 1962 military takeover.

Smith, Martin, *Burma: Insurgency and the Politics of Ethnicity* (London: Zed Press, 1991, 2nd edn 1999). An outstanding study of Burma's civil war and ethnic problems.

Thant Myint-U, *The Making of Modern Burma* (Cambridge: Cambridge University Press, 2001). A recent and excellent study of Burma's internal problems.

Tucker, Shelby, *Among Insurgents: Walking through Burma* (London and New York: The Radcliffe Press, 2000). An account of a trek from China through northern Burma to India in 1989.

Tucker, Shelby, *Burma: The Curse of Independence* (London: Pluto Press, 2001). A history of modern Burma, including its ethnic strife.

Yawnghwe, Chao Tzang, *The Shan of Burma: Memoirs of a Shan Exile* (Singapore: Institute of Southeast Asian Studies, 1987). A comprehensive study of the Shan, their history and rebellion against Rangoon.

11 Cambodia

Jan Ovesen and Ing-Britt Trankell

Cambodia is the country in Southeast Asia with the smallest ethnic minority population, both relatively and in absolute numbers. Among about 10 million inhabitants almost 90 per cent are ethnic Khmer.[1] Khmer dominance is ancient: for the Khmer, the kingdom of Angkor (ninth to fifteenth centuries) still remains very much the exemplary origin both of Khmer civilization and the Cambodian nation.

The ways in which governments, officials and elites in post-colonial Cambodia have perceived and treated the country's non-Khmer ethnic groups reflect an attitude of Khmer supremacy. This attitude is not so much directed against other ethnic groups (except for the Vietnamese), as manifesting a profound ethnocentrism, a conviction that Khmer culture is superior to others. This ethnocentrism puts the Khmer in line with the constructivist view, as opposed to the essentialist (see Chapter 1). Already at independence (1953) it was officially recognized that one could 'become Khmer' (*coul kmae*) by adopting the Khmer language and customs.

The Khmer see themselves as fundamentally agrarian, their primary crop, paddy rice, being not only the mainstay for all but an important symbol of the human condition in general. Consequently, the ideal society is one of rice-farming peasants. It was the Khmer Rouge that most explicitly pursued this ideal, but cities generally do not figure positively in the Khmer imagination. There is an implicit association between urban life and foreign, non-Khmer customs. From a Khmer perspective, the capital Phnom Penh is a place in some sense outside Khmer cultural space and inhabited mainly by 'foreigners'. The traditional 'foreigners' in Cambodia are the Chinese and the Vietnamese, and these have always to a large extent been urban populations. The rural–urban dichotomy is thus a significant dimension of ethnic relations.

Historically Cambodia has felt politically and territorially pressed between its two more powerful neighbours, Siam (Thailand) and Annam (Vietnam). Siamese armies contributed to the fall of Angkor in the late fifteenth century, and Cambodia was effectively under Siamese suzerainty for much of the period after this until becoming a French protectorate in 1863. Thailand temporarily annexed the northwestern provinces of Battambang and Siem Reap (where Angkor is located) during the Second World War; the name Siem Reap means 'Siam conquered', perhaps implying conquered both *by* and *from* Siam.

Nevertheless, since independence, the Cambodian governments and the Khmer educated elite have always regarded Vietnam and the Vietnamese as the big threat to Cambodian political, economic and territorial sovereignty, not Thailand and the Thais. Thus, the Khmer consider the Mekong Delta as *kampuchea krom*, a Cambodian territory unlawfully annexed by Vietnam. The Cambodian border provinces of Prey Veng and Svay Rieng have a significant Vietnamese rice-farming population who have settled ('encroached') in search of land. Vietnamese expansionism is a recurrent theme in Khmer propaganda.

The main cultural divide running through Indochina is that which divides mainland Southeast Asia between the 'Indianized' states of Burma, Thailand, Laos and Cambodia and the 'Sinicized' Vietnam. This cultural divide may explain why the attitude of the Khmer towards the Vietnamese is significantly different from that towards the Thai. So, also culturally speaking, both Vietnamese and Chinese are perceived as foreign. But in contrast to the Chinese, the Vietnamese in Cambodia are regarded by the majority of the Khmer as intruders, whose presence in the country many perceive as a threat to the Khmer-ness of the nation. Although the Vietnamese do not form one coherent ethnic community, the Khmer nationalist elite, who have pursued anti-Vietnamese propaganda since independence, have tended to ignore this fact, and little allowance has been made for the diversity of Vietnamese communities within the ethnic category 'Vietnamese'. Consequently, all members of this category have been victims of violent persecutions in recent Cambodian history.[2]

Ethnic minorities in the postcolonial period

The Kingdom of Cambodia (1953–70)

Besides his concern with territorial independence, Cambodia's first postcolonial ruler, Prince Norodom Sihanouk, launched a Khmer nationalist discourse aiming to promote national unity and counteract the perceived dominance of Vietnamese and Chinese elements. In the 1960s he devised an ethnic classification scheme according to which certain non-Khmer ethnic minorities were included as *bona fide* Khmers. These included, first, the indigenous minority groups of Mon-Khmer and Austronesian speaking uplanders, labelled *Khmer Loeu* ('upland Khmer') and found mainly in the northeastern provinces of Rattanakiri and Mondulkiri. Second, the Muslim Cham group, found in several areas of the central area, was given the label *Khmer Islam*. Third, the ethnic Khmer who live in the Mekong Delta on the other side of the Vietnamese border were rallied to the nationalist cause and called *Khmer Krom* ('lowland Khmer').

This status as 'honorary' Khmers implied not only recognition as part of the national population, but also the obligation eventually to become 'real' Khmers, especially among the uplanders. The aim of elevating the uplanders to *Khmer Loeu* was to create among them a national consciousness to replace their 'group or clan spirit'. To facilitate this process the government invited Khmer peasant and soldier families from the lowlands to settle in the sparsely populated hill areas in the northeast. In return for being allowed to help themselves to land,

Plate 11.1 While the French depicted the indigenous uplanders as 'savages' . . .
Plate 11.2 . . . they were welcomed by Prince Sihanouk into the Kingdom of Cambodia as Khmer Loeu

Source: Both photos courtesy of the National Archives, Phnom Penh.

these 'pioneers' were supposed to provide a good example for the uplanders to follow, such as cultivating paddy and wearing proper clothes. The government also targeted certain upland youths, calling on them to 'persuade their elders to transform their archaic way of life'.[3]

The Chinese and Vietnamese, on the other hand, were 'foreigners', and to distinguish them as such a law was promulgated in 1954 conferring Cambodian citizenship on children at least one of whose parents is a Cambodian citizen, as well as on anyone born in Cambodia after 1954 of parents also born in Cambodia, regardless of their parents' nationality. The law 'excluded from Cambodian nationality ethnic Vietnamese and Chinese residents who were either not born there, were born before 1954, or were born there after 1954 but not of a Cambodia-born parent'.[4] Such people could gain citizenship only by 'becoming Khmer' through undergoing ethnic tests proving their fluency in the Khmer language and their familiarity with Khmer manners, customs and traditions.

The Khmer Republic (1970–5)

Sihanouk's Prime Minister, General Lon Nol, took power through a *coup d'état* in 1970 and declared the Khmer Republic. In terms of policy towards the country's ethnic minorities, Lon Nol continued and greatly intensified the customary anti-Vietnamese sentiments among the Khmer. Lon Nol's combination of anti-communism and anti-Vietnamese policy resulted in a drastic reduction of the Vietnamese minority in Cambodia. Shortly after his takeover, Lon Nol ordered all 'Vietnamese communists' to leave the country within forty-eight hours. This unrealistic command spurred a general pogrom against all Vietnamese on Cambodian soil. Thousands of Vietnamese civilians were massacred and about 200,000 were forcibly repatriated to South Vietnam. In early 1970 the ethnic Vietnamese population in Cambodia was estimated at about 450,000, but five months after the *coup*, a further 100,000 had left the country, reducing the Vietnamese minority to about 140,000.[5]

Lon Nol's paranoid hatred of Vietnam and the Vietnamese was matched by his Khmer chauvinism and inflated sense of Khmer greatness. Having heard of the (linguistic) category Mon-Khmer, he promptly proposed the reversal into 'Khmer-Mon' in order that the rest of the world get their priorities right, and, as Marie Martin relates, 'in a burst of mental confusion the general arrived at the concept of the "Khmer-Mon race". The absurdity reached a pinnacle when he sent a delegation to Burma with the assignment of researching and reporting on the original Khmer-Mon dress'.[6] Lon Nol's attitude towards the Cham minority, on the other hand, was benevolent. In 1971 he proclaimed, in a characteristically muddled racial discourse, that 'the Chams are Malayo-Polynesian Khmer-Mons, thus also of our race but of a mixed culture, slightly differentiated'.[7]

Democratic Kampuchea (1975–9)

The Khmer Rouge regime (1975–8), led by Pol Pot and officially known as Democratic Kampuchea (DK), was responsible for probably the most intensive and terrifying atrocities committed by any political regime against any domestic or foreign group since the Second World War. Most of the just over one million victims – between 80 and 85 per cent – were ethnic Khmer, who constituted, and still constitute, almost 90 per cent of the country's population.[8]

Paradoxically, although the Khmer Rouge revolution represented a frontal attack on many Khmer cultural norms and values, it was also heavily based on Khmer cultural premises.[9] In Pol Pot's mind, the revolutionary reversal of core Khmer values was not only necessary for the exploited peasantry to consolidate its power, but also an instrument in the purification of the Khmer race, primarily from both Vietnamese and European contamination. The revolutionary rhetoric continuously emphasized the return of the original Khmer way of life, and the revolutionary utopia was a communist agrarian state, free of all corrupting foreign influences.

There can be no doubt that the Vietnamese were most viciously persecuted under Pol Pot, with roughly the same kind of fanaticism that Lon Nol had displayed from a very different political position. Within four months after the Khmer Rouge capture of Phnom Penh in April 1975, 150,000 were expelled, not many of the remaining 10,000 or so surviving the regime. When the paranoia of the Khmer Rouge leadership turned inward and the purges of internal enemies began (in 1977), targeted comrades were accused of having 'Khmer bodies but Vietnamese minds'.[10]

The DK regime basically represented a continuation of earlier ones in its attitude towards other ethnic minorities. The indigenous upland minorities in the northeast held a special place in Pol Pot's revolutionary imagination. They were the purest, the least contaminated by foreign influences, their society an example of 'primitive communism'. Pol Pot actually spent a year or so in the late 1960s among these people – who reputedly had to carry him around in a palanquin after the fashion of the French colonialists, since their country had not yet been contaminated with roads. However, Khmer Rouge admiration of the uplanders did not extend to general cultural acceptance and most of their religious institutions, notably animal sacrifices accompanied by enjoying large quantities of rice wine, were rigorously suppressed. Those uplanders who objected were killed.[11]

The People's Republic of Kampuchea (PRK, 1979–89)

When the Vietnamese army took the Cambodian capital Phnom Penh in January 1979, a ten-year period of military and political occupation began. Anti-Vietnamese sentiments disappeared from the official agenda. Article 5 of the PRK Constitution reads:

> The State carries out a policy of unity and equality among the people of all nationalities living in the national community of Kampuchea.
>
> All nationalities must love and help each other. All acts of discrimination against, oppression of and division among the nationalities are prohibited.
>
> The State takes care of ethnic minorities so that they can rise to the common level. The State pays special attention to the development of economy, education, culture, social affairs, health and communications in the mountainous regions and remote areas.[12]

With state help, functioning through Vietnamese technical, political and military assistance, people of all ethnic groups were allowed to return to their home areas and resume a semblance of normal life. As for the indigenous minorities, the PRK government largely continued Sihanouk's line of assimilation and Khmerization. The resolution from a Party conference on policy towards ethnic minorities in 1984 states that 'the minorities are always considered as an integral part of the Kampuchean nation' and they were supposed to show solidarity with the rest of the population in the interest of national defence. They should be introduced to the methods of 'more stable and modern agriculture', and, in line with the regime's general rural policy, they should be 'encouraged to participate in collectivization and to join solidarity groups'. Lowland Khmers should settle among the minorities, facilitating their transformation into 'good Khmers'.[13]

The State of Cambodia (SOC, 1989–93) and UNTAC (1992–3)

When the Vietnamese troops completed withdrawal in 1989, the nation changed its name to the State of Cambodia. There were no changes in policy towards ethnic minorities. All ethnic groups were still obliged to 'love and help one another', and, constitutionally, the minorities were still to be assisted 'so that they may reach the common level'.[14] At the same time, 'the languages and scripts and the morals and customs of ethnic minorities [were to] be respected'.[15] The main novelty was that Buddhism was now the state religion, as it had been up until 1975. The Constitution thus indicated a return to the emphasis on Khmer-ness, since none of the ethnic minorities are Buddhists. One result was that Buddhist temples all over the country were restored, and new ones built.

The 'liberalization' of the economy, combined with the general economic boom in Southeast Asia, led to an unbridled rush to exploit the country's natural resources; 'raw materials, especially timber, were being removed at breakneck pace' from 'the frontier zones . . . in the Northeast',[16] to the detriment of the ecology and possibly the social fabric of the indigenous minority societies. From its bases along the Thai border, the remnants of the Khmer Rouge troops were still an obstacle to security and peace in the country.

At the same time, international efforts were being made to bring enduring peace to the country. The result was the Paris Agreements of 1991, which stipulated a massive intervention by the UN, the United Nations Transitional Authority in Cambodia (UNTAC), leading to elections.

The question of who should vote in the elections was a thorny one, but the Paris Agreements conferred eligibility to vote on every person above the age of 18 who was either born in Cambodia or the child of a person born in Cambodia. This formulation enabled the international community to avoid the problems involved in determining ethnicity, citizenship and nationality in connection with elections.[17] Political participation would not be based on ethnic criteria.

Although the Khmer Rouge, represented by the Party of Democratic Kampuchea (PDK), had signed the Paris Agreements, they refused to demobilize once the UNTAC operation was deployed, and boycotted the elections. Instead they intensified their anti-Vietnamese campaign, presumably in the hope of winning over the other Khmer-nationalist parties. The objective was 'to engender en masse among Khmer a perception of all Vietnamese as not just the racial enemy, but the underlying cause of Cambodia's economic, political and social malaise'.[18] Massacres of Vietnamese peasants by the Khmer Rouge continued, while the Khmer-nationalist parties tacitly consented.[19]

The Kingdom of Cambodia after 1993

After the 1993 general election, which resulted in the coalition government of the Cambodian People's Party (CPP, successor to the Vietnamese-backed People's Revolutionary Party of Kampuchea) and the Sihanoukist royalists, the National Assembly adopted a new Constitution for the Kingdom of Cambodia. As Raoul

Jennar has noted, 'in many ways, the 1993 Constitution acknowledges the reestablishment of the order existing under the Constitution in force in 1953'.[20]

The Constitution says nothing about ethnic minorities. However, it does specify that: 'Every Khmer citizen shall be equal before the law, enjoying the same rights, freedom and fulfilling the same obligations regardless of *race, colour,* sex, *language, religious belief,* political tendency, birth origin, social status, wealth or other status'.[21] Although discrimination against minorities persists, it is not because of the Constitution but because of sociocultural practices.

Overview of contemporary minorities

Ethnic Khmer dominance in Cambodia is strengthened by the very marked identification among the Khmer as being primarily just Khmer. None of the minority categories display a similar inclusiveness with their ascribed ethnic identification. Thus, each of the numerically already insignificant ethnic minority categories is divided into a number of yet smaller groups or communities, making political mobilization along ethnic lines virtually impossible for any of them.

The indigenous upland minorities

Surrounding the flat lowland of central Cambodia are hilly and forested areas, unsuitable for paddy land and inhabited by the geographically marginal indigenous minorities. Today these minorities are mainly found in the northeastern parts of the country. But even the hilly forests of Kampong Thom, the Dangrek mountains in the far north of Siem Reap, and the Cardamom and Elephant mountains in Pursat and Koh Kong are populated by indigenous, Mon-Khmer speaking minorities, most of whom, however, are now presumably in more or less advanced stages of Khmerization. These latter groups include the Kui, the Pear, the Chong, the Samre and the Saoch. Virtually no research has been done on any of these groups. Slightly more attention has been paid to the northeastern minorities. They form part of a larger indigenous cultural area extending from the Boloven plateau (in Laos) in the north, through the Central Highlands of Vietnam to the east, to the Cambodian provinces of Rattanakiri and Mondulkiri.

The number of indigenous minority people in Cambodia is estimated at a total of about 100,000, of whom about 75 per cent are found in the northeastern provinces, Rattanakiri and Mondulkiri.[22] The main groups are the Austronesian- (Chamic-) speaking Jarai (in Rattanakiri) and the Mon-Khmer- (Bahnaric-) speaking Brao and Tampuan (in Rattanakiri) and Phnong (in Mondulkiri). Each of these groups number between 15,000 and 25,000 people. The Brao are divided into what is usually regarded as three separate ethnic groups: the Brao proper, the Kreung and the Kravet.

Apart from major linguistic differences (Mon-Khmer and Austronesian languages, respectively), the groups differ with respect to habitation and kinship organization. The Jarai and the Tampuan traditionally live in communal longhouses, several of which make up their fairly large villages; the others live in individual family houses arranged in a circle around the village communal hall. The Jarai and Tampuan have matrilineal descent and are organized in exogamous matriclans, while descent among the others is cognatic.[23]

Such ethnic and ethnolinguistic differences, however, are minor, in view of the overall social and cultural similarities between the various groups. They all subsist primarily on swidden cultivation of upland rice, supplemented by hunting and gathering. Until recently, swidden cultivation was sustainable, but population increase in combination with settlements by ethnic Khmer, and, most notably, logging and the establishment of palm oil and coffee plantations, have forced people to reduce the fallow periods, with the result that soil fertility is continually being diminished. In spite of the clan organization of the Jarai and Tampuan, traditionally there are no sociopolitical units beyond the local (village) community among any of the groups. The local community, on the other hand, is marked by strong bonds of social and spiritual solidarity. The cohesive nature of the local community is related to the subsistence mode. Each community traditionally occupied a common territory which they used for cultivation, gathering and hunting, in close cooperation with the spirits of the forests, mountains, streams and ancestors, to ensure the prosperity of the community. Prosperity is a central notion in the indigenous worldview, and it depends on the spirits' blessing. The spirits, in their turn, bestow their blessings if they themselves are happy. Feasts make them happy, so the indigenous cultivation cycles are punctuated by feasting during which buffaloes, pigs and chicken are sacrificed and lavish amounts of rice wine and liquor are consumed, to enhance the prosperity and well-being of both humans and spirits.

Although the spirits responsible for the prosperity of the community have traditionally been local, the uplanders are by no means parochial in their recognition of what spiritual powers may bring prosperity. Jonsson reports that at a major feast in his research area in 1992, King Sihanouk was among the spirits invoked.[24] This invocation, of course, reflects the increasing incorporation of the uplanders into the national society, which has alerted them to the material benefits accruing from national and donor-aided development. In the words of Frédéric Bourdier:

> the wish of the indigenous minorities is to preserve those elements of their life style that give them satisfaction, to have access to certain consumer goods, to be relieved of all economic insecurity, to live a peaceful life in relative freedom in the midst of a large kin group.[25]

To this end, they are quite prepared to accommodate certain elements of Khmer 'civilization', such as learning the Khmer language, wearing modern clothes, living a sedentary life and engaging in paddy cultivation where possible. But 'development' is inevitably channelled through Khmer cultural premises, and the Khmer are a lot more culturally absolutist than the uplanders. It never occurs to even the most well-intentioned Khmer, says Bourdier, that the 'uncivilized' uplanders may themselves have something to contribute to the development of their provinces. Their system of swidden cultivation is a priori deemed harmful to the environment, and their feasts are seen as wasteful – although, as Bourdier remarks, they are important occasions for the intensification of social relations and economically no more extravagant than the Khmer Buddhist ceremonies.[26]

The international aid community also tends to ignore the possibility that indigenous society may have positive contributions to development. The nation-wide programme for rural development, 'Seila', is a case in point. It is carried out – so far in eleven of the country's eighteen provinces – through the cooperation of a number of national ministries, with the assistance of the UNDP (among others) and to a large extent funded by international and bilateral aid organizations. The aim of 'Seila' is to create a decentralized structure for rural development planning and implementation. To this end, Village Development Committees are created whose task is to identify local development needs and submit project proposals to the district and provincial authorities. The committees replace the traditional system, with its high degree of community solidarity under the leadership of a council of elder men recognized as the social and spiritual authority, and are tantamount to reinventing a foreign version of the wheel to negotiate local terrain. The new method also sends the message to the uplanders that 'development' is something that can only happen through outside intervention, and that the 'language' of development is linguistically foreign (Khmer) as well as foreign to the indigenous cosmology, no matter how well the latter is geared to current concerns for sustainability and natural resource management. Among the Tampuan, for example, the introduction of new decision-making institutions has weakened community solidarity in general. 'Decisions to sell land . . . have been made individually by households without consultations. . . . This has eroded the communal approach to decision-making that has characterized Tampuan villages for ages.'[27]

The Chinese

A Chinese population has been present in Cambodia since at least Angkor. Most settled in the country as traders. Under French colonial rule, the demand for cheap labour led to increased Chinese immigration, primarily of plantation workers. In the early twentieth century, the French began to encourage the immigration also of Chinese women, contributing further to the vitality of distinct Chinese communities. Local Chinese communities were formed, not only in Phnom Penh, but also in the provinces, notably in Kampot, Kampong Cham and Battambang. Often these communities ran their own schools and published newspapers and journals in their respective dialects. At the same time, Cambodian Chinese have adapted to Khmer culture; intermarriage has been frequent. Today, as Penny Edwards has noted:

> most Chinese in Cambodia maintain their historical linkage to China through ancestor worship, embrace Khmer culture through attendance at [Buddhist

Plate 11.3 The Chinese have adapted to the Khmer Buddhist culture: Buddhist monks reciting over the coffin at a Chinese funeral in Cambodia (Photograph by Heng Kim Van, 2001.)

temples] and celebration of Khmer festivals, and maintain their ties to the Cambodian landscape through burial rites and worship of local territorial gods.[28]

Traditionally, the Chinese have totally dominated trade and commerce in Cambodia. But significant numbers have engaged in farming, notably non-paddy cultivation of vegetables, fruit, cotton and tobacco. Both the Khmer and the French felt paddy farming was associated exclusively with the Khmer, to the extent that in 1929 the French passed a law banning Chinese from owning paddy land. This legislation made still more Chinese turn to commerce.

In spite of having been very well integrated in Cambodian society, the Chinese suddenly became 'foreign residents' in Sihanouk's Khmer nationalist state. During the DK period, the Chinese suffered more than the average population, not because of their ethnicity, but because about two-thirds of them were urban dwellers, who were sent to work in the countryside and treated harshly. The DK regime employed numerous Chinese advisers from the People's Republic, but these new arrivals displayed little ethnic solidarity with the Cambodian Chinese, whom they scorned as evil capitalists.[29] Immediately after the Vietnamese invasion in 1979, many Chinese resurfaced as traders. But as the Vietnamese clamped down on urban markets, many Chinese made common cause with nationalist Khmers and fled across the Thai border.[30] After the Vietnamese withdrawal, the rights of the Chinese to observe their religious customs and celebrate their festivals were restored, and today 'ethnic Chinese enjoy greater freedom of cultural expression . . . than under any of the regimes in power from 1970 to 1993'.[31]

The current Chinese population in Cambodia is estimated at between 300,000 and 350,000, about 200,000 of whom are living in Phnom Penh.[32]

The Vietnamese

Most Khmer regard the Vietnamese in Cambodia as intruders. The Vietnamese do not form one single coherent ethnic community, whether in terms of occupation or the degree of adaptation to Khmer society. Nevertheless, the Khmer nationalist elite, who have pursued anti-Vietnamese propaganda since independence, have made little allowance for the diversity of Vietnamese communities within the ethnic category 'Vietnamese', and in recent Cambodian history the violence directed against them has often been indiscriminate.

The rice-farming settlers in the southeast, mentioned above, form one of the three main groups of Vietnamese in Cambodia. Another consists of primarily fisherfolk settled along the main waterways, the Mekong and Tonle Sap, often in 'floating villages'. These communities are long-established in the country and fairly well integrated in Cambodian society. Most are bilingual in Vietnamese and Khmer, and many frequent Khmer Buddhist temples. Their relations with the local Khmer population are generally friendly, but when anti-Vietnamese sentiments have been stirred up by nationalist propaganda, even these Vietnamese have been attacked.[33] The third group consists of the urban population who are either long-time residents or migrant workers. During the colonial period the French employed a fair number of Vietnamese as lower officials, believing them to be more suited to bureaucratic work than the Khmer. The migrant workers are mainly unskilled labourers in construction enterprises, and in the post-UNTAC period a substantial number of young females work as prostitutes.

The Cham

The name Cham indicates a purported origin in the 'Hinduized' kingdom of Champa that occupied the coast of present-day Vietnam until the Vietnamese destroyed its capital in 1471, reducing it to its southernmost principalities.[34] At this time the Cham underwent a gradual and partial conversion to Islam through the influence of the coastal trade of Arab, Persian and Indian merchants.

The ethnic label Cham in Cambodia covers virtually all the country's Muslims. They number about 230,000, many of them traders. The Khmer view the Cham with apprehension because of a reputation for possessing strong magic.[35] At the same time, both Khmer and Cham believe the latter belong firmly in Cambodian society, and as a well established Cambodian minority they are 'good to think with', as their land was once conquered by the Vietnamese and they thus exemplify a fate that many Khmer fear may one day become Cambodia's.

Three separate groups may be distinguished within the Cham ethnic category.[36] The Cham proper trace their ancestry to the Champa kingdom, but emphasize their religion (Islam) rather than their historical origins as their main defining

Plate 11.4 In the spirit possession cult among the Jahed Cham in Cambodia, the life at the ancient Champa court is reenacted in the ceremonies (Photograph by Ing-Britt Trankell, 2002.)

feature. Most still speak the Cham language, which belongs to the Austronesian family, but all are bilingual in Khmer. They are found mainly in Kampong Cham, Kampot and north of Phnom Penh.

A second group is referred to as 'Chvea', which is the Khmer word for 'Java', suggesting a penultimate origin in the Malay-Indonesian area. Today they speak Khmer. They prefer to call themselves not 'Chvea' but 'Khmer Islam' – stressing both their linguistic and national belonging and their separate religion, rather than their 'foreign' origin.

Both these groups are recipients of various forms of Islamic aid from the Middle East (Saudi Arabia, Kuwait and the Arab Emirates) as well as from Malaysia. The aid consists of schoolbooks and religious literature in Arabic, and contributions to building schools, mosques and wells. It also involves annual travel funds for some prominent members of local communities to go on the pilgrimage to Mecca. The Cham and Chvea welcome this attention from the world Islamic community, feeling it gives international recognition to their importance as Cambodian Muslims.

The third group of Cham are the Jahed.[37] Although Muslims, they identify themselves primarily in terms of their historical origins in the Champa kingdom. Their ancestors formed part of an exodus from a Champa principality after its ruler's defeat by the Vietnamese in 1692. Today they number about 23,000 people, all speaking Cham, but most being bilingual in Khmer. In terms of religion, the Jahed belong to a minority within the Muslim population. Their somewhat unorthodox version of Islam (superimposed on a basically Hindu type of cosmology and influenced by Sufi traditions) sets them apart from the other Muslims groups in Cambodia, the Chvea and the Cham. Their possession cult featuring the spirits of their royal ancestors in Champa still flourishes, another sign of their unorthodox approach to Islam.[38]

The Jahed are adamant in following the Muslim customs they have preserved from Champa. Central among these are the weekly prayer meetings at the mosque (instead of the five daily prayers of orthodox Muslims), the use of the Cham language (rather than Arabic) for prayers, and the preservation of their religious literature in the Cham script. In the long run it is doubtful that these traditions will survive, as orthodox Islamic missionaries exert pressure through promises of financial support for mosque-building and distribution of cheaply printed prayer books in Arabic.

Conclusions

In the late 1990s we were sitting with a group of young Khmer academics in Phnom Penh. The television in the background was showing CNN financial news, reporting that the shares of one company after another were down. One of our friends said, 'Yes, and Cambodia down!' The others applauded him, both for his wit and the pertinence of his comment. We were surprised, because this group of young people had grown up under the Khmer Rouge and Vietnamese occupation but had witnessed a very substantial influx of foreign aid and investments since 1993, giving them a greatly improved standard of living that included university education, making contact with international scholars, and changing their bicycles for motorbikes. A certain democratization had occurred, and construction of Buddhist temples was booming, indicating a cultural revival. Nevertheless the feeling was that the country was going down the drain.

This anecdote illustrates the general tendency among the Khmer to view their culture and society as having followed a path of continual decline since the glorious days of Angkor, a path that will eventually lead to Cambodia's territorial and cultural extinction. The French probably contributed to implanting this attitude. Their orientalist scholars documented the greatness of Angkorian achievements and paternalistically portrayed contemporary Khmer as descendants of a magnificent civilization, with a nature that is not only gentle and kind but also docile and lazy, so that they needed French protection against the Vietnamese. But for such gloomy sentiments to take root among the population, it is reasonable to assume that they also resonated with indigenous Khmer attitudes. Michael Vickery has pointed out that Cambodia sought French protection against the Vietnamese in the nineteenth century, 'even before the French were ready to impose it';[39] and he suggests that deeply ingrained sociopolitical structures of patronage may explain what he sees as traditional Khmer lack of self-reliance. In any case, postcolonial Khmer nationalists have adapted this view for their own purposes, with the result that 'giving Cambodian intellectuals (and semi-intellectuals, like Sihanouk, Lon Nol and Pol Pot) a grandiose, unusable past produced among them a *folie de grandeur*'.[40]

Given the comparatively modest size of Cambodia's minority population, it may seem a paradox that the dominant ethnic group is continually feeling both politically and culturally threatened. But since the historical Angkor kingdom was transformed (with French help) into the foundation myth of the nation, the postcolonial rulers, in their delusions of grandeur, have all had the ambition of restoring their Khmer nation to Angkorian magnificence. One of the ways of attempting to realize this imagined community has been the Khmerization of certain minorities and the externalization of certain others. So far, all rulers have failed in this grandiose ambition, and their failure has been interpreted as a confirmation of Khmer political and cultural decline, helped along by the perceived conspiracies of those whom they have themselves externalized.

Notes

1 Statistics on ethnic groups in Cambodia are unreliable. In 1995, the Ministry of the Interior published a list of twenty ethnic minority groups numbering a total of 442,699 persons, but grossly underestimating the number of Chinese and Vietnamese (47,000 and 95,600 respectively). If we replace these numbers with those of independent estimates (about 300,000 and 500,000 respectively), we arrive at a minority population of 11.4 per cent. Cf. Pen Dareth, 'Introduction', in *Interdisciplinary Research on Ethnic Groups in Cambodia*, mimeo, Phnom Penh: Center for Advanced Study, 1996, p. 13.

2 Jay Jordens, 'Persecution of Cambodia's ethnic Vietnamese communities during and since the UNTAC period', in S. Heder and J. Ledgerwood (eds), *Propaganda, Politics, and Violence in Cambodia: Democratic Transition under United Nations Peace-keeping*, New York: M.E. Sharpe, 1996, pp. 134–58.

3 Joanna White, 'The indigenous highlanders of the Northeast: An uncertain future', in *Interdisciplinary Research on Ethnic Groups in Cambodia*, Phnom Penh: Center for Advanced Study, 1996, p. 344.

4 Steve Heder and Judy Ledgerwood, 'Politics of violence: An introduction', in Heder and Ledgerwood (eds), *Propaganda, Politics, and Violence in Cambodia*, pp. 22–3.

5 Ben Kiernan, *The Pol Pot Regime: Race, Power and Genocide in Cambodia under the Khmer Rouge, 1975–79*, New Haven, CT: Yale University Press, 1996, p. 296.

6 Marie Martin, *Cambodia: A Shattered Society*, Berkeley: University of California Press, 1994, p. 130.

7 Martin, *Cambodia*, p. 130.

8 The exact number of victims is impossible to determine, even for demographers; see Patrick Heuveline, 'Approaches to measuring genocide: Excess mortality during the Khmer Rouge period', in D. Chirot and M. Seligman (eds), *Ethnopolitical Warfare: Causes, Consequences, and Possible Solutions*, Washington, DC: American Psychological Association, 2000, pp. 93–108. The figure of 1.05 million deaths that can be directly attributed to the terror measures by the regime, excluding demographically normal deaths due to illness and old age, has been suggested by Judith Banister and Paige

Johnson, 'After the nightmare: The population of Cambodia', in B. Kiernan (ed.), *Genocide and Democracy in Cambodia*, New Haven, CT: Yale University Southeast Asian Studies, Monograph No. 41, 1993, pp. 65–139.

9 See François Ponchaud, 'Social change in the vortex of revolution', in K.D. Jackson (ed.), *Cambodia 1975–1978: Rendezvous with Death*, Princeton, NJ: Princeton University Press, 1989, pp. 151–77.

10 Henri Locard, *Le 'Petit Livre Rouge' de Pol Pot: Les paroles de l'Angkar*, Paris: L'Harmattan, 1996, pp. 139–44.

11 Officially, the death toll for Rattanakiri province was 3,913, but it may well have been very much higher; Kiernan, *The Pol Pot Regime*, pp. 302–9.

12 Raoul Jennar, *The Cambodian Constitutions (1953–1993)*, Bangkok: White Lotus, 1995, p. 93.

13 Michael Vickery, *Kampuchea: Politics, Economics and Society*, London: Pinter Publishers, 1986, pp. 167–8.

14 Jennar, *The Cambodian Constitutions*, p. 113.

15 Ibid.

16 David Chandler, *A History of Cambodia*, 2nd edn, Chiang Mai: Silkworm Books, 1996, p. 237.

17 Heder and Ledgerwood, 'Politics of violence', pp. 23–4.

18 Jordens, 'Persecution of Cambodia's ethnic Vietnamese', p. 139.

19 Ibid., pp. 139–41.

20 Jennar, *The Cambodian Constitutions*, p. 1.

21 Ibid., p. 12, emphasis added.

22 This is the estimate by Frédéric Bourdier, 'Relations interethniques et spécificité des populations indigènes du Cambodge', in *Interdisciplinary Research on Ethnic Groups in Cambodia*, mimeo, Phnom Penh: Center for Advanced Study, 1996, p. 389. The government's list gives a total of 70,000.

23 See White, 'The indigenous highlanders of the Northeast'.

24 Hjorleifur Jonsson, 'Dead headmen: Histories and communities in the Southeast Asian hinterland', in I.-B. Trankell and L. Summers (eds), *Facets of Power and Its Limitations: Political Culture in Southeast Asia*, Uppsala: Uppsala Studies in Cultural Anthropology, No. 24, 1998, pp. 191–212.

25 Bourdier, 'Relations interethniques', p. 426.

26 Ibid.

27 John P. McAndrew, 'Indigenous adaptation to a rapidly changing economy: The experience of two Tampuan villages in Northeast Cambodia', *Bulletin of Concerned Asian Scholars*, 2000, vol. 32, no. 4, p. 47.

28 Penny Edwards, 'Ethnic Chinese in Cambodia', in *Interdisciplinary Research on Ethnic Groups in Cambodia*, mimeo, Phnom Penh: Center for Advanced Study, Phnom Penh, 1996, p. 110.

29 Ibid., pp. 140–3.

30 Steven Heder, *Kampuchean Occupation and Resistance*, Bangkok: Asian Studies Monographs No. 27, Institute of Asian Studies, Chulalongkorn University, 1980, pp. 23–5.

31 Edwards, 'Ethnic Chinese in Cambodia', p. 165.

32 Ibid., p. 109.

33 Jordens, 'Persecution of Cambodia's ethnic Vietnamese', p. 156.

34 Po Dharma, 'The history of Champa', in Emmanuel Guillon (ed.), *Cham Art*, Bangkok: River Books, 2001, pp. 14–27.

35 Michael Vickery, *Cambodia 1975–1982*, Boston, MA: South End Press, 1984, pp. 181–2.

36 William Collins, 'The Chams of Cambodia', in *Interdisciplinary Research on Ethnic Groups in Cambodia*, mimeo, Phnom Penh: Center for Advanced Study, 1996, pp. 15–107.

37 The authors have done anthropological fieldwork among the Jahed intermittently between 1996 and 2002.

38 Ing-Britt Trankell, 'Songs of our spirits: Possession and historical imagination among the Cham in Cambodia', *Asian Ethnicity*, February 2003, vol. 4, no. 1.
39 Vickery, *Cambodia 1975–1982*, pp. 13–14.
40 David Chandler, *Facing the Cambodian Past*, Chiang Mai: Silkworm Books, 1996, p. 316.

Further reading

Because of the turbulent political history of Cambodia since the 1970s, very little research relating to ethnic relations has been done. The only recent and comprehensive overview of the country's ethnic groups was a study carried out in 1995–6 by the Center for Advanced Study in Phnom Penh, on the initiative of the United Nations High Commission for Refugees; unfortunately this study was never properly published and is available only in mimeographed form, as *Interdisciplinary Research on Ethnic Groups in Cambodia* (Phnom Penh: Center for Advanced Study, 1996). Book-length studies of particular ethnic groups are equally scarce; the Chinese have been studied by William Willmott, *The Political Structure of the Chinese Community in Cambodia* (London: Athlone Press, 1970). A historical study of the Khmer is Ian Mabbett and David Chandler, *The Khmers* (Chiang Mai: Silkworm Books, 1995). Studies of Cambodia's political history, on the other hand, are numerous, not least on the postcolonial period. A general study is David Chandler, *A History of Cambodia* (Boulder, CO: Westview Press, 1992). Among the several studies of the Khmer Rouge period and its aftermath are Ben Kiernan, *The Pol Pot Regime: Race, Power and Genocide in Cambodia under the Khmer Rouge, 1975–79* (New Haven, CT: Yale University Press, 1996) and Michael Vickery, *Cambodia 1975–1982* (Boston, MA: South End Press, 1984). A brief overview of contemporary society is Jan Ovesen, Ing-Britt Trankell and Joakim Öjendal, *When Every Household is an Island: Social Organization and Power Structures in Rural Cambodia* (Uppsala Research Reports in Cultural Anthropology, 1996).

12 Laos

Minorities

Grant Evans

Laos is one of the most ethnically diverse countries in mainland Southeast Asia. A quick look at Map 2 (p. xviii) tells us why. Laos lies between the major states of the region: China on its northern border, Vietnam to the east, Cambodia to the far south, Thailand to the south and west, and Burma in the northwest. Populations from all of these neighbours overlap into Laos. Unlike these other countries, the lowland, ethnic Lao after whom the country is named, do not constitute an overwhelming majority of the population. The 1995 census shows the Lao making up around 2.4 million of a total population of just over 4.5 million, that is, just over half the population. If, however, an ethno-linguistic classification is used – lumping together all speakers of Tai dialects, of which Lao is one – then the Tai-Lao group rises to just over 3 million, or just over two-thirds of the population. By contrast, in all the neighbouring countries the dominant ethnic group – Vietnamese, Chinese, Thai, Cambodian, Burmese – make up 80 per cent of the population or more. The balance between the different ethnic groups in Laos is therefore unusual, with political attractions to particular ways of drawing the ethnic map.

History

For centuries the region was dominated by Theravada Buddhist kingdoms that waxed and waned until the idea of national states took hold in the nineteenth century, largely in response to pressures from European colonial powers.

Culturally the minorities in Laos apparently fall outside the framework of these Theravada Buddhist kingdoms. However, some of them, such as those around Luang Prabang or in Champassak, played a central role in various state rituals presided over by a Theravada Buddhist king or prince.[1] Besides the minorities directly caught up in traditional Lao state ritual there may also be important symbolic congruities between Buddhist polities and some of the upland societies. The overthrow of the monarchy in Laos in 1975, however, gutted the traditional symbolic forms of integration, with only less encompassing symbols of Lao nationalism substituted.

French colonialism (1893–1953) brought with it the trappings of the modern state, which demands much greater control over its citizenry than any pre-

Plate 12.1 Xieng Khoang Province felt the brunt of the war before 1975, as did the minorities living there. Since then, however, bomb casings have been used to build fences, as in this Hmong village

modern state. This often upset traditional arrangements, sometimes causing revolts. These revolts, however, were not 'anti-colonial' in any simple sense. For example, a 1914 revolt by Haw Chinese traders against the French occurred because the latter were trying to enforce their monopoly on the opium trade.

The Hmong were relative newcomers to Laos, their migrations beginning in the early nineteenth century, and therefore their growing presence finally demanded a redistribution of power in the highlands, which the French facilitated. They were also important economically because they grew opium. The centre of Hmong population was Xieng Khoang Province, and a dispute among clans there would ultimately lead one side into the arms of the Lao communists and the others to support the Royal Lao Government (RLG).

As the new Lao state took shape, the administrative integration of this important highland population gathered pace. In 1946 Touby Lyfoung became the assistant governor of the province, while in 1947 his brother Toulia became one of the province's representatives in the new National Assembly. Touby regarded the granting of citizenship to the Hmong in the 1947 Constitution as truly momentous. In 1965 he even became a member of King Sisavang Vatthana's Council. He encouraged Hmong participation in Lao national and annual festivals, and in particular the learning of Lao language and education. While social and cultural change among the Hmong accelerated in the 1950s, including the influence of Christian missionaries, it was not traumatic.

The war that swept through the highlands of Laos in the 1960s, and Xieng Khoang in particular, not only severely upset the highland habitat, but also led to high casualties among the minorities. One Hmong soldier, Vang Pao, rose to the rank of general and he and his multi-ethnic troops, many of them irregulars, spearheaded fighting against the Lao communists, and in particular North Vietnamese regulars sent against them. The military defeat of the RLG by the communists caused hundreds of thousands of minorities to flee as refugees after 1975.

Policy

There was no sharp break between the RLG and the Lao People's Democratic Republic (LPDR) on minority policy. Both regimes accorded minorities equal citizenship rights, and both regimes asserted that Laos was a unitary state made up of many ethnic minorities. However, with the overthrow of the monarchy, state propaganda has more forcefully proclaimed that the state is made up of all the minorities, 'Lao of all ethnicities'.

Yet, from 1975 to 1991 the new regime had no Constitution, and so minority rights or any other basic rights were not enshrined anywhere. Policies were elaborated primarily through speeches of party leaders and party statements. When proclaimed, the Constitution reserved no special rights for minorities.

The LPDR's attitude towards its minorities has been guided by orthodox communist views as transmitted to it by its main mentor, Vietnam. The key statement on minorities was given by Kaysone Phomvihane, Secretary General of the Lao People's Revolutionary Party, on 15 June 1981, later published as a booklet. This attempt to present a theoretical history of minority issues is, of course, a Marxist-Leninist view of the evolution of 'ethnic groups' and 'nations', whose line is that class lies at the bottom of ethnic problems:

> In every nation which has many nationalities the controlling class will come from the nationality which has progressed most quickly by oppressing the working people of all nationalities, the ethnicity that progresses slowly, which happens to all those developing small nationalities, have to struggle against the oppression of the larger ones. . . . The real cause of nationality problems is social class. . . . Each social class has their own aims and outlook and we need to realise this if we are to understand nationality problems. . . . The capitalists have divided the world into two types of nationality, such as the ruling nationality and the slave nationality. They think that the ruling nationality is 'precious and brilliant', and are the representatives of all that is 'civilized', as for the slave nationalities they are 'low and backward', and not able to be civilized.[2]

By contrast, he says, the socialist countries respect equality and, unlike the imperialists and feudalists, they promote solidarity rather than policies of divide and rule. A key issue for the LPDR was how to create a sense of national unity.

Plate 12.2 On 2 December 2000 the LPDR celebrated 25 years in power. Here a minority militia marches in the parade. On the left are generic southern 'Lao Thueng', in the middle generic northern 'Lao Theung', and on the right White Hmong whose dress has become generic for 'Lao Soung' in state representations of minorities

At the centre of this stands the ethnic Tai-Lao because they are the largest group in the country, and they also have the 'highest cultural development'.[3] Therefore:

> Lao culture must be the basic culture shared by all the ethnicities, and must be the one to provide the connections for the exchange of culture between all the ethnicities; spoken and written Lao is the common language and written Lao is the regular writing of all the ethnic groups; nevertheless, each ethnic group should still preserve its spoken language, and their separate customs.[4]

The most obvious Lao departure from communist practice elsewhere is the absence of autonomous regions for minorities. This idea emerged as a reluctant concession to Marxist-Leninist nationalities theory in states clearly dominated by one ethnic group – the Han in China, the Kinh in Vietnam. In China these autonomous areas remained in the firm grip of the Communist Party, and therefore under the clear control of the dominant ethnic group. In Vietnam autonomous regions were established in North Vietnam but abolished upon unification in 1976.

Kaysone and his comrades, on the other hand, were acutely aware that the ethnic Lao have no overwhelming majority in Laos. Furthermore, Kaysone and the LPRP were under no pressure from the Vietnamese to adopt a policy of autonomous regions. Indeed, given the ethnic distribution in Laos and the relative weakness of the state, they would have been seen as a potential source of weakness and division. The abolition of these zones in Vietnam in 1976 thereby placed both parties back in step with one another. Speaking directly on the problem of autonomous zones in his 1981 speech Kaysone says 'the views of our party have been for a long time that it is not necessary to have these for minorities in our country'.[5]

Since the revolution, the top leadership of the LPDR has remained lowland Lao-dominated. Indeed, as the new regime has entrenched itself in the lowland towns and cities it has become less dependent on minority support, and less responsive to their demands. However, the LPDR's propaganda claims to represent Lao minorities are pervasive, which ironically has produced its own problems because it has both made the minorities more aware of their ethnic differences and simultaneously raised their expectations about social advancement. Under the RLG the various ritual forms centred on royalty partially accommodated ethnic differences as hierarchical ones, thereby muting potential conflict, whereas the modern secular state traffics in equality. In this regard the Lao state, like many others, is found wanting for it is clear to everyone, especially the minorities, that they are not equal citizens. Rising expectations has been one source of disgruntlement with the new regime, especially among the few minority individuals who have managed to get into secondary or tertiary education.

Identification

The current Lao government often speaks of the multi-ethnic Lao nation, but the term 'minorities' generally refers to the non-Tai-Lao groups. The LPDR is sometimes considered to be more tolerant towards minorities than the former RLG because it has officially accorded them names acknowledging their 'Lao-ness'. The communist policy is to categorize the population into broad conglomerations: *Lao Loum* or lowland Lao, *Lao Theung* or mid-lands or uplands Lao, and *Lao Soung*, Lao of the highlands or mountains. The first applied to ethnic Lao and Tai groups, the second to a range of Mon-Khmer and Austroasiatic groups scattered throughout the country, while the third was generally reserved for Tibeto-Burman, Hmong-Mien groups.

In the early 1980s Kaysone Phomvihane called for more detailed categorizations of the ethnic groups in Laos. This task initially fell to the Lao Front for National Reconstruction and the Nationalities Committee, but was finally taken over by the Institute of Ethnography when it was established in 1988. Considerable confusion reigned about how many groups there were in Laos, but the Institute finally settled on forty-seven, a conclusion that was adopted in the 1995 census. The significance of this was that the disaggregation of the tri-partite system into its constituent ethnic groups ensured that each of them appeared less significant in relation to the dominant ethnic Lao group, placing the latter at the nation's cultural centre and apex.

Ethnologists may have constructed an idea of Lao ethnicity as distinct from Lao nationality, just as the Vietnamese have with the ethnic concept of Kinh or the Chinese with the concept Han, but none of these majority groups separates the two ideas in their minds, nor do they think of themselves as an ethnic group in the common use of the term, connoting minority, 'backwardness' and so on. This is despite the fact that some publications on ethnicity include references to the dominant group, and despite the fact that the census has a category under ethnicity for Lao. Consequently, at the official level, discussions of ethnicity in Laos invariably make clear that reference is to the 'ethnic minorities'; what is underlined is the idea of Laos as a country with many ethnicities, with the Tai-Lao ethnicity at its core.

This further highlights an important peculiarity of communist nationalism in Laos. In his various writings on nationalism Smith has argued that there are two roads to nationalism: a civic nationalism, which draws people together under one state as citizens regardless of ethnic affiliation, and an ethnic nationalism, which mobilizes a heroic memory or myth of an ethnic group in order to elaborate its claim to nationhood.[6] What we see in the case of Laos is a peculiar combination of both civic and ethnic nationalism. Due to tactical constraints and the de-mands of communist orthodoxy, they had to elaborate and act on a version of civic nationalism (expressed as a 'multinational' state), when in reality the funda-mental motivation of nationalism was a form of ethnic nationalism, a fact which became increasingly apparent after victory.

Urban minorities

Because minorities are mostly rural, cities are often ignored in discussions of Laos. Here we will briefly look at the Lao capital Vientiane (640,000 persons in the metropolitan area in 1999). Being the centre of government, Vientiane at-tracts individuals from all over the country, just as commercial importance draws migrants from all provinces. The two most important ethnic 'minorities' in Vientiane historically have been the Chinese and the Vietnamese. They established themselves there during the French colonial period functioning as merchants (mainly Chinese) or as part of the French colonial administration (Vietnamese). Indeed, in the 1940s over half Vientiane's population was Vietnamese and Chi-nese. The decline of French colonialism after 1945 meant that many Vietnamese returned home, but others replaced them when refugees fled from North Vietnam in the early 1950s. Up until 1975 both the Chinese and the Vietnamese popula-tions of Vientiane were relatively large. One writer claims that the Chinese population in Laos fell from around 100,000 before 1975 to around 10,000 in the mid-1990s,[7] and the 1995 census gives only 1,932 Chinese nationals living in Vientiane. Similarly, before 1975, Vientiane's Vietnamese population was thought to be in the tens of thousands, while after 1975 these numbers fell dramatically as many fled to Thailand or beyond, and the 1995 census registers only 3,460 Vietnamese nationals as residents of Vientiane.

If we look at the distribution of ethnic groups as described in the census we can gain or surmise some information concerning the city's ethnic composition. The categories sought by the census were contained in a list of forty-seven specific ethnic groups (including Lao, but not Indians, Thai, Chinese or Vietnamese, categories that were only included under a question on nationality), and there was a residual category 'other', and another category of 'do not know'. In some villages of Vientiane Municipality these latter two categories were sometimes quite large. It is likely that for Vietnamese and Chinese there is some ambiguity between 'ethnicity' and 'nationality', so we can interpret these 'other' and 'do not know' responses as giving some indication of the distribution of this population in the city. And, indeed, in villages that were traditionally known to be Vietnamese or Chinese, these two categories were as high as 28 per cent, suggesting that these villages retain Chinese or Vietnamese populations. What this also reveals is significant concentrations of particular ethnic groups in some parts of Vientiane.

Despite its limitations, a Vientiane social survey also provides some interesting information on ethnic patterns of marriage. Among the Lao, 98 per cent marry Lao, 62 per cent of Phu Tai marry Phu Tai while the remaining Phu Tai marry only Lao, thereby giving some credence to the category 'Lao Loum' for these two groups. A similar statement could be made for the small number of Tai Lue in Vientiane who only marry either Lao or Lue. The Khmu men in the survey overwhelmingly married Lao or Phu Tai women, while only 15 per cent of them had Khmu wives.[8] Chinese men married mainly Lao or Phu Tai (75 per cent), or other Chinese. Vietnamese men mainly married other Vietnamese (60 per cent), or Lao women. Other groups in this survey, such as Hmong, Phu Noy or Katang, who only represented very small numbers, mainly tended to marry within their group, but around 30 per cent of Hmong men married either Phu Tai or Lue women, while about half of Phu Noy married either Lao or Lue. Within this configuration it is mainly 'Lao Loum' women who are being 'transacted' and they are therefore key agents in drawing other ethnic groups into a Lao cultural orbit.

We know relatively little about the ritual and religious practices of the both the Chinese and Vietnamese communities in Vientiane. Both communities maintain separate temples, but a shared Buddhist tradition also allows some easy overlap into the Lao temples, which follow Theravada Buddhism. Similarly, there appears to be considerable ritual syncreticism when people from either of these groups marry ethnic Lao.

Both the Vietnamese and Chinese maintain separate schools, though since 1975 both have been tied tightly to the central curriculum. Nevertheless, these schools do teach Vietnamese and Chinese language. In its enquiries on language use in the home the Vientiane Social Survey found that while a small proportion of Vietnamese or people of Vietnamese descent use Vietnamese in the home, nobody of Chinese descent reported using Chinese. This probably results from the repression and surveillance inflicted on the Chinese population from the late 1970s until the late 1980s due to political problems between the LPDR and People's Republic of China (PRC). These people, therefore, are reluctant to reveal their Chinese identity, even though it has begun to re-emerge in the 1990s.

There is a small south Indian Muslim minority in Vientiane maintaining their mosque in the city centre. The so-called hill-tribe minorities are not as visible as the Chinese or Vietnamese. In terms of institutional religion they tend to gravitate towards either Catholicism or another of the various Christian churches in Vientiane. There are no formal schools where any of these minority languages are taught. A certain amount of ritual syncretism can also been seen among them when marriages occur between any of these groups and the Lao.

Cities are extremely complex social and cultural arenas allowing for highly diverse ethnic interactions and processes of ethnic change. Capitals like Vientiane are also among the most fast-changing areas of the country, so minorities residing in them or migrating to them are subject to greater pressure towards cultural change and perhaps conformity with the dominant culture – which, one should add, is also in the process of change.

Population

The Lao population, which stood at some 3.5 million in 1975 after long years of war and disruption, grew by two million over the next twenty years, and by 2000 was thought to number 6 million. No full census was taken during the French period, and war during the period of the RLG ensured that no proper census could be conducted. Indeed, the census of 1995 was the first full and fairly reliable census of the Lao population.

Broken down according to broad ethno-linguistic criteria, the Tai-Lao group (six subgroups, including ethnic Lao at 52.5 per cent) came to 3,029,154 persons or 66.2 per cent; the Mon-Khmer (27 subgroups) came to 1,037,655 or 22.7 per cent; the Hmong-Mien population was 338,130 or 7.4 per cent; the Tibeto-Burman group had 122,653 persons or 2.7 per cent; the Viet-Muong 4,071 persons or 0.1 per cent; while 'others' made up around 1 per cent.

In many provinces ethnic Lao are in a minority, such as in Oudomxay or Sekong. One ethnic group dominates in some districts: in Nong Het district in Xieng Khoang Province the Hmong are over four-fifths of the population.

Infant mortality rates, which remain high by world standards, are worst in the countryside and in the mountains where most of the minorities live. This is generally because of low education levels and poor health facilities. Nevertheless, some progress has been made. Infant mortality has decreased from 104 per 1,000 in 1995 to 82 in 2000. There are small regional differences, but in 2000 mortality dropped dramatically in urban areas to 41.7 per 1,000.

Economy

Around 90 per cent of the Lao population are engaged in rural production, much of it close to subsistence level. A major aim of development has been to transform this natural economy and re-orient it towards the market. The majority of ethnic minorities are engaged in agriculture of some kind.

Along the Mekong and its tributaries with their alluvial plains one finds paddy-rice field systems. Farmers also fish and raise livestock. In these areas are some of the few dry season irrigation schemes that allow double-cropping. Vegetables grown along river banks provide cash income, and there are also field crops like cotton, sugar cane and tobacco. Much of the country's food is produced in these plains. It is overwhelmingly Tai-Lao peoples who inhabit the lowland areas and it is also here that one finds the country's major cities.

Rotational dry-rice shifting cultivation and maize found on the rolling hills and mid-level mountain slopes. Livestock is important to the economic system, particularly among people in the south of the country, who also rely heavily on forest hunting and gathering. Where possible, this upland agriculture is supplemented by paddy fields on scarce narrow valley floors, but there is little terracing. The people here are mostly from the broad Mon-Khmer groups, but Tai-Lao peoples also participate in this system.

In the highlands and mountains we also see upland rice, maize and tubers, and in some cases opium. Gardens and livestock are important. Many of these people practise pioneering (non-rotational) shifting cultivation. It is here we find Hmong-Mien, and also Tibeto-Burman groups.

Since 1975 the government has regularly issued edicts and targets for the eradication of shifting cultivation, which is alleged to be ecologically harmful through soil erosion and the destruction of forests. Population relocation of minorities has been proposed as the solution, and in the revolution's early years this was often carried out by force. While the proclaimed motivation at that time was economic, politics predominated as the new government became concerned with population control. Furthermore, during its brief attempt at collectivized agriculture (1978–85) the government forcibly integrated minorities into lowland cooperatives, causing hardship for everyone, and even localized inter-ethnic conflict.

Pioneering cultivation is generally considered the most destructive. That is where villages move into a new area, frequently densely forested, denude the forest and use the soil until it is depleted, and then move on. Rotational shifting cultivation, on the other hand, involves sedentary villagers who manage the rotation in such a way that the system is sustainable, in contrast to pioneering modes. This is the most common form of shifting cultivation in Laos. Often government policies have upset these relatively stable systems to nobody's advantage, leading to some resentment. Since the early 1990s, international advice and a move away from this orthodoxy have resulted in more practical solutions to the problem.

Opium has long been both a cash crop and integral to the lives of many minority peoples. International aid donors with a political agenda have sometimes encouraged opium suppression programmes that provide few alternatives to the upland minorities and simply leave them poorer.

Overall, the nation's minorities participate only marginally in the national market economy, and while there is exchange at provincial and occasional markets in the highlands, it is a small percentage of the GDP.

New economic policies in operation since the early 1990s have brought about increased economic exchange in the countryside, and an improvement in the standard of living. Nevertheless, low production levels and sparse cash limit minority participation in the market economy. Large wealth differentials have appeared, and predictably the most wealthy are urban-based Lao, and people of Chinese and Vietnamese descent.

Education

In 1975 over half the population of Laos was thought to be illiterate. Inevitably, literacy was much higher in the towns than in the countryside, where most minorities live. This measure of illiteracy most often refers to literacy in the Lao language. However, significant numbers of Hmong were literate in a writing system devised for them by missionaries, and Iu Mien men had literacy skills in Chinese characters. Nevertheless, the common measure of literacy underlines the fact that for almost half the population of Laos the Lao language is not their mother-tongue.

Before 1975, influenced by their Vietnamese and Chinese mentors, the Lao communists produced some Hmong booklets written in Lao script. From then until the turn of the century, however, the LPDR resisted the idea of mother-tongue education for minorities. Only then did they begin to relent, realizing that this policy inhibited minority education. Yet there are still no major programmes to deal with this issue.

Mass literacy campaigns launched after the revolution and continuing into the 1980s had a negligible impact on overall literacy. Indeed, many Lao and most minorities entering schools for a few years soon regress to illiteracy after leaving because of the general absence of reading materials. In other words, reading is peripheral to their lives.

In the 1990s, and with assistance from the United Nations Development Programme, non-formal education projects at the village level began to provide education appropriate to local concerns and so help to sustain literacy. Foreign aid developed a programme aiming to assist the education of minority girls. Educational reforms in the 1990s have seen a slow rise in overall literacy.

Also in the 1990s, with Vietnamese assistance, authorities established special high schools for minorities in Oudomxay in the north, in Thakhek in the centre of the country and Pakse in the south. While these schools cater for fairly small numbers, they do provide privileged access to high school education for some ethnic youth. A fast track for minority students is also provided in some cases through the privileges granted to minority members of the Party and the army.

Society

Religion

There are no easy ways to generalize about the religious beliefs of the non-Lao minorities. Much discussion contrasts the 'world religion' Theravada Buddhism of the ethnic Lao with minority beliefs characterized by the catch-all of 'animism'. This contrast, however, is misleading as popular Buddhism in Laos contains many beliefs one can call animist. Beyond Theravada Buddhism, supernatural belief systems arguably vary from one ethnic group to another. Forms of 'ancestor worship' are widely found, but these too vary from the more obviously Sinitic beliefs of the patrilineal Hmong, through to the more clear recognition of female ancestors among some other more matrilineal groups, particularly in the southern highlands. It is already clear from this brief description that belief varies with social structure, so an adequate account of minority beliefs would require a description of each social structure.

After 1975 there were attempts to 'cleanse' Theravada Buddhism of 'superstitious' beliefs and bring it more into line with 'scientific socialism'. Most minority belief systems were seen as 'superstitious'. With regard to Buddhism, this campaign collapsed in the late 1980s, with 'superstitious' practices flourishing among Theravada Buddhists since the 1990s. However, the state places some cultural value on Buddhism, and beliefs held by the minorities are still more likely to be labelled 'superstition' than practices associated with Buddhism.

Missionary activity by Christians before 1975 did attract some members of minority groups, such as the Hmong or Khmu. In outer-lying areas there have been occasional crackdowns on Christianity and, in some cases, the destruction of local churches because of what are seen as 'divisive' beliefs.

Family

The family is central to social structure in most minorities but there are important variations across all minorities. However, beyond that, there are no easy generalizations to be made about family structures among minorities, which range from patrilineages among Hmong or Iu Mien, to matrilineages among the Katu, or simply weaker forms of patrilineal or matrilineal reckoning for aspects of social and cultural activity, through to nuclear-style families with relatively weak lineal interest. Whether people live matrilocally or patrilocally depends on social structure.

Secessionist movements, rebellions

After the 1975 revolution, accounts of continuing, sporadic fighting in the mountains emerged in early 1976, and in July there were reports of the use of napalm against resistance strongholds. While soldiers loyal to Vang Pao made up part of this resistance, another group came to prominence, the Chao Fa, perhaps best rendered as 'Soldiers of God'. This was a millenarian movement that had emerged in the early 1960s, a result of the disruption of Hmong culture and society. Its leader Yong Shong Lue promoted his own messianic script for the Hmong, believed in the coming of a Hmong king and that he could protect his followers from enemy bullets. There had always been some overlap between these two groups, and indeed Vang Pao had tried to suppress the Chao Fa's influence among his men. In the chaos that followed the flight of Vang Pao the influence of the Chao Fa appears to have grown dramatically and fuelled Hmong resistance to the new regime. With the collapse of US support, Hmong drew on their own cultural resources to maintain resistance. These forces, however, had little ammunition and did no more than harass the new government. Nevertheless, any opposition was intolerable to the new leaders in Vientiane and in 1977 they decided on a showdown with the Hmong resistance. This coincided with a treaty drawn up with Vietnam legitimizing the use of Vietnamese forces against the resistance; perhaps upwards of 30,000 Vietnamese troops were used in the large-scale operation launched against the Hmong in 1977. The fighting was ferocious and included shelling and aerial bombing with napalm. Because the Hmong resistance fighters lived with their families, operations against them entailed indiscriminate civilian casualties, leading to charges of genocide when these people staggered into the camps in Thailand and told their stories.

It is clear that the campaign against the Hmong at times degenerated into the savagery associated with 'ethnic cleansing'. Even though the LPDR and its ally Vietnam broke the back of the resistance by 1978, they had killed and mistreated so many people in the process that resentment continued to fester, finding sporadic expression in outbreaks of fighting against the government. In early 2000 long-standing tensions with ethnic Lao in Xiang Khoang over such problems as land disputes and resettlement programmes suddenly boiled over into intense and extensive fighting. Vietnamese troops were called back into the country for the first time since the late 1980s to help quell the insurgents. Reporters who visited the area not long after saw burnt-out houses and found residents shaken by the sudden attacks. The government denied that there was a serious problem and blamed 'bandits'.

The relaxed policies on movement in the 1990s have not only allowed Hmong, for example, to visit their refugee relatives in America, but also those relatives to visit Laos. Through this channel debates over the Hmong past and future, which are vigorous among the overseas Hmong, have made their way back into the Hmong communities in Laos, setting up a parallel discourse to the one promoted by the government. If anything, Hmong desires for autonomy have been hardened by their exposure to the politics of ethnicity in America, but it is unclear what impact these ideas have when they reach Laos. Less visible, but equally important minorities, such as the Khamu, are also quietly voicing their discontent. They are an important part of the national army and some of their members have risen through the ranks, though few hold high positions outside the army. One influential Khamu spoke to me in 2000 of his unhappiness:

During the revolution it was all about how the Party supported the people, now it is the people who must support the Party. Look around Vientiane, the Lao people are rich, but go to the countryside, the Khamu there are poor. They can't get into the university, unless of course their father is a colonel who can get them through the back door. It is not right.

It is unlikely that such rumblings are going to go away in the near future.

Foreign policy and the minorities

In his 1981 address, Kaysone referred to attempts by 'reactionaries' to 'encourage some ethnicities to create self-governing regions of ethnicities such as an auto-nomous region for the Lue, the Hmong . . . in order to break them away from the lineage of the Lao nation'.[9] Not only was he referring here to Lao and Hmong exile groups in Thailand, but in particular to China whose autonomous regions, he claimed, 'are merely pretentious hollow structures to show off to the outside, that's all'.[10] Kaysone's special sensitivity to China at this time comes no doubt from his understanding of communist tactics vis-à-vis minorities in the

Plate 12.3 Black Tai women in the mountainous northern province of Houaphan. In the past they were often referred to as 'tribal Tai' partly because they were non-Buddhist, something that set them clearly apart from ethnic Lao. Reference to linguistic affinities rather than religion, however, places them in the 'Lao Loum', lowland Lao group

Lao revolution, whereby the Vietnamese often chose their advisers in Laos from among minorities who straddled the borders, such as the Black Tai or Hmong. Kaysone was aware of Chinese attempts at the time to use minorities straddling their borders to foment unrest in Laos, or in Vietnam.

Since the crushing of the resistance inside Laos, incursions from camps in Thailand have fallen dramatically, and there have only been minor incidents. Moreover, since Vietnam and China patched up their differences in the early 1990s the Lao-Chinese border has not been problematic. Of course, smuggling across borders is another matter, but that is endemic to the whole region.

Conclusion

The role of the nationalist state is cultural standardization, and the education system is one of the main instruments for teaching ethnic minorities in Laos about a Lao standard culture. In fact, in the crop of textbooks for schools released in the 1990s one finds fewer references to minorities than one did in those released immediately after 1975. In the history of the creation of modern nations, however, there is nothing exceptional about the Lao state's attempt to promote such a standard culture. There are, however, some forces moderating this. First, ethnic diversity can be sold to international tourists, and to a degree this has created some sense of pride amongst the more 'colourful' groups concerning their culture, thus offsetting their sense of inferiority in relation to the dominant culture. Second, 'ethnic identity' has become a touchstone for many people in our globalized world by presuming to give people a sense of 'roots'. Generally, the world is more sensitive to ethnic issues than in the 1970s, and governments like the LPDR are aware of this. Many international aid organizations in Laos now insist, often to the annoyance of their Lao counterparts, on paying attention to 'ethnic minority needs' in their aid programmes. Some Lao clearly feel that this attention to minorities creates national 'disunity', when in fact it provides a check on the power of the dominant group in the absence of democracy. But many of the confusions which occur in debates between Lao and foreigners about ethnic minority rights also arise from the fact that not only Lao, but foreigners themselves, often swing confusingly between ethnically based views of the nation and those based on citizenship rights.

One suspects that minority issues are going to loom even larger within Laos in the future, especially as minority peoples become more highly educated and demand greater access to power and wealth. Here the role of long-distance nationalists among the Lao minority diasporas will no doubt come to play an influential role.

Notes

All Laos photographs taken by Grant Evans.

1 See the chapter 'Minorities in state ritual' in Grant Evans, *The Politics of Ritual and Remembrance: Laos Since 1975*, Chiang Mai: Silkworm Books, 1998.

2 Kaysone Phomvihane, *Reinforce and Expand the Basic Trust and Solidarity between Various Ethnic Groups in the Lao National Family, and Strengthen Unity. Resolutely Uphold and Strengthen the Country and Build Socialism to its Completion*, Vientiane: National Printery, 1982, pp. 48–9.
3 Ibid., p. 47.
4 Ibid., p. 49.
5 Ibid., p. 69.
6 For a good overview of his views see Anthony Smith, 'The politics of culture, ethnicity and nationalism', in Tim Ingold (ed.), *Companion Encyclopedia of Anthropology*, London and New York: Routledge, 1991, pp. 686–705.
7 Florence Rossetti, 'The Chinese in Laos', *China Perspectives*, September/October 1997, no. 13, p. 26.
8 *1997–1998, Vientiane Social Survey Project*, Vientiane: Institute for Cultural Research, Ministry of Information and Culture, 1998.
9 Kaysone, *Reinforce and Expand*, p. 60.
10 Ibid., p. 71.

Further reading

General

Batson, Wendy, 'After the revolution: Ethnic minorities and the new Lao state', in J. Zasloff and L. Unger (eds), *Laos: Beyond the Revolution*, London: Macmillan, 1992, pp. 133–58.
Carol, J. and W. Randall Ireson, 'Ethnicity and development in Laos', *Asian Survey*, 1991, vol. 31, no. 10, pp. 920–37.
Chazée, Laurent, *The Peoples of Laos: Rural and Ethnic Diversities*, Bangkok: White Lotus Books, 2002.
Evans, Grant, 'Apprentice ethnographers: Vietnam and the study of Lao minorities', in Grant Evans (ed.), *Laos: Culture and Society*, Chiang Mai: Silkworm Books, 1999, pp. 161–90.
Vatthana Pholsena, 'Nation/representation: Ethnic classification and mapping nationhood in contemporary Laos', *Asian Ethnicity*, 2002, vol. 3, no. 2, pp. 175–97.

Specific studies

Chazée, Laurent, *The Mrabri in Laos: A World Under the Canopies*, Bangkok: White Lotus Books, 2001.
Evans, Grant, 'Reform or revolution in heaven? Funerals among Upland Tai', *Australian Journal of Anthropology* (formerly *Mankind*), 1991, vol. 2, no. 1, pp. 81–97.
Evans, Grant, 'Ethnic change in Highland Laos', in Grant Evans (ed.), *Laos: Culture and Society*, Chiang Mai: Silkworm Books, 1999, pp. 125–47. (On Black Tai and Sing Moon.)
Izikowitz, Karl Gustav, *Lamet: Hill Peasants in French Indochina*, Bangkok: White Lotus, 2001 (originally published 1951).
Khampheng Thipmuntali, 'The Lue of Muang Sing', in Grant Evans (ed.), *Laos: Culture and Society*, Chiang Mai: Silkworm Books, 1999, pp. 148–60.
Ovesen, Jan, *A Minority Enters the Nation State: A Case Study of a Hmong Community in Vientiane Province, Laos*, Uppsala Research Reports in Cultural Anthropology, No. 14, 1995.
Proschan, Frank, '"We are all Kmhmu, just the same": Ethnonyms, ethnic identities, and ethnic groups', *American Ethnologist*, 1997, vol. 24, no. 1, pp. 91–113.
Yang Dao, *Hmong at the Turning Point*, Minneapolis: World Bridge Associates, 1993.

Index